D0044891

THE BONE AND SINEW OF THE LAND

THE BONE AND SINEW OF THE LAND

AMERICA'S FORGOTTEN
BLACK PIONEERS
& THE STRUGGLE FOR EQUALITY

ANNA-LISA COX

PUBLICAFFAIRS

New York

PublicAffairs
Hachette Book Group
1290 Avenue of the Americas, New York, NY 10104
www.publicaffairsbooks.com
@Public_Affairs

Printed in the United States of America

First Edition: June 2018

Published by PublicAffairs, an imprint of Perseus Books, LLC, a subsidiary of Hachette Book Group, Inc. The PublicAffairs name and logo is a trademark of the Hachette Book Group.

The Hachette Speakers Bureau provides a wide range of authors for speaking events. To find out more, go to www.hachettespeakersbureau.com or call (866) 376-6591.

The publisher is not responsible for websites (or their content) that are not owned by the publisher.

Print book interior design by Amy Quinn

Library of Congress Cataloging-in-Publication Data
Names: Cox, Anna-Lisa, author.
Title: The bone and sinew of the land: America's forgotten black pioneers and the struggle for equality / Anna-Lisa Cox.
Other titles: America's forgotten black pioneers and the struggle for equality
Description: First edition. | New York: PublicAffairs, [2018] | Includes bibliographical references and index.
Identifiers: LCCN 2017056938| ISBN 9781610398107 (hardcover) | ISBN 9781610398114 (ebook)
Subjects: LCSH: African Americans—Northwest, Old—History. | African Americans—Indiana—History—19th century. | African Americans—Ohio—History—19th century. | Frontier and pioneer life—Northwest, Old. | Frontier and pioneer life—Indiana. | Frontier and pioneer life—Ohio. | African Americans—Social conditions—Northwest, Old. | Northwest, Old—History—1775-1865. | Northwest, Old—Race relations.
Classification: LCC E185.925 .C64 2018 | DDC 977/.0496073—dc23
LC record available at https://lccn.loc.gov/2017056938

ISBNs: 978-1-61039-810-7 (hardcover), 978-1-61039-811-4 (ebook)

LSC-C

10 9 8 7 6 5 4 3 2 1

For Leora
and
Stephan
With hope for the future

Contents

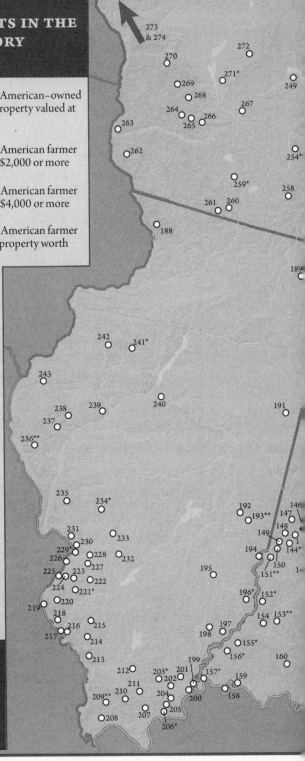

AFRICAN AMERICAN FARMING SETTLEMENTS IN THE NORTHWEST TERRITORY STATES, 1800–1860

○ Settlement with at least one African American–owned farm no larger than 199 acres with property valued at less than $1,999.

* Settlement with at least one African American farmer owning 200 acres or more or worth $2,000 or more

** Settlement with at least one African American farmer owning 400 acres or more or worth $4,000 or more

*** Settlement with at least one African American farmer owning 1000 acres or more or with property worth $10,000 or more

TOTAL SETTLEMENTS

OHIO:	95
INDIANA:	92
ILLINOIS:	56
WISCONSIN:	31
MICHIGAN:	64
TOTAL:	338

Note: Each numbered dot on this map represents one settlement, which often included more than one farm. The values denoted by the asterisks represent the value of individual farms in the settlement, not the combined value of all the farms.

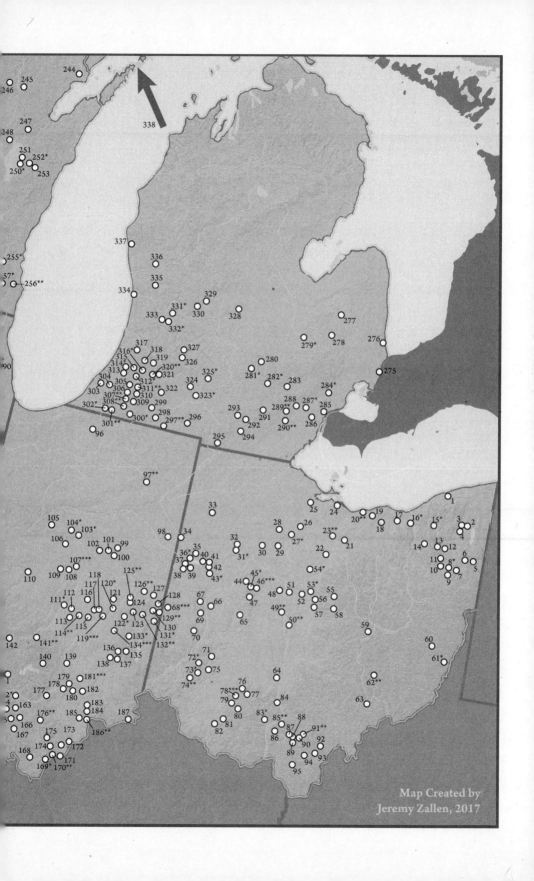

African American Farming Settlements in the Northwest Territory States, 1800–1860[1]

[No asterisk] = Settlement with at least one African American farmer owning less than two hundred acres or with property valued at less than $2,000

* = Settlement with at least one African American farmer owning two hundred acres or more or worth $2,000 or more

** = Settlement with at least one African American farmer owning four hundred acres or more or worth $4,000 or more

*** = Settlement with at least one African American farmer owning 1,000 acres or more or with property worth $10,000 or more

Ohio

1 Painesville, Lake County
2 Bloomfield, Trumbull County
3 Mesopotamia, Trumbull County
4 Farmington, Trumbull County
5 Youngstown, Mahoning County
6 Austintown, Mahoning County
7 Goshen, Mahoning County
8 Smith, Mahoning County*
9 Knox, Columbiana County
10 Lexington, Stark County
11 Atwater, Portage County
12 Charlestown, Portage County
13 Ravenna, Portage County
14 Stow, Summit County
15 Bainbridge, Geauga County*
16 Independence, Cuyahoga County*
17 Middleburgh, Cuyahoga County
18 Grafton, Lorain County
19 Russia, Lorain County
20 Brownhelm, Lorain County**
21 Fitchville, Huron County
22 Sharon, Richland County
23 Greenfield, Huron County**
24 Perkins, Erie County
25 Sandusky, Sandusky County
26 Tiffin, Seneca County
27 Seneca, Seneca County*
28 Big Spring, Seneca County

165 Paoli, Orange County
166 Stampers Creek, Orange County
167 Southeast, Orange County
168 Harrison Township, Harrison County
169 Franklin, Floyd County*
170 New Albany, Floyd County**
171 Jeffersonville, Clark County
172 Charlestown, Clark County
173 Silver Creek, Clark County
174 Lafayette, Floyd County
175 Wood, Clark County

176 Washington, Washington County**
177 Driftwood, Jackson County
178 Jackson, Jackson County
179 Redding, Jackson County
180 Spencer, Jennings County
181 Geneva, Jennings County***
182 Vernon, Jennings County
183 Lancaster, Jefferson County
184 Smyrna, Jefferson County
185 Republican, Jefferson County
186 Hanover, Jefferson County**
187 York, Switzerland County**

Illinois

188 East and West Galena, Jo Daviess County
189 Wheeling, Cook County
190 Maine, Cook County
191 District 32, Iroquois County
192 New Albany, Coles County
193 Grandview and Embarrass, Edgar County**
194 Darwin, Clark County
195 Newton, Jasper County
196 Pinkstaff, Lawrence County*
197 "Not Stated," Wabash County
198 "Not Stated," Edwards County
199 Wabash, Gallatin County
200 Shawnee, Gallatin County
201 Cane Creek, Gallatin County
202 Equality, Gallatin County
203 Curran, Saline County*
204 Eagle, Gallatin County
205 Monroe, Saline County

206 "Not Stated," Hardin County*
207 Miller Grove, in the Shawnee Hills, Pope County
208 "Not Stated," Pulaski County
209 District 2, Union County**
210 District 2, Johnson County
211 Stonefort, Saline County
212 Township 8/"Not Stated," Williamson County
213 Township 8, Jackson County
214 T6S R5W, Randolph County
215 T4S R5W, Randolph County
216 T6S R7W, Randolph County
217 T6S R8W, Randolph County
218 Prairie du Rocher, Randolph County
219 Mitchie, Monroe County
220 New Design, Monroe County
221 Turkey Hill, St. Clair County*
222 Lebanon, St. Clair County

Wisconsin

Michigan

Author's Note

At the front of this book is a map of a reality that no one thought existed, of a population that most have considered impossible—a population of successful African American pioneers integrating America's first free frontier.[1]

The territory on this map became part of the United States in the revolutionary days of the early republic, and it was truly revolutionary, for this is the Northwest Territory—the largest piece of land in the New World to be set aside as free of slavery and to offer equal voting rights to American men regardless of the color of their skin. Before California or Texas, before Wyoming or Oregon, this territory was known as the Great West, a region of tremendous importance that shaped the nation before the Civil War. The pioneers featured in this book grew their farms and families on the frontier while also keeping alive the dream that had given birth to their new homes and their new nation, a dream of a country where all men are created equal and there could be liberty and justice for all.

The map reveals the activities inspired by this dream, but it is limited in a few ways. It does not represent all African Americans in the Northwest Territory states, only African American farming settlements, so none of the many African American urban entrepreneurs are shown. And even in the rural areas, it excludes all the African American businesspeople who were not property-owning farmers, such as blacksmiths, general store owners, and mill owners.

My definition of a successful landowning African American entrepreneurial farm is based on the following criterion: a man of any skin color owning at least two hundred acres of property would have been eligible to run for office based on the Northwest Ordinance of 1787. Having that much acreage would represent considerable economic success: Loren Schweninger points out in *Black Property Owners in the South*, by the mid-1800s a farmer with property worth between $2,000 and $5,000 was in the top 13 percent of wealthy landowners in the United States at that time, regardless of skin color. Many of these settlements included farmers with such wealth, and some were even wealthier.

What's more, the number of landowning African American farming settlements on this map is conservative, and so is the value of the farms. African American farming families often did not want themselves or their farms counted on federal documents before the Civil War. This is unsurprising given the anti-immigration laws, the fugitive slave laws, and the unjust taxation policies in these states. The first African American lawyer in Ohio would not allow the federal census to record the value of his large and successful Ohio farm in the 1850s; it is recorded only in local land deeds and tax records.[2]

Because of settlement patterns, I drew information about Ohio, Indiana, and Illinois farms primarily from the 1850 federal census, while Michigan and Wisconsin data came from the 1860 federal census. Although some of these settlements had disappeared by 1860 and others only existed for a decade, they are still counted, for they had an impact both on the African American farmers themselves and on the white pioneers moving in and around them. Each of these pioneer farming families and each of these settlements testifies to the truth that people of African descent had the ability, courage, and perseverance to rise in America. This is the story of their rising and what happened when they rose.

Introduction

Boston, Massachusetts, 1853

William Lloyd Garrison left Boston in early October 1853 to travel to the Great West. He headed first to Albany, New York, where he would catch a train that would take him hundreds of miles west. By 1853 Garrison was one of the most widely recognized and revolutionary white abolitionists of his day, and he had been publishing his newspaper, the *Liberator*, in Boston for over twenty years, filling its pages with reports from the region he was now on his way to visit.[1]

The Great West, the Northwest territories, the frontier. Today these words conjure up images of the Rocky Mountains or the wild ranges of Texas. But the "Great West" was the name commonly given to the first territory created by the new nation of the United States, in 1787. Most of this region would become the states of Ohio, Indiana, Illinois, Michigan, and Wisconsin in the first half of the 1800s. Maps from the early nineteenth century show the nation ending at the Mississippi River, as if that waterway were a cliff at the end of the world.

And even as the nation expanded, this image of the Northwest Territory stayed strong in the minds of many Americans.

In 1853, Garrison did not plan on visiting all five of those states, just Ohio and Michigan. He was not getting any younger, and the new train lines now connecting the East Coast to Michigan and Ohio made travel there much easier. But he also had to be careful to visit what he deemed the safest parts of the Old Northwest Territory states. He knew of vicious attacks against abolitionists in some of these regions—he had

1

reported on them in his newspaper for years. Of course, Boston was not exactly safe either. In the 1830s Garrison had nearly been tarred and feathered as well as lynched in his hometown of Boston. And tarring and feathering continued to be a favored means among pro-slavery men of torturing those struggling against the tyrannies of bondage and prejudice, even in the Northwest Territory states.[2]

Garrison wrote accounts of his journey soon after returning. He wrote of traveling around Michigan and Ohio, speaking to crowds large and small, of being barred from speaking halls in Detroit and almost attacked there. He wrote of his meetings with white and black abolitionists, as well as their enemies. He wrote with good humor of the time a young white man on a train platform in Ohio had warned him that an antislavery meeting was to be held in the area and "the nigger man from Boston was going to be there," referring to Garrison himself. Garrison wrote, "This was really a very fine compliment, and I was as much gratified as amused by it."[3]

But he devoted his first article upon his return, when his memory was freshest, to certain facts about the region that moved him and gave him hope:

> Is it not on the American soil that the "Great Debate, the Conflict of the Ages," is to be settled . . . as to the equality of the human race— human brotherhood—the value of man as man? Settled, not as an abstract theory, but by a practical recognition of the world-reconciling fact; settled, not with mountains or oceans intervening, but with people of every clime and race standing side by side, grouped together in one common locality, literally neighbors, daily looking each other in the face, and continually interchanging the kindnesses and courtesies of civilized life![4]

As Garrison wrote about "people of every clime and race standing side by side" as neighbors, he was not envisioning some grand imagined experiment, some ideal future; he was describing a reality that he knew existed across most of the Great West. He was writing about a population in that region that most historians today do not know existed. But it did.

At the very time when the United States was forming itself, when the young nation was opening its first free frontier, there was a pioneering movement so massive and successful that it changed the legal and social landscape of our country. This movement consisted of free people of African descent.

Long before the Great Migration of the twentieth century, there had been another Great Migration, one that spanned the first half of the nineteenth century. This was a migration, in wagon trains and on foot, of tens of thousands of African American pioneers who became some of the earliest settlers of the Great West. Most of these pioneers had not come to cities; instead, they had flung themselves at the wildest edges of the frontier. Highly visible, assertive, and brave, they scattered themselves across the land in hundreds of farming settlements.

But the full scope of these pioneers' accomplishments has been lost, for even the best historians have assumed that there were very few successful African American farming settlements across the Northwest Territory before the Civil War.[5]

Of course, historians have long known that by 1860 the federal census counted over 63,000 African Americans as living in the five Northwest Territory states. And as Stephen Vincent pointed out in his important work on African American farmers in antebellum Indiana, 73 percent of those counted in those five states in 1860 were living in a rural setting.[6]

To put this number into context, the Northwest Ordinance, completed in 1787, stipulated that a region could become a state if it had 60,000 non–Native American settlers. This meant that by 1860 more than a state's worth of African-descended people were living in the Great West. Much has been written about the move of African Americans to the African colony of Liberia starting in the nineteenth century; yet by the early twentieth century the descendants of those American immigrants only numbered around 15,000.[7]

Until recently, we have known little about the lives of African American pioneers in the Great West. Some historians have argued that the frontier was too dangerous and challenging for African Americans, who faced many social and legal adversities beyond the inherent difficulty of building up a farm from nothing.[8]

But before William Lloyd Garrison was even born, African Americans had settled in the region, guarding its forts and homesteading their farms in the earliest days of American expansion.

Most African American pioneers faced a brutal irony. They could only enjoy some freedom and equality at the far edges of the nation, where its laws and culture lay lightly on the land. But there was also something about timing—about the fact that these pioneers were able to settle a region created at the height of the young nation's fervor for freedom. And these earliest pioneers, some even joined by whites who continued to hold on to the ideals of liberty and equality, were able to carve out spaces in the rural Old Northwest where astonishing levels of equality were possible at a time when most of the rest of the nation—south or north—was growing hostile to those ideals.[9]

While some of the first African-descended people in this region had arrived before there was even a United States and lived harmoniously with Native Americans, later pioneers of African descent were sometimes different. Some were even Indian agents, taking up arms during the War of 1812 to battle Native Americans in the Northwest Territory.[10]

The violence on this American frontier—the brutal battles, forced removals, death marches, and genocides—is truly horrifying. This was no virgin territory free for the taking. However, African American pioneers before the Civil War did see the Northwest Territory as a place of fresh hope. They understood how dangerous it was, how violent it was, how their settlement would displace Native peoples, with whom they might even come into conflict. But they sought success, and before the Civil War that meant owning good land and farming it well. And they intended to succeed on the frontier. The Northwest Territorial

Ordinance of 1787 promised that this region would not only be free of slavery but offered equal voting rights to any man who owned at least fifty acres of land.[11]

While free African-descended people had long owned farms from Vermont to Virginia, this movement of African Americans onto the frontier created a wholly new situation. They came to settle where they wished to, around the people they wanted to be near. Determined to be equal, these pioneers defined their own goals, working independently and with whites to further the causes of liberty and equality.

They used their position as free homesteading pioneers across this portion of the nation to assert their rights and push for change. As their numbers, their farms, and their communities grew, they refused to lie low.

And they managed to succeed in extraordinary ways. They organized successful conventions that brought pressure against state governments, helping to roll back prejudiced laws. They founded and funded successful schools open to girls and boys, black and white, in the cornfields of 1840s Indiana, when attempts to create such schools in the Northeast were being violently opposed. And it was in the rural spaces of this region that the first African American was elected to political office in a free and open election before the Civil War.

No wonder a group of African American farmers from Carthagena, Ohio, wrote to African Americans in Cleveland, urging them to leave the cities where they were being oppressed and attacked to come to the rural areas and farm. As they wrote, "Those who live in towns and follow those precarious occupations for a livelihood, which prejudice has assigned to you, would you not be serving your country and your race to more purpose, if you were to leave your present residences and employments and go into the country and become a part of the bone and sinew of the land?" Of course, these rural African Americans discovered that in some regions their very successes could cause prejudiced whites to attack them. In the years before the Civil War, the rising of African Americans in the Northwest Territory states led to incidents of legal, political, and social violence. But while achieving success may not have been a solution to prejudice, prejudice could not erase the fact that African Americans were succeeding—were rising—in much of the rural and frontier spaces of this region.[12]

These pioneers reflected almost all the faces of African American freedom. Some were first-generation free. But some came from families who had been free for centuries and were literate landowners in the slave South. Many of these long-free families could trace their liberty back to the seventeenth century and had fathers or other relatives who had fought as patriots in the Revolutionary War. But while some were freed, some had purchased their freedom, and some were generations free, all of these successful landowning pioneers chose to be farmers.

They understood that by colonizing the newest portion of the nation, they were laying claim to citizenship in powerful ways. Today, most Americans' identity has little to do with land ownership, but in the early United States a man could only vote if he owned property, so ownership of land was key to being considered a full person, a full American. And as they scattered across the frontier, these propertied black farmers were keeping alive a national discussion about the meaning of freedom and equality.

These were pioneers in the purest sense, willing to risk their freedom and their lives for the chance to gain not just land but their rights. This is their story, the story of African American pioneers who became the bone and sinew of the land.

1

"Life, Liberty"

Gibson County, Indiana,
Spring 1818

Keziah and Charles Grier strapped their axes onto their backs before going up to hitch up the oxen for their first day of plowing together. Once they got to the starting place, Charles would have adjusted the lines, glancing at Keziah, who held the team's head up front, then called out for the team to start.

They had their axes ready, but not for trees. Those were already gone on this little patch of land that they planned to work this spring. Charles had already been clearing the trees and underbrush since he purchased his forty acres in 1815. Some trees he set alight until they crashed to the ground, smoking. Others that looked good he had felled for building the small cabin that was now their home.[1]

If he was lucky enough to find some chestnut trees on his land, then he had his fence wood. Once he had felled the tree, his back damp and sore from the effort, he would have to cut through the thick trunk in long lengths of roughly twelve feet. Then there was the splitting of that green wood. Making the first split was always the hardest, a task requiring patience, time, and exhausting effort. The fence was necessary to protect the kitchen garden from the deer and to keep the hogs penned before slaughter. But this work was so hard that many pioneers either paid strong young men eager for money or forced their bonded laborers to do it.[2]

Until recently, Charles had been one of those men forced to do this kind of labor. But this was his frontier. And now, this was his labor, his life, his land.

He must have shown Keziah his likely land as he was courting her, all forty acres of it.

It was the best land. Already it was highly prized, for it was rich river-bottom land where almost anything would grow. It was close to the Patoka and Wabash Rivers, so they could easily find transportation for themselves or anything they might want to sell. But it was also high enough to avoid the yearly flooding that struck so many other areas nearby. It was almost perfect. It had to be.[3]

The Griers knew that their lives depended on this land, for this soil was to grow their food and support them, and more besides. Of course, they wanted a family, but they hoped for more than mere survival. Had Charles already told Keziah that he wanted to be able to grow not only their family but their farm? He wanted to leave behind a legacy, an investment in this new nation to pass along to their children. Not just freedom but a future full of success.

But that was the future. That was their dream. First came the plowing.

The oxen were fresh, but Keziah and Charles knew that their team was tender and the land hard. For they were not just plowing, they were clearing the frontier—the first people to ever put a blade into this particular patch of earth and turn it to cultivation.

So they adjusted the axes on their backs and started walking. There would be a lot of walking that day, and every day, until the field was plowed. Even on cleared land, plowing one acre with a single-blade plow required nine miles of walking on rough mud.[4]

And the Griers were starting with forty acres. If they had been farming outside New York City and decided to drop their traces and set off for Boston, the plowing of that forty acres would have walked them there and back every spring. Those farmers lucky enough to have a hundred acres under cultivation might just as well have been walking from New York City past Chicago every spring. But there was no city of Chicago yet in 1818; there was just water and wilderness.

But walking behind a plow was only possible once the earth underneath had been cleared. To clear not what grew above but what grew below, however, was a different challenge. Charles and Keziah did not own long-cultivated earth; their land had been virgin forest up until recently, and everything had grown on it but crops. Trees, bushes, brambles, ferns, vines, wildflowers, and more had thrived there. And all of them, all of them, had roots.

Within a few feet the team hit the first big root. The oxen put their heads down and pulled, groaning a little. Charles would have called to them, whistling, cajoling, encouraging, until the root snapped and they jerked forward. The next root was bigger, and as the team pulled Charles would have had to call to Keziah. But she certainly already had the axe off her back, walking towards Charles as he reversed the team clear of the root, so he could dig around it. It could well have been as thick as his leg. Once he had cleared around the root Keziah would have lifted the axe high above her head and brought it down hard, hacking into the earth as shoulders strained and the blade dulled on the dark dirt.[5]

Once she was through the root, they started off again, knowing they did not have long before the next root, for roots lay under the earth like a second forest. In this rich, newly cleared land, they would hit a sizable root about every eight feet, or every half a minute. And each root stopped the team.

Even if all went well, after half a day of this labor they would all be in pain. The oxen's shoulders, where the yoke lay, would be so sore that the beasts would flinch if Keziah laid her hand even gently on their tender skin. Only two creatures have the strength, patience, and courage for this labor: oxen and humans.

This work stretched ahead of Keziah and Charles, not just that year, but for years to come. It generally took at least twenty years to clear forty acres of virgin land, twenty years before most of the roots and rocks were gone. And those twenty years depended on surviving droughts, floods, infestations, and early frosts. But their farming was an act of hope.

There were other options. The white settlers pouring into their region would have been glad to hire Keziah to do their laundry or cooking. And Charles could have become a blacksmith or woodworker or set up shop in Vincennes as a barber. And there was always the river. He could have bought or built himself a boat and become a river man—they knew enough people of African descent who had done that. But this was their land, their life together, their choice.

As they turned the oxen toward home, the sun would have been high overhead. But though they were weary and warm, there was a freshness to that first spring.

Everything was fresh—their marriage, their love, their land, even their freedom.

As Keziah led the team back, the sun would have glinted on her skin, shining like the wings of the crows that clamored round them on the newly turned earth.[6]

Did Charles catch his breath with the wonder of her—the wonder of his wife? For this was not her first frontier. She may have been younger than he, but she had already helped found a farm in this territory.

But that farm was not hers. Keziah had been brought in bondage from South Carolina by a family of white pioneers who believed that settlement on the American frontier was impossible without the aid of forced labor.

Keziah's owners were not unique in this belief. Many a slave-owning family was making a similar argument to the politicians back east, some of whom seemed open to their pro-slavery arguments. True, the Northwest Ordinance of 1787 clearly laid out that this was to be a free land where slavery could not take root. But there were already some loopholes. There was one for the French slave owners just up the Wabash River in Vincennes, whose cooperation the new United States desperately needed in the Great West. And there were a few other loopholes besides.[7]

But most slaveholders were supposed to free the people they held enslaved once they entered the Northwest Territory. Of course, they could always ask those enslaved people if they wanted to become indentured servants, to labor for a set period before being freed with some small reward for their labors. But this system quickly became rife with corruption, and enslaved people often had little choice about their indenture. Indenture bonds could last seventy years or more—long outlasting the actual lives of those they held in contract.[8]

And then there were families like Keziah's owners, who assumed that there would be little oversight or interest in upholding freedom laws out there on the frontier. And for a while they were correct in this assumption.

So Keziah was forced to leave her home in South Carolina. She must have remembered the sea—the sea that separated her from everyone. She would have remembered all that she had been forced to leave behind, kin, friends, community.

And then Keziah had been forced to do frontier work as a pioneer girl in bondage. She had to learn how to hitch a massive felled tree to an ox team and drag it out of the woods to a building site. She had to learn how to notch a log with an axe so it fit snug and sure atop another and then another until a cabin was complete. She had to learn how to find the best patch of woodland in which to tether the milk cow so it could feed on oak leaves when there was no grass to be found.

All this while war waged, making this a more dangerous frontier than those to the south. The rumblings of the War of 1812 had started in 1811 in the Northwest Territory. In that year the Battle of Tippecanoe, just up the Wabash River from where Keziah was living, helped bring the nation toward war with the British and their allied Native Americans. Before she knew it, Keziah was on the front lines of the battle. She and the family who owned her may well have had to flee to nearby Fort Allison to keep from being killed.

They had all survived; they had all stayed, despite the war, even though the pioneer population on the western side of the Wabash River had plummeted during the conflict.[9]

But even after the war ended, there were still so many dangers.

There were always the wolves. Keziah would have heard them howling close on a winter night, those same wolves that had so terrified the English explorer William Faux, who had risked a trip to this wilderness around the same time Keziah and Charles were married. Faux had stayed in the more settled town of Evansville, close to the Ohio River. But even there the wolves "howled and prowled into town" till the explorer had shivered with fear in his bed.[10]

But Keziah did not have the luxury of shivering inside, in bed or anywhere else. She would have had to be up and out in the cold darkness of a winter morning to empty the chamber pots, bring in the wood, and build a fire to warm the white people who still slept under thick blankets. The others who labored with her would have been up as well, all of them people in bondage north of the Ohio River.

Of course they were supposed to be free in this free land. But they were living on the frontier, and the men responsible for upholding the ban on slavery had little interest in doing so. Many of the administrators of the Northwest Territory moving into Vincennes on the Wabash River were avid pro-slavery men. This meant that the people who held Keziah in bondage—asleep in the cabin while she worked—were bringing their own laws north with them, trampling her rights just as surely as Keziah trampled down the fresh snow to make a path to the barn.[11]

Oh, it was cold—colder than she could have ever imagined.

Did she remember her first glimpse of snow when she had arrived from South Carolina? Had she tried to catch the delicate flakes that first winter as they flew through the air like petals in springtime? Now they only stung her face like a swarm of frozen bees, blown so thick and fierce by the wind that she could not have seen any wolves even if they had stood just a few feet away, watching her trying to survive.

Years later, as more and more people in America who called themselves white began to make viciously prejudicial arguments about the inherently inferior nature of people from Africa, did Keziah wonder at the illogical world they seemed to inhabit? As an enslaved laborer she was considered an appropriate settler on the frontier, but as a free woman she was not. The contradiction was hard to miss.

Then again she may have shrugged her strong shoulders, not surprised at what little sense people made when driven by their baser passions—whether greed, jealousy, fear, or hate.

At least she could know that, no matter what others thought of her, she was loved by Charles.

He was her own. There was no family to introduce them, no fussing aunt or grandmother to arrange a meal after church. No cousin to vouch for his character. She only knew him after he had come north.

But she would have watched, and she saw him weather what would make most men founder.

Word must have gotten around when Charles bought his first forty acres in 1815 from the federal land agent's office in Vincennes. That first growing season on his land may have been a good one. But then the world came to an end.

The weather had already been running cold for years, but in 1816 summer disappeared entirely. Few knew that in a place now called Indonesia a volcano had erupted, blowing ash into the upper atmosphere, shadowing the earth. The sunsets were wonderful, but then spring never came. The frost lay heavy on the ground, refusing to loosen and thaw. And then it snowed in June.

This cold was not merely uncomfortable; it was deadly. Many people in the United States were subsistence farmers like Charles, and the lost summer meant lost crops. And with no crops, people starved from New York to the frontier.[12]

At least there was the forest filled with animals. They too were starving, but a squirrel or pigeon could make a passable stew, seasoned with the tough wild onions that could still be found under the snow. But Charles must have been gaunt when he courted Keziah, his clothes cinched tight and bunching around his waist, his bones sharp against her hands when they first embraced.

Maybe it was the fact that he had survived that terrible year without starving or turning to despair or to drink. Maybe it was the fact that even though he had seen so much, survived so much, he still had a heart to give. And so they got married in 1818.[13]

Like Keziah, Charles had lived most of his life enslaved. He had been born in Virginia in 1782 to an enslaved woman. This meant that from the moment Charles took breath, he was in bondage. However, he was proud that he knew the exact day of his birth.[14]

Charles might have stayed an enslaved person until death but for the death of the man who owned him. The will handed Charles down, like a piece of furniture or a farm animal, to a pastor by the name of James Grier. The Reverend James Grier then made the astonishing decision to free the man given to him—a deliberate decision to sacrifice his financial gain, for Charles was walking wealth, either sold or kept. Many men did not have the courage to do this, but James did, and Charles would take his last name in recognition of the Reverend James Grier's extraordinary act.[15]

But just because James Grier wanted to free Charles did not mean that he could easily do so. As early as 1691 the leaders of the Virginia colony had passed a law making the manumission of enslaved people more difficult. And while Virginia had softened some of those laws during the Revolution, by 1813 it had put back numerous legal hurdles in place to block freedom—an ironic truth during this time when the nation was trying to preserve its freedom from British bondage.[16]

One of the most challenging legal hurdles was an 1806 law stating that anyone freed in Virginia had to leave that state within twelve months or risk reenslavement. This was a dreadful requirement for anyone with an enslaved family, and Charles may have had to leave behind beloved kin to come to the Indiana Territorial frontier. Perhaps he was still grieving their loss when he met Keziah. And she would have been grieving losses as well, because being enslaved meant facing constant loss, not just of freedom but of family and community.

Beyond the surprise of freedom was the surprise of the location of that freeing. Most Virginians who desired to free the people they held in bondage headed due north to Ohio because it was the closest portion of the free frontier. But by 1807 Ohio had already created laws hampering the settlement of recently freed people like Charles. These Black Laws insisted that all African American settlers had to prove they were free and, worse, had to find two men on the frontier willing to deposit a bond totaling $500, supposedly to ensure that free people of African descent would not hamper the local economy. In reality, this law discouraged free African American immigration into the state, for $500 was a crippling sum.[17]

Whatever the reasons, in his thirty-first year Charles was brought to the western edge of the Indiana Territory to be free. And once brought, he had to survive.

Keziah had seen him do just that. And she had grown to love him.

There must have been affection, an attachment, an understanding between them. They were not forced together; they chose each other.

Even in their portion of the Great West, there were choices. This was not about blood or color; this was about the human heart and sympathetic minds. And there were certainly others of a similar mind to either Charles or Keziah. Marriage between people of different backgrounds, different colors, different languages was not unheard of out on the frontier. But Charles and Keziah had a good deal in common. The sorrow for one thing. Both had endured the hardship of being brought to the wilderness from a home place.

Now they had each other, and their church—Elder Wasson's New Lights congregation—and there were others around them as well who shared their ancestry and some of their hardships. Everyone would have known about the Morrises, Andersons, Tanns, Goinses, Coles, Portees,

Caseys, Byrds, Days, Pettifords, and others in and around Fort Allison, just across the Wabash River. They were also pioneers of African descent, but they were the earliest, and they were the freest. And they and their friends were bringing a radical vision of freedom and equality to the Northwest Territory frontier.[18]

This group had arrived free around 1800 to help to build Fort Allison. The Northwest Territory was a dangerous place to build anything in 1800, much less a fort. It is little wonder that this small group of Americans started gathering to pray together.[19]

They were only a small group of Americans living along the Wabash River, trying to lay claim to a territory where the United States was barely recognized as having dominion. Indeed, their new nation barely existed. The Revolutionary War was over, but many in the country were unsure about the break with England, and the United States was having a hard time staying united, much less laying claim to its vast new Northwest Territory. And the local peoples were none too pleased with these upstart Americans trying to take what the British and the French had previously agreed were the sovereign lands of the First Nations.

But this small band of families had made the long and difficult journey west in order to stake a personal and national claim to this frontier. Among them were the free African American brothers Sian and John Morris and their families.

Despite their endangered and uncertain lives, the families of Fort Allison held a strong belief about what America should look like. Indeed, their group symbolized their hopes for an integrated, free, and equal America.

By 1806, John Morris helped to found the Maria Creek Baptist Church. He and all the members knew that people were enslaved all along the Wabash River, their bondage legalized through loopholes in the Northwest Ordinance. But his integrated band of frontier folk was intent on making clear that the United States should be a place for freedom and justice for all. So when writing their church's charter, John Morris and his white and black brethren included the stipulation that their congregation would grant slave owners neither membership nor communion.[20]

Of course, they were still intent upon fighting the Native peoples of the region to clear them from the land so that immigrants from the east could purchase and farm it. By 1818 free African American Indian scouts were already the stuff of legend. Austin Tann had worked out of Fort Allison as an Indian scout. In 1810, when only nineteen, he had watched as the Indiana territorial governor, William Henry Harrison, met with the Native American leader Tecumseh.[21]

However, their belief in the equality of people of African and European descent put these African-descended people at Fort Allison on the front lines not only of the new nation but of the debate that was already tearing apart the fragile fabric of the American territorial settlement. Just up the river from them was Vincennes, a town founded by the French in the eighteenth century, and many of its elite French-descended residents owned slaves. They were soon joined by the new members of the territorial government, including Governor Harrison who was appointed as governor of the Indiana Territory in 1800 at the age of twenty-seven. The Indiana Territory at that time was a region covering almost all the Northwest Territory except for a portion of what is now the state of Ohio. Harrison was a man who put his ideals into action. The young Virginia-born politician illegally brought enslaved people into the territory and forced them to support his life there while he waged his battle to make slave labor legal in the region he was governing. Harrison was determined to make his stand on the frontier to force the issue of slavery.[22]

Yet the Morrises, and the other families at Fort Allison, both white and black, were also determined to hold to their ideals, even if it meant angering or alienating powerful people in the settlement nearest to them.

While the Maria Creek Baptist Church would have welcomed them, Charles and Keziah belonged to a different congregation, a little outpost of the New Lights order led by Elder Wasson, an ardent abolitionist who had come from Virginia with James and Charles Grier. All these

Virginians, black and white, brought with them opposing positions on slavery and the future of their new nation. But they were intent upon making their vision a reality by living it out—Governor Harrison by forcing illegally enslaved people to build him mansions while the Griers and Elder Wasson worshipped together and supported each other.[23]

So, Keziah and Charles were far from alone, even when they were first married.

This meant much.

Starting out as a pioneer is hard, no matter what the color of one's skin. But doing so as a newly freed person brought its own challenges, even with friends nearby. There were no kin to come along and settle around, offering help with building a cabin or birthing a baby. There was no one back home who could hearten with letters or send support—in either money or food—when times got hard. And times always got hard.

But this was 1818, and the Griers had hope for a good harvest. It must have been hard to plant on that hard-won ground without fearing frost and famine. These were some of the hardest farming times ever known, and the recent freezes would have scared everyone. Even finding starter seeds to sow in the spring would have been challenging.

And both knew that even if everything went well, crops growing to ripeness in their fields, their work was barely begun. If they grew corn, then they had to pick each ear, making sure it was stored so that it stayed dry over the winter. True, some kept the corn in the fields, if they had a dog or two to keep the wildlife away, for the field of standing corn could become a pantry place, with the corn gathered when needed.

But grain was the hardest work of all. Some pioneers were so eager to plant on the land they had cleared that they seeded too much and watched their bounty rot in the field, unable to harvest it quickly enough. Even the strongest and most skilled men could only harvest about a quarter acre a day, using a technology that had changed little in thousands of years. When the crop was ripe and ready for harvest, Charles and Keziah would sharpen their scythes and move out into the field, swinging low and hard to cut the stalks. But cutting the stalks was not enough; the stalks then had to be raked and bundled quickly so they could dry and be protected. It took at least two people to harvest grain. Often it was considered women's work to rake and gather the fallen stalks, but necessity would have required that Charles and Keziah trade off, as shoulders burned and arms trembled from the hard hacking.[24]

Yes, Keziah and Charles had strength and hope. They had created their own home and were creating their own lives rooted deep in their land. By summer the woods were full of racket, everything growing louder at twilight. As evening drew on, only the bats were quiet, flitting above the clearing Charles and Keziah had created near their cabin, while the fireflies glowed green above the growing buckwheat.

Their plow was put away near to them in the cabin, safe and enclosed, for they had learned that creatures from bears to squirrels would gnaw on the handles soaked with their sweat and salt.

They had planted in hope, and they hoped they would soon harvest.

But something else was growing to the south of them that must have been troubling. That second frontier, the Louisiana Purchase, had been opened to slavery. Some had argued that it would thin slavery out to the point that it would disappear. After all, the nation had moved to ban the international slave trade in 1808, and many had dreamed that ending the importation of enslaved people would finally drive the tyranny of slavery out of the United States.[25]

But it was coming back to life.

And soon, Charles and Keziah would find themselves working to assure others could also be free, for they were an African American farming family close to the border of slave states that were fast filling with misery. More people were crossing the Ohio River, refugees from bondage, willing to grow their own liberty, even if many whites in the nation seemed intent on expanding slavery.

2

Interlude:
"We hold these truths to
be self-evident"

Why was there a space called the Northwest Territory? And how did it start out as the largest piece of land in North America to be free of slavery and to allow equal voting rights for black and white men?

It certainly did not seem like a place suited to nurturing high ideals, especially those connected to liberty and equality. The region later known as the Northwest Territory had long been a difficult frontier wracked by conflict—conflict that would lead to the birth of the United States in 1776. The French and Indian War raged there for years. The British defeated the roughly 60,000 French loyalists who lived in that region, along with their Native American allies, in 1763, allowing them to claim the French lands stretching to the Mississippi River. The British colonists had wanted to make this realm their new frontier. Already, colonists were moving in. But King George III snatched it from their grasp, setting aside a large portion of it for its rightful owners—the Native Americans. Powerful and wealthy fur companies, counselors to the king, saw the region as a source of fur rather than farmland.[1]

Much has been made of a Tea Party in Boston, but the loss of the Northwest Territory infuriated colonists far outside that city, leading even the most loyal British subjects to consider rebelling. And when they did rebel, winning the Northwest Territory was considered one of the Revolution's greatest triumphs, practically doubling the size of the new nation. Almost as soon as the British gave it up in 1783, the United States made certain that it would be available for settlement, and plans were soon being made to divide the entire region into plots and sell it.[2]

But African-descended people had been living in this region long before the signing of the Declaration of Independence. Some of the earliest known people of African descent in this region were the enslaved people brought by the Frenchman Philip Francois Renault in 1720. Renault was well known to King Louis XV, who had given him permission to explore north up the Mississippi River. Renault hoped to make his fortune by forcing the hundreds of people he brought with him to dig lead mines in the wilderness of what would later be western Illinois. Renault may have been a sophisticated and successful French courtier, but the people he brought in chains may have also been well traveled. Renault had purchased them on the French colonial island of Saint-Domingue in the Caribbean, on his way from France to the American continent.[3]

The people he purchased could have been born in Europe, the New World, or various nations on the African continent, for Saint-Domingue was home to people of many cultures and backgrounds. But in 1720 the people whom Renault brought with him held a common kinship—the chains of bondage and the success of survival.

There is no record of how many of these people died or managed to escape from the mines and farms Renault tried to establish. As Renault must have found, forcing people to labor is much easier on an island flanked by weapon-wielding Europeans and surrounded by the sea. It was another situation entirely trying to keep people in bondage in the middle of a vast uncharted land that was home to various nations, many of them hostile to colonial ambitions. Philip Renault gave up in his attempts after a few years, heading back down the Mississippi and selling the last people he held enchained before heading back to France, where he must have been vague about just how many people he had lost in the New World.

But people kept bringing enslaved African-descended peoples into what would become the Northwest Territory, and the region continued to be a haven for freedom seekers. Of course, because they intended to stay free, they would not have been eager to allow themselves to be counted by French officials wandering through that wild region trying to get accurate census counts of the non-Native peoples living there. By the late eighteenth century, people of African descent were scattered across this unsettled territory, fluent in French, English, and numerous native languages, adept at surviving and flourishing, often living closely with Native Americans.[4]

When the first American surveyors came to plat the Northwest Territory, one even noted a settlement of free African-descended people in the Wabash River valley in today's Indiana. The settlement was so extensive and established that he could not resist noting it—drawing a fancy curled circle around his notation with his quill pen.[5]

And in a shocking move, in 1787 the Northwest Ordinance, the governing document of this region, ordered, "There shall be neither slavery nor involuntary servitude in the said territory," making the territory the largest piece of the continent ever to be set aside for freedom since colonization. This was a hard-won and difficult decision. Powerful white men knew the profits enslaved people could make in the New World, and men like them had been working people to death doing just that since the earliest colonial days. Instead, the Northwest Territory became a haven for freedom, although not in the way that many people imagine.[6]

The iconic traveler of African descent moving into and through the antebellum Old Northwest has long been imagined as enslaved, a refugee in rags, relying on white people for help and for liberty. But most of the African American pioneers to the Northwest Territory and states—at least those who allowed themselves to be counted on the federal census—were already free. Indeed, they likely had to prove their freedom to settle and purchase land in this territory.

True, millions of whites were joining them. The Northwest Territory states saw one of the largest movements of human beings from one region of the planet to another. Within fifty years of the territory's opening for sale, it went from being the home to its original peoples—the Native Americans—and a few thousand immigrants from other lands to over 4 million settlers.[7]

But in those early years of nationhood, the land that Keziah and Charles Grier were working was part of a larger project in the nation, a project worked through with words. Words that spread ideas like roots through this young nation, words that were growing ideas of something new and strange.

> From the first dawning of the human mind,
> Children should be instructed to be kind:
> To treat no human being with disdain,
> Nor give the meanest insect useless pain. . . .
> Our blessed Lord descended to unbind
> Those chains of darkness which enslave the mind;
> He draws the veil of prejudice aside,
> To cure us of our selfishness and pride. . . .
> The same eternal hopes to all are given,
> One common Savior and one common heaven.
> When these exalted views th'ascendant gain,
> Fraternal love will form a silken chain,
> Whose band, encircling all the human race,
> Will join the species in one large embrace.[8]

These may sound like words to a nineteenth-century hymn written during the rise of a new abolitionist movement in the 1830s or during the difficult days of the Civil War, but they were written remarkably early—in 1805. They come from a poem written by a white woman, Isabella Oliver, who lived in Pennsylvania, and she was writing for an audience hungry for the themes of liberty and equality. For she was writing during a period that saw the new nation swept by a fervor for freedom.

But this fervor was born of earlier poems, earlier writings. Beautiful, clever, and funny words that had very real power. One of America's first great poets, the African-born Phillis Wheatley, had written these words while enslaved in 1773:

No more, America, in mournful strain,
Of wrongs and grievance unredressed complain;
No longer shall thou dread the iron chain
Which wanton Tyranny, with lawless hand,
Has made, and with it meant t'enslave the land.[9]

Phillis Wheatley wrote those words before the Revolutionary War, and now that war was over. The colonies had managed to survive and win it. But that bloody and nasty conflict had been riddled with division and prejudice. Some may well have been fighting to preserve and grow slavery, while many others were encouraged to fight by forming a hostile bond of hatred for those of African descent and Native Americans, even as those of African descent and Native Americans fought as patriots alongside them.[10]

As the new nation emerged from that war, there was little solid ground left to stand on. There was not even a constitution. There was, however, the Declaration of Independence. And this was one of the most radical statements in that revolutionary document: "We hold these truths to be self-evident, that all men are created equal, that they are endowed by their Creator with certain unalienable Rights, that among these are Life, Liberty and the Pursuit of Happiness."[11]

The men who crafted this document had been born into a world where most people assumed the exact opposite: that God had decreed that some men were born to rule and some to be ruled, that the order of the world was monarchy, not democracy, and that some people would always enslave others. While the men who actually signed the Declaration may not have had the imagination or courage to envision a nation where all men were truly free and equal, others around them were acting on these ideals, their imaginations sparked by a new way of thinking about people and societies, a movement called the Enlightenment.[12]

Not all these Enlightenment thinkers were antislavery, but many were. And some of these thinkers opposed not just slavery but prejudice.[13]

James Otis was one of the best-known and most influential American writers of the revolutionary period. He wrote formal letters of complaint to the British government that were printed and read throughout the colonies. In 1764 he wrote, "The Colonists are by the law of nature free born, as indeed all men are, white or black. . . . Does it follow that tis right to enslave a man because he is black?" He added with irony that people of prejudice liked to point to physical differences between Africans and Europeans as a reason for enslavement. But, he argued, "will short curl'd hair like wool, instead of Christian hair, as tis called by those, whose hearts are as hard as the nether millstone, help the argument?"[14]

Otis also referred to the brilliant and satirical arguments against prejudice and slavery of the French philosopher the Baron de Montesquieu, whose work from 1748 was popular and well known in revolutionary-era America. Montesquieu was already familiar with the many arguments slavers made to defend their enslavement of people from Africa. And knowing this he wrote a devastating and very funny attack on every defense of slavery they put forth.

One of Montesquieu's arguments goes straight to the heart of a defense of slavery made by enslavers and their allies in the United States even a century after he wrote. Those prejudiced enslavers in America in the 1800s were hauntingly like their counterparts in the 1700s, arguing that slavery was not an evil but a kindness because those they enslaved were lacking in essential human traits that would enable them to care for themselves or live independently. Montesquieu addresses the argument at its face, stating that if slavery "is pretended to be beneficial" because enslaved people are at least "provided subsistence," then it follows that only those people "incapable of earning their livelihood" should be enslaved. Montesquieu then asks why anyone would want to employ such a diminished worker. He does admit that babies could possibly fall into the category of those "benefitting" from slavery because they require assistance to live. But as he points out, "Nature" has supplied to infants "mothers with milk" for their food, so they need not become enslaved to be cared for.[15]

And Montesquieu criticized not only slavery but prejudice based on skin color and ancestry, which he saw as dangerous to society because "prejudices eradicate every tender disposition." He also led his readers to see both how ridiculous and how deadly prejudice was by presenting a story about the ancient Egyptians (whom he called "the best philosophers in the world") being so prejudiced against people with red hair that they killed them.[16]

In addition to these European and American writers, African-born and African-descended writers were also writing powerful critiques of slavery and prejudice. Olaudah Equiano, one of the most internationally renowned African-descended writers of the Enlightenment, wrote a moving narrative of his capture and enslavement as a child and his life in bondage. He knew that many Europeans defended enslavement of Africans on the grounds that they were "uncultivated." But, as he wrote, "let the polished and haughty European recollect, that *his* ancestors were once . . . uncivilized, even barbarous. Did nature make *them* inferior to their sons? And should *they too* have been made slaves?"[17]

These were not just fine and funny words. These were powerful new ideas, and they were being used to make revolutionary changes, for Americans were acting on those ideals in a way that the Western world had never seen.[18]

People started to give up slavery.

When the Declaration of Independence was signed in 1776, there was no North or South. There were no slave and free states, there were just slave colonies. Every single colony allowed slavery and had enslaved people.

The Declaration voiced an almost insane hope for a different kind of government, a different kind of nation, one ruled by the people, where all would be born with the opportunity for "life, liberty and the pursuit of happiness." Some of the writers of that document had wanted even more. They wanted to condemn slavery. They knew that creating a truly free nation would not be easy. But they believed, with many Americans at the time, that slavery must end.[19]

Indeed, many of the men who signed the Declaration of Independence thought that the system of slavery was evil. They may have thought it was essential but not good. Even Thomas Jefferson, already deeply prejudiced and hungry for the wealth that enslaved people could bring him, wanted to include the stain of slavery as a reason for the country to become independent. He wrote a statement later cut from the Declaration of Independence, accusing King George III of waging "cruel war against human nature itself, violating its most sacred right of life and liberty in the persons of a distant people who never offended him, captivating them and carrying them into slavery in another hemisphere, or to incur miserable death in their transportation thither. This piratical warfare, the opprobrium of infidel powers, is the warfare of the Christian King of Great Britain, determined to keep open a market where men should be bought and sold."[20]

Jefferson, like many Americans at that time, held conflicting views about slavery and equality. Unlike Jefferson, however, many Americans during these revolutionary times were moving beyond words and acting on the best ideals of the nation, moving it toward the goals of freedom and equality in concrete ways. And even before the war was won, the revolution for freedom had begun.

True, when finally signed in 1787, the Constitution included much meant to strengthen the power of enslavers to keep people in bondage—even if those people tried to run or rebel. And patriots with printing presses had done everything they could to foment hate and prejudice to rouse the fighting spirits of white men. But even before there was a constitution, the fervor for freedom had started. Enslaved people knew of the words of the Declaration of Independence, those words about the self-evident truth that all men are created equal and that all those equally created men have a right to life, liberty, and the pursuit of happiness. And their white lawyers knew those words. And their white judges knew those words. And, together, they were acting on them.[21]

Around 1781 an enslaved man called Quok Walker sued for his freedom in a Massachusetts court. Other enslaved people were petitioning for their freedom as well, including a woman called Mumbet. And when they won in 1783, they won freedom for their entire state. For the judge agreed that—among other things—slavery was at direct odds with the words of the Massachusetts constitution about the equality of men. As a group of enslaved people in New Hampshire argued to a judge in 1779, while the Revolutionary War still raged, "Freedom is the inherent right of the human species."[22]

But it was more than the courts, it was the idea of liberty. Enslaved people had been suing for and even winning their freedom for a while, without effecting more than their own individual freedom. But that was before the Declaration of Independence. That was before the Revolution.

Some white Americans had been turning toward freedom because of their faith. Quakers, many of them from the southern slave colonies, had decided that human bondage was a sin. And they had been working to free hundreds of the people they held enslaved. The Episcopal Methodist Church, at its first conference in 1784, took a firm stand on slavery and the equality of all people, regardless of the color of their skin, stating, "Slavery is contrary to the laws of God, man, and nature, and hurtful to society; contrary to the dictates of conscience and true religion; and doing what we would not others should do unto us." And in 1794 the general assembly of the Presbyterian Church resolved that any person who "keeps, sells or buys" a human being is a "man stealer," which is "the highest kind of theft" and a violation of the Eighth Commandment.[23]

As the ideas of freedom and equality were gaining power, whole states started tipping toward freedom.

Vermont was first in 1777, before some even thought of it as a state, and then more started joining the cause. By 1804 seven more states had followed Vermont's lead, including Pennsylvania, New Hampshire, Massachusetts, Connecticut, and Rhode Island. This meant that a total of eight of the nation's original thirteen colonies had voluntarily decided to end slavery by 1804.

These were not easy decisions, for they had an impact not only on those who owned enslaved people but on those who were involved in the lucrative slave trade. And when the slave state of New York finally decided to gradually abolish slavery in 1799, the other slave states must have been stunned.

New York Harbor is today filled with boats of tourists traveling past a statue dedicated to liberty. But once those same waters carried massive ships filled with people in chains. And the sale of those who survived the brutal and often deadly journey was making some New Yorkers very wealthy. In 1785, after fierce resistance, New York decided to end the sale of enslaved people imported into the state, effectively closing its ports to those massive ships. And in 1799 that state decided to slowly end slavery. This turning away from wealth toward liberty must have been a shock to the remaining slave states. True, it was a slow turning, and for years an incomplete and far from perfect one. But it was still a turning.[24]

In other states where whites could not be convinced to officially give up enslavement, granting freedom was made easier. Colonial Virginia had long had laws intended to make manumission very challenging. But this was a new time and a new nation, and even Virginia eased its restrictions on liberation. Between 1782 and 1806 roughly 10,000 people were recorded as freed in that state. And North Carolina's free African American population rose from roughly 5,000 in 1790 to over 10,200 in 1810, despite its much stricter manumission laws. We may never have an accurate count, however, of the men and women freed, as many were never counted and others, like Charles Grier, were leaving slave states in order to be freed.[25]

Other states, like Maryland and Delaware, made new laws not only encouraging freedom but also discouraging the removal or sale of an enslaved person out of the state. This meant that by the time the Civil War broke out, most people of African descent in Delaware were free.[26]

This was an extraordinary time, full of confusion and conflict but also hope.

And moves were also being made toward equality. The Northwest Territory almost doubled the landmass of the new United States, and that region was designated slavery-free. But another clause in the Northwest Ordinance was significant—a clause for equality. For the ordinance gave all freemen the right to vote.[27]

To be sure those freemen—or anyone else who wanted to vote almost everywhere in the nation at this time—had to be men. And they had to be property owners. The writers of the ordinance decided that a man must own fifty acres to vote and two hundred acres to run for office. There were other caveats as well, but none of them, not one, mentioned skin color. This was not an omission; this was knowing inclusion. It was understood that if skin color was not mentioned, then any property-holding man over the age of twenty-one could vote.[28]

Indeed, the wording of the ordinance was very similar to North Carolina's 1776 constitution, which also stated, among other lengthy requirements, that "all freeman of the age of twenty-one years" could vote. But none of those requirements used the word "white." And soon, free propertied African American men were voting in North Carolina.[29]

And North Carolina was not alone. By 1792 ten other states had similar constitutions, refusing to use color to confine the vote, including the newly created state of Kentucky, which had entered the union that year. Of course, in that same year whites in Delaware, in a backlash against the growing number of free people of African descent in their state, worked hard to exclude all but whites from the right to vote. Still, in 1792, on the eve of the nation's second election, as it stood poised to reelect George Washington as president, the entire Northwest Territory as well as eleven of the nation's fifteen states had decided to use inclusive language regarding voting rights in their constitutions.[30]

Of course, this was not a perfect time or a perfect period of freeing. While this passion for liberty may have been popular, and social pressure was being brought to bear on white enslavers to give up the wealth they had amassed by owning people, not everyone was enthusiastic. Most states, regardless of whether some might have been thought of as southerly or northerly, had active abolitionist organizations, but Georgia and South Carolina never did. And some of the states that had officially abolished slavery decided to end the practice so gradually that it would take decades before all people were free. Indeed, some whites in New Jersey were so loath to encourage the course of liberty that they still held people enslaved when the Civil War broke out.[31]

Today we can easily view slavery as such a poisonous institution that its demise was all but inevitable. But in early America, its ending required tremendous social and economic change and was far from certain. Nothing about freedom was fated. It faced fierce resistance.

As Manisha Sinha points out in *The Slave's Cause*, her magisterial book on the struggle to end slavery in America, almost every case in which a state abolished slavery at this time involved the efforts of both people of African descent and their white allies to challenge the system of bondage. They were rarely loved or lauded for their resistance; instead they were often punished for their work.

And even as people were working together to end slavery and fight for equality, prejudiced whites were working to diminish or eliminate equality and freedom. But African Americans and their white allies were aware of this backlash. They understood that they had to constantly renew, reinforce, and defend the fervor for freedom, and equality. Nothing was guaranteed, not even the clause in the Constitution that seemed to promise the end of the slave trade in 1808.

And the members of abolition societies across the new United States knew of this resistance as well. That was one reason why roughly two dozen of these revolutionary abolitionists decided to meet in Philadelphia in 1794. They had been active in their own states but had never convened like this before. Maybe they had been inspired by another revolution. Just a few months earlier, representatives from Saint-Domingue had landed in Philadelphia. They represented the leaders of the most successful slave revolt in the new world—a war that had been fought and won in Saint-Domingue in 1791. They arrived in Philadelphia with their French white abolitionist allies, who had just formally announced that the entire island was free of slavery. One of those allies was the French-born abolitionist August Polverel, who had been the one to make the official proclamation of the abolition of all slavery on the Caribbean island of Saint-Domingue. In that proclamation, Polverel stated, "The slavery of a single individual is incompatible with the principles of the Republic." The nations acting upon these revolutionary ideals had a relationship so intertwined that the ship Polverel traveled on, in order to make his proclamation to the residents of Saint-Domingue, was named *America*. But America, France, and Saint-Domingue had long had intertwined histories, bound together by slavery as well as freedom. For this was the same Caribbean island that the French Philip Renault had come to in the 1720s to purchase people to work the lands that would later become the state of Illinois. Now, seventy years later, delegates from Saint-Domingue—European-born, African-born, and Saint-Domingue-born—had stopped in America on their way to Paris to announce this important emancipation to the new Revolutionary National Convention now trying to lead the radical Republic of France—because France was now a revolutionary nation as well.[32]

News of the Saint-Domingue revolution of 1791 and the French Revolution had swept Europe and the Americas. But there was already resistance, and when the delegates from Saint-Domingue landed in Philadelphia, they were physically attacked by French sailors as they disembarked from their ship. The African-born delegate Jean-Baptiste Belley bore the brunt of the attack.[33]

But the delegates survived, made it to New York, and sailed for France. Arriving in Paris they went to the Convention Hall, where one of the French deputies rose to greet them, announcing that these revolutionary men from across the Atlantic—African, Caribbean, and European—were making it possible to complete the project of the Revolution. The French deputy added that while the French revolutionaries had succeeded in dismantling the hierarchies of the monarchy and the church, these delegates from Saint-Domingue would help France overcome the "aristocracy of skin," to win the battle against prejudice directed at African-descended people.[34]

And when the French National Convention affirmed that slavery was "abolished throughout the territory of the Republic; in consequence, all men, without distinction of color, will enjoy the rights of French citizens," the African-born revolutionary leader Jean-Baptiste Belley stood up amid the applause and, in a voice loud enough to be heard above the noise in the hall, proclaimed that his actions over the decades since he had made himself free by purchasing himself made him a true revolutionary and valuable citizen of the new republic.[35]

Many at that first abolitionist convention in Philadelphia were also working toward these same two goals: ending slavery and abolishing inequality based on skin color. They worked hard for days to write a petition to the federal government, arguing for many causes, including the immediate end of slavery, a halt to the sale of enslaved people from the United States for export to other nations, and the defense of the rights of all free American men, no matter what their skin color.[36]

These American revolutionary abolitionists wrote in that petition, "Many reasons concur in persuading us to abolish domestic slavery in our country. It is inconsistent with the safety of the liberties of the United States," for "freedom and slavery cannot long exist together"— echoing the words and sentiments of August Polverel in his speech on Saint-Domingue.[37]

Even if the abolitionists in Philadelphia in 1794 had not heard Polverel's exact words, they understood the context for their statement. So the convention of delegates of this early abolitionist organization carefully put together their petitions, urging the federal government not just to join with the revolutions in Saint-Domingue and France but to lead the charge for liberty and equality. As they wrote, "What people will advocate freedom . . . while they view the purest republic in the world tolerating in its bosom a body of slaves?" After all, this was "America, dignified by being the first in modern times, to assert and defend the equal rights of man."[38]

While these abolitionists praised the work done to give free property-owning African American men the equal right to vote in some states, they urged that all forms of racial prejudice be overturned, arguing that the new nation should have an "exploding of the general opinion that the color of a man is evidence of his deprivation of the rights of man." They added that the fervor of freedom that was already sweeping the nation, causing whole states to abolish slavery, would not be a complete project without equality, for in "removing the sorrows of slavery, what do we effect, if the new-made man is relieved from the power of one, only to be sensible of his hopeless inferiority to all?" Criticizing unjust and prejudiced laws, the petitioners asked how a free man of color could own property and start a business if "the law does not spread its defense around him?" And they were quick to remind the federal government that equal protection under the law was a right, not a "privilege" or a "favour."[39]

These men were writing this during a time of great uncertainty and instability in the United States. The new nation was deeply in debt, and pirates were even attacking its ships and taking white Americans into slavery. If ever there were a time for the federal government to use any excuse it could think of to avoid living up to the expensive and difficult ideals of liberty and equality, this would be it. This would have been the time to ignore abolitionists' petitions. This would have been the time to pass gag laws to silence anyone petitioning the federal government to end slavery.

But instead, the federal government responded constructively. In almost apologetic language, it reminded the abolitionists of the limits of the federal government's jurisdiction. But it did agree to end the sale and exportation of enslaved people from the United States. It was a small gesture, given that the institution of slavery persisted, but in a young nation, the profits from the slave trade were a real economic sacrifice in the name of moral progress. The nation's leaders were willing to take at least a limited stand.[40]

It certainly seemed like a stand to the DeWolf family, one of the wealthiest in the United States at that time. Their wealth was based on slave trading—bringing shiploads of horror in and out of Rhode Island, which like New York and other eastern coastal states had made a fortune from that trade. And the DeWolfs used every tactic, most illegal, to continue their lucrative trade even after its official abolition.[41]

The fight against freedom was not limited to such tactics.

Even with their success, the abolitionists gathered in Philadelphia knew that they—and many others—would need to continue to work hard to move forward against the powers that were opposing the goals of liberty and equality.

Already whites in the section of the Northwest Territory now called the Ohio Territory were going to court to complain about the ban on slavery, and there were rumors that other states would soon join Delaware in excluding African Americans from the right to vote. Then, in 1799, possibly in response to the new state of Tennessee's decision to allow voting rights for all, prejudiced whites in Kentucky denied African Americans equal voting rights just seven years after becoming a state with equal voting rights. In 1801 whites in Maryland followed suit. And in 1807, New Jersey's white residents, who had only decided in 1804 to take the slowest path to ending slavery possible, were already so concerned about the weakening of their status that they actually reversed the state's constitution and barred black New Jersey citizens from voting.[42]

More troubling still, the slave powers had their sights on the Northwest Territory, and they were working hard to grow slavery and diminish equality there. For they could see that the two were connected—that with equal rights came equal power, and that power might undermine slavery.

In 1802 whites in Ohio petitioned to make it a slave state as soon as it applied for statehood, and for a brief period it looked like they might win. That same year, pro-slavery activist William Henry Harrison, the first governor of the Indiana Territory, joined forces with some of the enslavers around him to petition that the territory allow slaves, even temporarily. This was not an unimportant petition, for the Indiana Territory at that time covered a vast area. However, Harrison and his allies knew they had to tread carefully, for popular opinion was still against slavery at that time. So, they put a great deal of thought into their petition, delicately explaining that they understood that there were a "variety of opinions" on the subject of slavery and that while some thought it "decent and just" to hold people enslaved, many in America thought the practice evil. Indeed, they went to great length describing the disgust Americans felt toward slavery, adding that most thought of it as "a crime of the deepest stain; that it is repugnant to every opinion of natural justice, of political rights, and to every sentiment of humanity." In the end, they begged that the evil of slavery be laid lightly on the territory only for a brief period so that it could be more quickly settled.[43]

They would have said none of this if they did not believe that the sentiment against slavery was popular at that time, for only a fool states a counterargument in a debate unless it has very real weight and power against his claim. And Harrison and his men were no fools. But Harrison would have sent his petition off with some hope, for he also knew he had a terrible practicality on his side.

First, he asked only for a temporary period of ten years. Over and over he stressed that the enslavement of people was awful but suggested that using small groups of enslaved people to clear the frontier might be slightly better than working them to death on a large rice plantation in South Carolina. But, as Keziah Grier and others like her knew, separating children from their families, bringing them lonely and heartbroken to the frontier, and forcing them to clear land for their enslavers was not exactly a kindness.

Still, William Henry Harrison knew that the federal government wanted the land he governed controlled and cleared. This was no easy task in a place where Native Americans had been in contact with Europeans for over a century, were armed and sophisticated, and had no interest in seeing the new young nation of the United States usurp their land. Harrison knew that the politicians back east expected him to control this territory and open it to settlement, and so he was arguing that, distasteful as it might be, forcing enslaved people to clear the forests, even if many were lost (as many probably would be), was better than losing the region so recently won from the French and now the British. Yet even Harrison's delicately worded petition, with its veiled threat about losing control of the Indiana Territory, could not win. Though sent to a committee headed by a congressman from Virginia, his petition was rejected.[44]

Still, while the federal government managed to fend off these larger attempts to legalize human bondage in the Northwest, it did not protect equality. There was a fervor for freedom, but what little dedication white Americans had for the project of equality was beginning to weaken. And not just Americans' dedication. Within only ten years of abolishing slavery and declaring equality among mankind, France turned its back on those ideals as well. Just as in the United States, there had been an almost immediate attempt to restore slavery, with French slave powers making a failed plea for a return to the practice in 1795.[45]

Just eight years later much had changed, and in 1803 France went to war to reinstate slavery in all its colonies. Napoléon Bonaparte's colonial minister Denis Decrès defended the moves, arguing, "Liberty is a food for which the stomachs of the negroes are not yet prepared." The island of Saint-Domingue only managed to stay free by once again fighting the French for its liberty. But the people of the French island of Guadeloupe lost their battle and were reenslaved.[46]

American enslavers had also made the argument that enslaved people were not fit for freedom and equality, and they would turn to it with even greater enthusiasm some years later. But whether in French or English, it employed the same language of prejudice to justify a return to a prerevolutionary culture of hierarchy that assumes some people are fit only to be ruled, whether that ruler is a king or a plantation owner. Yet Decrès and the French who were empowering enslavement and prejudice, as well as their American counterparts, knew just how successfully people of African descent could stomach liberty. They had seen just how ably they could create, defend, and further it.

Meanwhile, the men of color who had stood up at that 1794 convention in Paris as supposedly full and equal citizens—those revolutionaries from Saint-Domingue—were being arrested. Some were deported while others died in French prisons. And in 1804 Napoléon Bonaparte was crowned emperor.[47]

Of course, France and the United States were very different places with different cultures. For one, the United States managed to hold on to its fervor for freedom—which affected not just its government but its churches and many of its citizens—for an entire generation. It had started down a path of freeing tens of thousands of people and set aside a vast region of its lands for freedom. But this did not immunize the United States from a backlash of its own; it just looked different and grew more slowly. But this did not make it less terrible or destructive.

But even as that backlash was brewing, people of African descent, long free or recently liberated during the fervor for freedom, would make the Northwest Territory and states their home. And as they settled the Great West, these African American pioneers and their white allies preserved and grew the vision of liberty and equality that had once stirred the nation.

That backlash manifested itself in many ways across the nation, from the southeast to the northwest, from the cities to the rural regions. But a particularly terrible form of this backlash against equality arose in the Northwest Territory as the region settled, its territories became states, and more people of African descent moved onto that frontier. Whites decided to take away equal voting rights.

Ohio was the first state carved out of the Northwest Territory, and whites in that state were also the first to reverse the Northwest Ordinance of 1787, using the word "white" in their first state constitution as a criterion for full citizenship when Ohio became a state in 1803. By all that was just, these states should have held the right to vote as sacred as freedom from slavery. And many whites still believed that America should be ruled by a free and equal citizenry. The discriminatory wording was not added to the Ohio constitution without debate, but in the end it was included. Every new state created out of the Northwest Territory would follow suit. But this did not destroy the hopes of African Americans and their allies that the dreams of equality could still become a reality.[48]

After all, the fervor for freedom was one reason there were free people who could come to the frontier of the Great West. In 1790 there were roughly 58,000 African-descended people counted as free in America's first census, but by 1810 there were roughly 186,000. When New York finally decided to pass legislation officially ending slavery in 1827, the number stood at roughly 320,000. This was the largest number of free people of African descent existing in any New World or European nation at that time, except for that revolutionary island of Saint-Domingue, which was now being called Haiti. This was a blossoming, a blighted one to be sure, but still bearing fruit.[49]

This was the nation that Keziah and Charles Grier were helping to create. These were the ideals that their freedom, their frontier, and their lives were founded on. And they would nurture and grow those ideals on their Northwest Territory farm, in their family, and in their community even as those ideals came under attack.

3

"The pursuit of Happiness"

Gibson County, Indiana,
Spring 1828

Sometimes she woke before it was light.

Keziah Grier always had reasons for waking early. Until she was free she had been forced awake before most others, and the body can carry long habits.

But now there were so many other reasons for waking. The child coughing, the baby hungry, Charles turning to hold her.

The cabin was crowded, but she could go outside.[1]

Her bare feet might feel dew, cold enough, but not sharp frost. This was a goodness. Even in May every clear night brought the fear of frost. And there was no snow. The rain was better, but it still could be tiresome. It must have seemed that it would never stop, coming straight down or driven hard by winds that grew into storms.

But finally there was a clear morning.

As she stood there, Keziah would have heard her own breath in the stillness, watching that bright star that always hung low in the east over the trees at the edge of their field—their field so much bigger than when they had started working it ten years before. There were fewer wolves now but more people—and those people could also be a trouble.

Many were just passing through. Illinois to the west was drawing many. Keziah would have heard so many different voices, languages, and accents. A lot of English pioneers were coming to New Harmony, that odd place on the Wabash full of people with more dreams than sense. But most of the English preferred river travel, arriving on boats that could bring them west still wearing silk slippers. The big spaces of grassland west of the Wabash River were being promised as easy land for settlement to city folk from London. But Keziah knew that while trees might have roots to battle, they offered all that was necessary for life on the frontier.[2]

The forest gave them so much: the wood to build all their fences, to build barns, to add to their home and then heat it in the winter.

Then there were the berries, the greens, and the wildlife. Even in the coldest months Charles could shoot something for the stewpot when they were all tired of preserved pork.

Their pigs were fine in the forest. Most of the settlers had figured this out and would let their hogs roam. Hogs could grow, if not fat, then at least larger, for they would eat just about anything—acorns, roots, even an old deer carcass rotting by the river. In fact, the forest was increasingly full of hogs, and Charles may well have needed to strengthen the fences against the wandering beasts that could wreck a field of sprouting corn in minutes.

Now, in the spring, they could let the cow forage in the forest as well. That cow loved the fresh green leaves, stretching her head up, her neck seeming to grow longer, her tongue reaching and wrapping around the tender leaves. That cow could strip a branch bare in minutes. Did Keziah ever feel that same hunger in the spring? Her own belly seemed to be ever growing large with babies, and after the long winter the green of any growing thing must have made her mouth water.

Their lives had settled somewhat. The summers had not frozen their crops, and the ground that Charles chose had proven good. The earth was so rich that everything they sowed seemed to grow. There was the squash, ranging its heavy vines over mounds of earth, wonderfully huge. And the corn, though thin and weedy, was tall and full of ears. Even the grain, the bit they dared to plant, ripened fine and heavy at the end of the summer.

And now they had a family. Did Keziah laugh to see Charles closely followed about the yard by their children as they all went out in the morning? They followed him like chicks after a hen as he walked to the barn to feed the livestock.

But for now, alone in the dim light, it was still.

Soon the rooster would crow or the cow would complain, but for now she could stand there.

Then a warm hand tucked into hers, small and soft. Her absence had been noticed; she was missed.

Malinda was her oldest, now ten years old and growing so fast.[3]

Malinda still might have that troublesome cough, worse in the morning, trying to get clear from her winter illness. The very things that made their crops grow also seemed to make people die. The wet, the water, the flooding, and the rich mud that made this such good growing land also made for sickness.

This was such a tender age. If the cow ate the wrong weed, the kettle spilled, the ice on the river broke, the cart tipped, the cut festered, the snake struck. Or more people came.

New people were a danger to them until they could figure out otherwise. If Keziah heard a noise, she had to discover what had made it, and fast.

Was it someone lost? But there are all kinds of lost.

There were those white folks who were now flooding in, their wagons everywhere—thousands of them. Some were fine with Keziah and Charles, but others were not. Seeing the Griers' cleared land and snug home, some of those pale faces would get that pinched look, their light eyes narrowed.[4]

Some settlers into the Northwest Territory states did not think of fairness or hard labor, for they were already poisoned by prejudice.

Ohio was filling up even faster than Indiana, and the malice directed against African American pioneers like Keziah was already growing. In 1821 the young white abolitionist Benjamin Lundy came across a sizable African American settlement on his way to Michigan, about three miles from the village of Somerset. When he visited with them he found the residents furious—"wonderfully wroth" as he put it—over their treatment by the whites who were settling around them.[5]

Closer to home, some whites in the Griers' own Gibson County, Indiana, had petitioned the territorial government in 1814 to ban any free African Americans from settling there. Indeed, some of the earliest African American pioneers to the Northwest Territory were already leaving.[6]

The African Americans who had settled around Fort Allison, just across the Wabash River from the Griers, were being urged to leave the United States entirely. George Flower, a wealthy and influential Englishman who had recently arrived in the United States, was now trying to people the prairie with English pioneers. He was pressuring the African Americans who had been there when he arrived, to leave for Haiti, the land of fresher revolution, urging them to make a new start there.[7]

Flower hated slavery, but he was not overly fond of people of African descent either. He reviled slavery because it combined "the degenerate European aristocracy, and a full-blooded African barbarism." In the same breath he accused white Americans of prejudice because they "retain the old colonial feeling of hatred toward color" and praised Englishmen for having "no feeling of superiority or inferiority as connected with a cuticle of any color."[8]

He hired African Americans to work his land and publicly professed to admire their work ethic and skill. But over time he decided that it would be better if they were gone from his lands and what he considered to be his country.

Of course, he passionately defended his actions. He mentioned local white hostility and an attempt to kidnap one of his laborers. Finally he admitted to seeing "no hope of just treatment for the free colored people that lived on my lands, or relieving myself from the trouble of defending them, I proposed that they should go to Hayti."[9]

George Flower was one of a new breed of abolitionists. He despised the system of slavery but was not warm toward free people of African descent. He was a colonizationist.

All those states giving up slavery, all those now free, had created a response, and one of the most popular was the colonization movement. Called by its founding members the American Colonization Society (ACS) and formalized in 1816, it supported an extreme form of segregation: the removal of all free people of African descent from the United States. Its motivations ranged from pure prejudice to a worry that free African Americans would give enslaved people ideas about the joys of liberty—as if a person had to see someone else of the same skin color enjoying liberty in order to long for it.[10]

It didn't matter whether they were newly freed people like Keziah and Charles or belonged to those families with free roots deeper in the New World than the founding members of the ACS had. They could be newly arrived from Ghana or descended from every kind of person now living in the United States—Dutch, Narraganset, Nigerian, Irish. The ACS did not care; it just wanted those Americans thought of only as "African" gone.[11]

Maybe it was because those free people revealed their lies—all those twisted words the prejudiced wrote and spoke about inferiority, monkeys, and sons of Hamm to support their prejudice. But in the end it was just a return to the old ways of thinking that some men were not created equal—a way of thinking that the Revolution was supposed to have put an end to.[12]

Of course, many of the men who started the ACS were also extreme pro-integrationists. They thought it a lovely thing to have their babies nursed at a black breast, to eat food grown and cooked by dark-skinned people, to have African-descended women in their beds—so they could be very intimate with them indeed—as they raped them.

Of course, those people all had to be enslaved to be worthy of such integration.

Now, George Flower did not own any slaves, but he was certainly new to the United States. And now he had convinced the Jones family, an old American family of African-descended patriots, who had built and later defended Fort Allison through the War of 1812, that they should leave the nation they had helped to create.[13]

Bishop Richard Allen would have been furious.

Bishop Allen was an influential and respected African American preacher based in Philadelphia who had started off preaching to both blacks and whites. But with the growing prejudice in the Northeast and the segregation of the Methodist Church, he left and created the African Methodist Episcopal Church. And he utterly opposed the ACS and its attempts to remove free African Americans from their homes. In 1829 he wrote, "Why should they send us into a far country to die? See the thousands of foreigners emigrating to America every year: and if there be ground sufficient for them to cultivate, and bread for them to eat, why would they wish to send the *first tillers* of the land away? . . . This land which we have watered with our *tears* and *our blood*, is now our *mother country*."[14]

In the end George Flower did not manage to convince many of the African Americans in his region to leave their land in Illinois. Keziah must have been relieved. Indeed, some worried that Flower's plan was a hoax to get all of them on a boat to New Orleans, where they would be sold into slavery.[15]

Being a dark-skinned pioneer brought so many unique dangers, and Keziah and her family were so very dark. Whites not only hankered after their farm but wanted their bodies.

No matter how free they were, their skin made them a commodity in the right market, and there were men, both white and black, who took advantage of free families like theirs, deep in the northern woods. And they often hunted in secret, at night, trying to catch people while they were asleep. New Orleans seemed a long way away, but there were auction blocks with people on them much closer than Louisiana. Louisville and Saint Louis were both just spitting distance away on one of those newfangled big steamships now running on the Ohio River.[16]

Perhaps Charles took her down to the Ohio River to see those ships. Their wheels thumping the water, the noise so loud it must have felt like it was moving right through her body. And all that power, that force, being used to carry that cargo they would have been able to see clearly on the open decks—people in chains, mothers like her, being taken south and west.

Keziah knew that for some the Ohio River was a crossover into the promised land of freedom, but for most it held nothing but misery. Once there had been ships packed with people in chains, being forced across the ocean to America's shores, destined to be sold. But now rivers had replaced oceans, and steamships had replaced sailing vessels. Those steamboats on the Ohio ran south into sorrow, traveling deep into slavery. Anyone on its waters would hear the weeping.[17]

And the hunger for enslaved people was increasing.

The trade that had brought her people to these shores had been stopped officially, but slavery was growing. It was supposed to be dying, and many people assumed—with all those states abolishing slavery, all those people freed, and the importation of slaves banned—that it would die. But all that fine land included in the Louisiana Purchase had added to a massive demand for enslaved labor.[18]

Then in 1820 the unthinkable had happened: Missouri became a slave state. For so long almost everyone had talked about slavery as a curse on this new land. All those states that had ended slavery, all those people freed, even this frontier—their own Northwest Territory—free. But something was shifting.

It must have seemed that so many people of European descent who had been revolutionaries alongside people of African descent were turning their backs on the ideals of equality and freedom.

Keziah could not read, but she had friends who could, friends who were still sympathetic to the causes of freedom and justice. She and Charles still worshipped with Elder Wasson, and he may have told them the shocking news about Missouri. It was practically next door to them, and now it was a new slave state.[19]

This was not just politics for Keziah, not just an issue of how many white men could sit and vote in the federal government; this was a change in her whole world. Saint Louis, Missouri, was less than two hundred miles west of them. Due west of them, a short trip down the Ohio River and then up the Mississippi River. If Charles did not go there himself to trade their goods, he could have easily sent their goods down to that city's markets.

This deliberate extension and growth of slavery was being championed by men who were rejecting the founding principles of the young nation. The Maryland senator William Pinkney, who fought so hard for Missouri to become a slave state, dismissed the revolutionary ideals of his forefathers. He scoffed, "The self-evident truths announced in the Declaration of Independence are not truths at all, if taken literally."[20]

It took a few more years for the politician John Randolph from Virginia to state his feelings about his fight to grow slavery in Missouri and the nation, but only a few. By 1826 he was publicly voicing his opinion that the Declaration of Independence was a risky document, for it clearly asserted that "all men are born free and equal," an idea he rejected "for the best of all reasons, because it is not true."[21]

Neither William Pinkney nor John Randolph had the Griers successfully homesteading nearby. But they must have been very myopic to miss all the free and successful African Americans who inhabited Washington, DC, at the very time they were fighting to extend slavery into Missouri. By 1819 the city had a thriving free African American community, and a number of schools had already been started by—and for—African Americans in the city. Ann Maria Hall, herself educated at an integrated school in Alexandria, Virginia, had her school right on Capitol Hill, a region of the city that was home to the "best colored families of Washington."[22]

Slavery's advocates would go to amazing lengths. They seemed willing to ignore the obvious and even the law.

The Griers' friend Jacob Hawkins knew this all too well, for he had been enslaved illegally in Indiana. He now lived just a few miles away in Daviess County, but he had also come from South Carolina—Charleston to be exact, once the busiest slave-importation port in the United States and still a place of great wealth and suffering.[23]

His enslaver, Eli Hawkins, was part of a group of pro-slavery people joining around the territorial governor, William Henry Harrison, as he made one attempt after another to grow slavery in the Indiana Territory.

Long before she was married, Keziah may well have known Jacob and his sister, Ann. They may have even traveled together from South Carolina, catching a ship in Charleston that would take them out to sea to the mouth of the Mississippi River, then up north to the Ohio River, then up that river to the Wabash River, and finally up the Wabash to Vincennes. Vincennes, that town where Harrison was already forcing enslaved people to help build his huge brick mansion in the wilderness—trying to replicate the plantation homes of his birthplace just as he tried to replicate a culture of slavery, inequality, and privilege.[24]

But the governor knew that popular opinion was against him. Even his own father-in-law, John Cleves Symms, a judge in the stretch of the Indiana Territory west of the Wabash River, was freeing enslaved people who were coming before him and complaining that they were being illegally held in bondage in a territory meant to be free.[25]

Still, when Harrison's petition to extend slavery into the Indiana Territory was denied, he was furious. So he decided to turn his back on the federal government and create a slave state, passing a law with the help of local judges that stated that while enslaved people could not be brought into the territory to live and work there, they could be brought in as indentured servants, and their enslavers could pick the length of their indenture bond without their agreement.[26]

And in 1806 Eli Hawkins, the man who held Jacob Hawkins in bondage, had been first in line at the deed office in Vincennes with Jacob and Ann in tow. Once they were in front of the clerk, Jacob became the first person recorded in the new deed book. The language was formal and made it look as if Jacob and Eli were in agreement, but there was no chance of that. For Eli Hawkins decided that an appropriate indenture term for Jacob would be ninety years. And William Henry Harrison, who would become the United States' ninth president, made sure that Jacob could do nothing about it.[27]

Next was Jacob's sister, Ann, who also had to listen to the clerk tell her that her bond was for ninety years of unpaid service.[28]

Jacob and Ann had been taken away from their parents and family and brought to this cold and wild place. Were they told that they would be freed? Were promises made to their parents?

But everything was being broken, their family and now their future.

Most indenture bonds, even on the Northwest Territorial frontier, lasted a much shorter time than this, especially if the bond servant was white. They also included the guarantee that the indentured person would get something in return for their unpaid labor—schooling in a trade and sometimes even a formal promise that they would be taught to read. And when the indenture bond ended, some form of material reward was also promised, usually a gun, some items of clothing, some money, and the tools of the trade they had learned.[29]

But Eli Hawkins promised nothing to Jacob and Ann, for he knew both would be dead by the time their bonds expired.

Others were recorded that day, almost all of them recorded as being in their teens, although many may have been much younger. Their enslavers were dreadfully pragmatic: they were traveling to the very edges of the new nation where there were very few laborers, enslaved or free, so they wanted to bring with them the healthiest, strongest, and youngest people they could—even if taking them destroyed families and devastated children.

And most of those children and young people in that deed book were signed up for indenture bonds of between ninety and ninety-nine years.[30]

Governor Harrison had won. He had effectively extended slavery for almost a century in the vast territory he governed, and Jacob and Ann left Vincennes for Eli Hawkins's homestead knowing they would not be free until 1896.

Yet this same Governor Harrison, just a few years later, must have been grateful for the truly free African-descended people in his territory when he mustered a regiment of free African Americans to defend that far western border of the nation during the War of 1812.[31]

Maybe this was about usefulness.

And Harrison would continue to have a sweet tooth for the forced labor of African Americans. Indeed, in 1830, when he was no longer governor and had moved to Ohio, he continued to use every legal loophole to create something that looked like slavery in his home. In that year he placed an ad giving notice of a reward for the capture and return of "George W. West," a young man "bound" to him by the overseer of the poor in Miami Township, Ohio.[32]

But in 1816, the passion for liberty was still strong in the Indiana Territory. And when in that year Indiana became a state, its freshly written constitution made clear that slavery would forever be banned within its borders.

Some people took this to heart. But others refused. Eli Hawkins must have felt safe in the fact that Jacob and his sister were indentured servants and thus, in the eyes of the law, technically free. But most could see the cynicism of his position. Indeed, years later when county histories were being written, those interviewed remembered Jacob and Ann as slaves.[33]

Then five years later everything changed, and it was all because of Polly.

Polly had been born into bondage in the Indiana Territory, as had her mother, around 1800, for their enslavers were the Lasselles, an elite French family in Vincennes that had managed to survive many wars and changes along the Wabash River since the 1760s.[34]

This complicated Polly's situation, because her bondage was allowed; the new United States did not want to anger the local French population whom it was trying to cultivate as allies in controlling the region.

But for Polly and her mother these political decisions meant that, while others were being liberated, they continued to labor in bondage.

Even so, when Indiana became a state in 1816, they were supposed to be free. But their enslaver, Hyacinthe Lasselle, was not going to give up so easily.

Everyone knew Hyacinthe—how could they not? His father had been one of the original settlers of Vincennes. But Polly was determined to make Hyacinthe and the state of Indiana face up to forced labor and face her. And she had found a young white lawyer to represent her. Amory Kinney had just come to Vincennes from New York. Like her, he believed that freedom was the right of every person. So he took Polly's case, even if it meant going against the powerful Lasselles.[35]

Once the court agreed to hear Polly's case, however, Hyacinthe did something terrible that forced Polly to sign an indenture bond. He must have been hoping he could take advantage of the same loophole that Eli Hawkins had used so successfully.

It was not an easy case; in fact, it was legally impossible. Even before statehood, Governor Harrison had made sure that the Indiana Territory barred all people of African descent from taking a white person to court or even giving testimony as a witness in a trial involving a white defendant or a white plaintiff. Luckily, the state supreme court was unwilling to uphold that legislation and decided to hear Polly's case.[36]

And Polly refused to give up, even though she may have been tortured. The violence and threats that were made to force her to sign that indenture bond can only be imagined.

When a young indentured African American woman called Phoebe, across the Wabash in Illinois, thought she was free because her bondholder had died, she discovered that she was not. Instead, like an enslaved person, she had been gifted in her bondholder's will to his son. When she complained, the son brutally punished her, although he would later admit to only using "a little force and beating." So Phoebe took him to court.[37]

But Phoebe lost her case in Illinois. And now Polly hoped she would not lose hers in Indiana.

Finally, in July 1820 the Indiana Supreme Court, in its new stone building on the central green of Corydon, Indiana, made its decision.

It was considering politics as well. Chief Justice Isaac Blackford may have heard about the arguments for the Missouri Compromise that were attacking the Declaration of Independence. And there was the Missouri Compromise itself, bitterly contested in Washington, DC, since 1819.

Justice Blackford would have known of all the ways in which Illinois courts were making a mockery of the Northwest Ordinance's ban on slavery, including Phoebe's failed bid for freedom. In Illinois, once a part of the Indiana Territory, many whites were intent upon making a success of forced labor, and they were deciding against every plaintiff like Polly, even making it legal to buy and sell African American indentured servants in the state.[38]

With all of this in mind and more, the court decided in Polly's favor.

In his opinion the chief justice quoted a section of the 1816 Indiana constitution that he thought relevant to the case, even before he argued that the constitution outlawed slavery: "That all men are born equally free and independent, and have certain natural, inherent and unalienable rights, among which, are the enjoyment and defense of life and liberty."[39]

Polly had won, and she had won freedom for everyone in that state who had been forced into indentured labor, including Jacob and Ann.

In pursuing her case, Polly joined a courageous group of African Americans who had risked similar moves for liberty. Indeed, most states that ended slavery during and just after the Revolutionary War only enacted those laws when an enslaved person argued for their freedom in court. And often they were women, like Polly—women willing to risk the worst torture and torment their owners could inflict to gain freedom for themselves and all others in their state.[40]

Jacob and Ann must have thought they would finally be free.

Then again, they must have had hopes for liberty when their bondholder, Eli Hawkins, had died a few years before Polly's case was won. But Jacob and Ann, like Phoebe in Illinois, found themselves still in bondage to Eli Hawkins's widow. And now Eli's widow had remarried and seemed even more intent upon keeping her unpaid laborers, despite the state supreme court's decision.[41]

But Jacob decided to fight. Maybe it was for his sister, Ann. Or maybe it was for Ellen Embry. Ellen had also come from South Carolina, and she and Jacob wanted to marry. But Jacob could not, not when his own life and body was contracted into bondage.[42]

Did Jacob consider just running? That was an option.

But it would mean leaving Ann and Ellen behind. And Daviess County was home to him now. He had spent almost half his life there. He knew this land, and he must have believed that he and Ellen could make a good life there, if only he were free.

So Jacob decided to fight for the best ideals of the Revolution with his very life, because his life depended on them.

He was not alone. Jacob and Ann had now been joined by Isaac, whom Eli Hawkins had "purchased" before he died.[43]

Jacob and Isaac must have had to do everything in secret, but they had an ally. Polly's lawyer, Amory Kinney, had moved to Daviess County—possibly because things had gotten a bit too hot for him in Vincennes after he won his supreme court case against one of that city's most powerful families.

And Kinney was trying to build his practice when Jacob and Isaac came calling.

Now, Kinney knew that what Eli Hawkins's widow was doing was illegal. He also knew that many of the wealthiest and most powerful white families in the area were of a like mind to that widow, and they would not be too pleased with his taking on Jacob and Isaac's case.

Kinney had been through a lot with Polly, and he was again trying to make a living as a lawyer. He could have told Jacob and Isaac to leave, insisting that since the state did not allow an African-descended person to take a white person to court, he could not represent them in their suit against Eli Hawkins's widow. Or he could have just told them that he was not interested in yet another court battle that would damage his reputation and business.

But Amory Kinney took their case, even if it meant he might be unpopular for a time in Daviess County.

Did he ask about the safety of the men, how they would protect themselves and Ann while pursuing their freedom? He knew the risk they were taking. He might lose some clients, but Jacob and Isaac could be very badly hurt. In his heart did he wonder if they might back out? Eli Hawkins's widow had married a harsh man, and he could do horrible things to Ann, things that could cause any brother to drop a case.

Maybe they had managed to get Ann away, or maybe she had been the one urging them to go to court, for the worst may have already happened to her, and her life could have been a misery.

Somehow, they decided together—this white lawyer and these three African Americans—that they would all take the risks before them. But none of them knew how bad it could actually get.

The death threats started as soon as Amory Kinney filed his motion at the Daviess County Courthouse. He later recounted his shock at this turn of events, that his own neighbors—and possibly some of his own clients—would sooner kill him than see freedom, justice, and the law upheld.[44]

If a famous white lawyer like Kinney—who had just won a state supreme court case that had changed state law—faced such threats, the two young men and Ann must have had a terrible time of it. But they stood firm, and when Kinney argued their case before two judges, both decided in favor of freedom. Indeed, they extended their decision, making clear that no one was to be held in any kind of bonded labor in that county.

They were all free. Jacob, Isaac, Ann, Ellen, everyone.

Within a few months, Jacob and Ellen married. Now, in 1828, they were farming their own land and growing their family in Daviess County, right next to Gibson County, where the Griers lived.[45]

But not everyone was so lucky. The Illinois courts continued to reject all pleadings for freedom from African American indentured servants, and even in Vincennes—Polly's old home—people continued to keep others in bondage, even in outright slavery, and no law would stop them.[46]

And the land to the south of them, over the Ohio River, was filling up fast with enslaved people. And while many tried to run, not everyone made it out.

Keziah Grier would have heard Elder Wasson preach that love was stronger than death. And some of those people fleeing through their woods were willing to risk death rather than lose those they loved.

It was love that made John and Eliza Little willing to risk everything to be free together, as they made their way north and across the Ohio River. This young couple from Tennessee had both been sold away from their parents. John Little was originally taken from his home in North Carolina and forced to walk enchained in a coffle for hundreds of miles until he arrived in western Tennessee.[47]

Once they decided to run they were betrayed, shot at, beaten, imprisoned, and betrayed again.

At one point, John was captured and jailed, chains binding his hands and feet. His cell was on the top floor, so he broke through the ceiling, jumped off the high roof, and crawled for miles on his hands and knees, while the stunned jail keeper searched the building, convinced that no man in chains would jump to certain death off that roof.

When Eliza's shoes wore out on the long walk north, John gave her his own to protect her bare feet while his feet bled. She walked in them until they fell apart. But still they walked north.

Later, they both agreed that the most terrifying part of their journey was trying to cross the Ohio Bottoms, a heavily forested swamp that bordered stretches of the Ohio River. Walking across the more settled lands along the riverbank would have meant certain capture, so they had to travel through a region that most people avoided. John remembered, "The water was black and deep. I bound our packages on my wife's back, placed her on a log as a man rides on horseback, and I swam, pushing the log, holding it steady, to keep her up. Had the log turned right or left, she would have slipped off, and the packs would have sunk her. It would have been death, sure." Eliza added, "The water in some places was very deep,—it was black, dirty water. I was scared all but to death." John admitted, "I almost repented I had started, but on I went." After all, both agreed, "worse than death was behind us, and to avoid that we risked our lives."[48]

Keziah would have known about people just like John and Eliza, people willing to risk death for freedom. There may have been mothers, like herself, with children the age of Malinda, now too exhausted to walk. Keziah could well have seen children carried by parents whose backs still bled from the whip, their arms still bruised from beatings—those parents willing to endure any pain to see their children safe and free.

These refugees from slavery had come far, but they knew that even the Griers might not be trustworthy. Some refugees and their allies in the region reported that even men of African descent would betray and hunt others.[49]

Keziah knew that as a woman she would seem safer, and with Malinda at her side, she would look safer still.

It is hard for children to keep secrets. But Keziah knew that when she and Charles decided to help people find liberty, all their children would have to become secret keepers as soon as they could talk, for talking of helping the hungry, the thirsty, the terrified could kill them all.

How do you explain that to a child?

Their life was so fragile. And helping the refugees did not make them any safer.[50]

There was not much that Keziah could give to those who were running from bondage. Some food, some comfort, some warmth and directions. She would have to explain that even though they were in a free state, the refugees had to keep walking north. The Griers would have known that in 1815 eight people who had escaped bondage and had been living nearby in the Indiana Territory had been denied their freedom when they had pled their case in the Gibson County Courthouse. Even this wilderness north of the Ohio River was too far south to be safe.[51]

But the Griers could always provide some warm cornmeal from the pot over the fire, and sometimes they could spare a little smoked meat.

By this time they had learned to gather the sweet sap from the maple trees around them, rendering it down into thick syrup or a brown sugar that could cure meat or sweeten their food.[52]

And they could give refugees something to keep them warm as they continued their journey north.

Wool from their sheep was safest. Anything purchased could bring suspicion. Not that she and Charles had the money for fine linen, and cotton came from a tortured source. But she had sheep, so she had wool, and no one need know how many sweaters and shawls she was knitting, or for whom.

Shearing took effort from both Keziah and Charles, one of them holding the sheep, the other carefully clipping the mass of wool that had grown all year. And the sheep would complain—grinding out their rough cries, some even fainting in distress as Keziah held their sagging weight.

Then her work could really begin.

First the wool had to be washed. It must have looked an impossible task, the raw wool sitting in a massive mound, fluffy and filthy. The pile would have tempted the children, who probably didn't mind that it was caked with mud, full of burrs and bugs, for it was so soft and bouncy.

The water involved would have been more than they used to bathe the whole family. They had to haul gallons and gallons to the house and heat it. Keziah used soap she had made from the rendered fat of their slaughtered pigs. The wool resisted getting wet, it was so full of the oil that coated each strand and protected the sheep from the rain and cold. So she had to push it down hard and work it into the warm soapy water. After some tough kneading and squeezing, she could pour off the dirty water and do it all over again, and again, until the water ran clear.

Once the wool was clean she had to dry it, squeezing it out as best she could, then hanging it in the sun or by the fire. But it was still a mess, all tangles and knots. So it had to be carded.

She would have taken two wooden paddles lined with sharp little nails pointed outward, like a torturer's idea of hairbrushes. She would work a small bunch of wool between the two paddles, the repetitive motion hard on arms and shoulders, getting every tangle out and fluffing the wool into large soft puffs ready for the spinning wheel.

There was not much on the farm that Keziah and Charles did not work on together, but spinning had long been women's work. It was a valuable skill—allowing Keziah to clothe all of them and create yarn and knitted items for sale. The thump of her spinning wheel as she pushed the treadle with her foot over and over again to make the wheel spin must have been as constant and familiar to her children as a heartbeat, pulsing throughout the day and into the evenings in the dying firelight. Later, as she checked each of them, pulling their blankets up and tucking them in, her hands would have been soft from the grease that still clung to the wool she had been working with.[53]

Now Keziah would have been teaching Malinda how to spin. The shawl Malinda would certainly have worn so proudly may well have been her first, made from wool Malinda had spun into yarn and knitted. It may have been a little lumpy, the yarn a bit uneven, but it was warm, and Malinda could have held it close around her small shoulders as she watched the woods with her mother in the morning.

Standing there in the half light, her daughter beside her, Keziah must have looked like help. She must have seemed safe. And she would have been.

Despite the danger, despite the risk, she was choosing to help—they all were.

Did a person come slowly out, moving into the light? Hoping for charity, for survival, for freedom? Keziah made her choice once more—they would be met with kindness and comfort.

But not everyone north of the Ohio River made such a choice.

Keziah knew as well as anyone that crossing that river could mean freedom, but for some that crossing took them to a life of sorrow and terror beyond imagining.

"And secure the blessings of Liberty"

Southern Illinois, 1819

The first thing that Cornelius Elliott would have seen was the smoke. As they got closer to the Ohio River, the smoke would have filled the entire northern skyline. It must have looked as if the whole world was on fire.

In some ways it was. The smoke was from the massive bonfires on the Illinois side that were constantly alight, blackening the sky by day and lighting it by night, to extract salt from water.[1]

This may have been the frontier, but the salt springs of southern Illinois were among the most profitable enterprises in the new state. And the man bringing Cornelius Elliott into Illinois was the leaseholder of the largest of the mining operations.

By 1819 the salt industry had burned so many acres of woodland that the territorial government had become alarmed and legislated how many acres of forested land could be burned a year. But the laws were pretty much ignored—as were most laws in that area.[2]

Timothy Guard, who had just purchased Cornelius Elliott, was familiar with this fact. He would have been making sure that certain laws in the region were not upheld, for Timothy Guard's salt spring was making a lot of people a lot of money, himself included.

Salt springs: the term seems innocent enough. But some of the earliest work done by the newly created American government involved these salt springs. By 1803 Congress had already given the Treasury Department the right to lease the land out to individuals for 10 percent of the salt produced and a portion of the profits. Between 1807 and 1818 alone, the government received 158,394 bushels of salt in rent, and profits for that period were modestly estimated at $28,165. This was a formidable sum. When the mines were turned over to the newly formed state of Illinois in 1818, the leaseholders contributed nearly 25 percent of the state's tax revenue.[3]

Out there on the Illinois frontier these massive operations produced the wealth-generating salt that the mine owners, the state, and the newly created nation so desired. Soon the salt industry of Illinois was ruled by greed and infected with death.

It hadn't always been that way. The springs had long been valuable, even to the local indigenous people, offering a steady supply of salt almost 1,000 miles from the sea. The Native Americans of that region had figured out how to harvest it by carefully carving out large wooden pans where the water could be collected and allowed to evaporate in the sun, leaving behind the gleaming crystals.[4]

But this was too inefficient a technique for the new American owners of the salt mines. To extract a higher yield, the water had to be evaporated from the salt at a faster rate. The leaseholders needed fire. So they started burning everything they could, cutting down the forests to create massive bonfires. But green wood is full of sap and does not burn clean, and the air was always thick with dark, wet smoke.

Some of the earlier leaseholders had been happy to work with the salt water bubbling up to the surface, but Timothy Guard had a more ambitious plan: digging underground to get to the source of the salt springs. There was a problem, though: as any child who's been to the beach knows, digging a hole in wet sand is difficult, for every shovelful is replaced with mud.

No one wanted this brutal job, with the constant danger of drowning in salt muck. So Guard forced people to do the work for no pay. By the time he brought Elliott to Illinois, Guard and the other "salt barons" of the region were well on their way to owning more slaves than anyone else in the state.[5]

Slavery was technically outlawed in Illinois, but where massive profit was concerned, loopholes were found, exceptions granted, blind eyes turned. Soon the forests were not the only things being destroyed around the salt springs of Illinois. Freedom was as well. By the time it became a state in 1818, Illinois had the highest number of people in bondage of any of the Old Northwest territories or states, thanks in large part to the salt works.[6]

Guard and the other leaseholders were not particular about whom they forced to work to create their wealth. Native Americans, white indentured servants, and enslaved African Americans all toiled together. But it would have been hard for anyone watching to tell them apart as they worked the pits, all of them covered in mud, all of them stained from their wounds.

But the easiest and most readily available workers were African American, and soon one of the pits was given the vile nickname "Nigger Spring." Working at Guard's salt springs was to exist in a hell that seemed straight from Dante's imagination, complete with whippings, fire, smoke, and a muddy, ever-deepening pit.[7]

In Timothy Guard's hell, however, those managing the tortures stayed well away from the pit, for drowning was not the only danger; there was the salt water itself.

As the pit deepened, it yielded water with a higher salt content. This meant more profit for Guard and worse conditions for his enslaved workers, for too much salt in water has an unfortunate effect on the human body. There are few firsthand accounts from that period by those who actually survived the worst of the salt industry. Mary Prince was one survivor. She was enslaved in the British Caribbean, made to work the drying "ponds" that lined the ocean's edge. She was soon suffering from "salt ulcers," a condition caused by spending too much time in extremely salty water. Mary described them as "dreadful boils, which eat down in some cases to the very bone, afflicting the sufferers with great torment."[8]

Mary's torments occurred in the Caribbean, where conditions differed from those in Illinois. In Illinois, rather than salt ponds in the hot
sunshine, there were fires in the forest. These created the smoke that
Elliott had first seen when he got close to the salt works. By the time he
arrived in 1819, the salt-work managers were piping the salt water from
the pits to the rapidly receding edges of the forest. It was actually easier
to bring the salt water to the fuel than to bring the massive trees, heavy
with sap, to the springs. When he finally got close enough to the fires
themselves, Elliott would have seen the massive pots, called "kettles,"
hanging above them. Filled with the piped-in salt water, the kettles were
kept over the fires until the water had boiled off, leaving the salt behind.
This rendering process often caused the kettles to fail, spewing scalding
sludge on the people tending them.[9]

Why would someone work another human being to death? It
doesn't make sense. Indeed, some pro-slavery advocates before the Civil
War argued that the horrors described by those who had witnessed the
slave system firsthand were exaggerated. Any sane slave owners, they
reasoned, would preserve the health, life, and even happiness of the people they owned. But this argument does not take into account the fact
that when human beings are worth less than what they produce, their
lives have terrifyingly little value.

Timothy Guard understood just how deadly it was to work in his
pit, but he was willing to make the investment, to buy lives for little
money and turn deaf ears to the screams of the dying.

No accurate count was kept of those who died in the salt works of
Illinois—it behooved no one to do so. But Elliott, and all those who
worked there, were witnesses to this terrible economy.

Luckily Elliott was only a witness to the worst of it, for he was both
blessed and cursed to be a skilled man whose body and its labors were
worth a great deal to Timothy Guard, for Elliott was a cooper. As a cooper he made many of the tools that Guard needed: barrels for salt, buckets for hauling mud, and wooden pipes to bring salt water from the pits
to the fires. Elliott had been about twenty-eight years old when Guard

visited his enslaver (and possibly father), John Elliott, in Maury County, Tennessee. Guard must have hunted hard for an enslaved person like Elliott, skilled and available for sale, for without a cooper he could not grow his works. Elliott had been born in North Carolina around 1790, but before the birth of his younger brother, Aaron, his mother and brothers had been moved to Tennessee by John Elliott.[10]

Like many enslaved people, Cornelius was unsure of his own birth year, but he knew that his skills made him a valuable man. This made his sale price high, $1,000 in 1819—an immense sum at a time when a healthy young man sold for around $300 and the wage for a free laborer in that region was about thirty-seven cents a day. Back east in more settled Sturbridge, Massachusetts, a farm with a home and all barns and outbuildings on almost a hundred acres of land could be purchased for $985. But Timothy Guard was a wealthy man, and with Elliott's labor he planned on making himself even wealthier. He paid John Elliott the full amount.[11]

Once in the Salines, surrounded by their horrors, no one could have blamed Elliott for losing heart, for giving in to despair, or for fleeing. The salt works were not a place to encourage dreams of freedom. But as Elliott trudged across the burnt lands checking the wooden pipes for leaks, as he hauled wooden staves out of the soaking bucket and forced yet another metal band over bent wood, he held on hard to hope—not just for his own freedom but for the freedom of his whole family. He dreamed beyond survival to success. He dreamed of his own land, his own farm, his own life.

But to gain all of this, Elliott had to become a freedom entrepreneur—a person willing to negotiate and work to purchase himself and the people he loved. And to do this he had to bargain with Timothy Guard. But Elliott had courage; after all, he had already survived the end of the world.

In 1811, when Elliott was around twenty-one, the world seemed to start on a path toward destruction. First, a total solar eclipse darkened the middle portion of the American continent. Soon afterward, everyone could see a comet, hanging continuously in the sky for the whole fall and early winter. Then on December 16, the earthquake hit. Now called the New Madrid Quake, for the Missouri village at its epicenter, it is still the worst quake east of the Rockies in American history. But those who felt its full force were not thinking of history but of survival as the earth tore itself apart beneath their feet.[12]

The noise was deafening, and the settlers who heard the sound of cracking and rumbling would have had little to compare it to. No bombs that powerful existed in 1811. Fountains of mud and sand spewed high into the air, and massive chasms opened up and swallowed people and animals. The earth rose so high under the Mississippi that sections of the river ran backward. The tremors shook the ground in Washington, DC, and rang church bells in Charleston, South Carolina. At the time Elliott was living less than two hundred miles away from the epicenter.[13]

He escaped the worst of the devastation but would have soon heard reports of the quake and understood its terrors. And December was not the end of it. Two more earthquakes hit in January and February. No mere aftershocks, these were huge quakes in their own right—the actual aftershocks numbered in the thousands. By early March everyone in that region must have wondered if the world was going to be constantly shaken until nothing was left standing or alive.

Instead, the earth settled, and war broke out. The War of 1812 brought more death and terror, threatening the new nation's existence.

Somehow Elliott survived these traumatic years. Though he and his mother and brothers were still together, they were still in bondage, and their existence held no certainty at all. Years later, in 1850s Canada, a man by the name of Christopher Nichols recalled the terror of this aspect of enslavement. As he recounted, "I have seen parents and children, husbands and wives, separated by sale. . . . All the time I lived in slavery, I was in dead dread and fear. If I slept it was in dread—and in the morning it was dread—dread night and day." And in March 1819, Cornelius Elliott had to face his worst fears: he was being sold and separated from most of his family, for Timothy Guard had come calling.[14]

It was not unheard of for slave owners to bring enslaved people into a Northwest Territory state, though legally those people were supposed to be made free. Cornelius Elliott knew he was a valuable man and that his owner would drive a hard bargain, but he may have hoped to get his freedom out of the deal. Then again, Timothy Guard, and those like him in Illinois, knew just how to exploit every loophole and legal (or illegal) advantage to force people to work in bondage.[15]

But Elliott may have had other reasons to hope. He knew that Timothy Guard badly needed his skills, and that fact alone would keep him from the deadliest and most dangerous work in the Salines. Also, Guard needed Elliott to be mobile while he worked the pipelines. Guard knew that people would run from the terrible labor he was forcing on them, and the wilderness offered them a place to hide. After all, this was not New Orleans or Providence, with people and an infrastructure in place to catch a runaway. So these salt-work owners used many means to ensure their forced laborers stayed put. Chaining them to their beds was not unheard of, and the ladders into the pits would have been closely guarded. But Guard knew he could not keep Elliott constantly chained, so he had to think of other ways. One may have been the promise of freedom, however expensive. And it would be very expensive.

While Elliott's value protected him from the pits and probably saved his life, it also meant that purchasing himself must have seemed almost impossible. But Elliott was undaunted, and Timothy Guard agreed that Elliott could buy his freedom. Guard's agreement did not come cheap, however, for he insisted that Elliott reimburse him for every penny of the $1,000 he had paid for him.[16]

This was the frontier, far from banks or any access to gold or cash. Even the owners of the salt works paid their taxes not in gold but in salt. A thousand dollars was an almost unimaginable sum. But Elliott dreamed of freedom, and nothing was going to dissuade him.

But how does one buy oneself? There are the relatively straightforward challenges, like earning extra money while enslaved. Once that problem was solved, then where could one store the money? Only the rare bank would agree to hold money for such a business, and for most of the enslaved, their owners also owned the places they might hide money. Finally, the entire process rested on the notion that an owner could be trusted to uphold a promise.

How could a negotiation between people with no legal rights and their owners ever be fair? To secure their own freedom, enslaved people would have to promise to work harder than ever, in unbearable conditions, to earn money that legally belonged to their owners. If an owner agreed to such an arrangement, the temptation to break a promise and keep the handsome profit must have been strong, and the enslaved person would have no recourse.

The stories of such deals going bad were common. Alfred T. Jones knew this all too well. When he opened negotiations with his owner in 1833, he had lived all twenty-three years of his life in bondage in Kentucky. Here is how Alfred describes what happened next: "I made an arrangement with my master to purchase my freedom for $350. . . . But before the business was completed I learned that my master was negotiating with another party to sell me for $400." Realizing that his owner had decided to steal his $350 and any hopes of freedom, Alfred Jones fled to Canada.[17]

Luckily, he knew how to read and write. This meant that he could write his own pass, a document saying that he was traveling under the permission of his owner. Twenty years later, the owner of a successful apothecary shop in Canada, the entrepreneurial Alfred Jones admitted that the pass "was not spelled correctly, but nobody there [in the United States] supposed that a slave could write at all."[18]

The papers Alfred refers to were part of the powerful and complicated legal structure that protected the system of slavery and prejudice in America at that time in both the South and the North. A person held in bondage had to have a pass from his or her owner to move freely. By the nineteenth century, prejudice and the law had become firmly intertwined in America. The legal and social assumption across white America was that a person of African descent was enslaved unless proven otherwise. This meant that free people of African descent, especially on the Northwestern frontier, had to have "free papers," legal documents proving that they were owned by no one but themselves.

Every single one of the Northwest Territory states had white residents who created Black Laws requiring any person of African descent entering that territory to show such papers to any white authority who demanded them. And meeting those demands came at a great cost. These whites instituted anti-immigration laws often under the guise of so-called Black Code bonds. Only people of African descent had to pay them, and they were made cripplingly expensive to discourage free African Americans from settling in these territories and states. Most territories required a $500 bond, but Illinois demanded $1,000. Whites in Illinois were making it brutally clear that they did not mind having people of African descent in their state as long as those people were not free.[19]

These bonds were not just a formality; they were a threat. Every free person of African descent in the Northwest Territory states would have known someone who had been forced to pay the bond, and those who hadn't knew they could be financially destroyed at any moment if a local white person decided to enforce the bond law. In Elliott's home county, a free man by the name of George Shockley had to submit a $1,000 bond when he arrived there to settle in 1834.[20]

Of the three border states of the Northwest Territory, Illinois had the harshest Black Codes in place during the period that saw the highest migration into the Old Northwest, and a strongly pro-slavery elite created indenture laws that all but legalized slavery in the early nineteenth century. By 1810, African Americans made up 5 percent of Illinois' territorial population. This was too many for some whites. So an 1813 code barred any new free African Americans from entering the state and required those who lived there already to register with local officials. Failure to abide by the code could result in a whipping of the offender "on his or her bare back not exceeding thirty-nine stripes nor less than twenty-five stripes." Six years later, the state passed a law forbidding assemblage by any people of African descent—including for worship. Admittedly, in 1829, Illinois decided to allow African Americans to enter the state as long as they recorded free papers and paid a bond. While that bond was technically not raised to $1,000 until 1845, George Shockley's experience showed that any county could decide to make the bond as high as it liked well before 1845.[21]

If Elliott wanted to stay in Illinois or any portion of the free Northwest Territory, he would have to have his free papers and be prepared to pay that bond. Yes, he could flee to Canada, and many free people of African descent did. But Elliott must have seen himself as an American, and he wanted to stay in America, making his home and his future there. And he had another reason for wanting to be legally free in America—for only with freedom papers in hand would he be in a position to buy the freedom of the people he loved.

So Elliott must have promised Guard he would stay in the salt works and labor to buy his freedom, hoping Guard would keep his word.

But Guard now knew that Elliott had freedom on his mind, and this could make him more of a flight risk. Guard would have known of other freedom entrepreneurs like Alfred T. Jones, who when cheated escaped to Canada. Guard meant to keep Elliott in Illinois for the time he needed him, even if Elliott came up with $1,000. So Timothy Guard bought some insurance—he purchased Guard's little brother, Aaron.[22]

Aaron Elliott was much younger than Cornelius and probably had no highly valuable skills to keep him out of the pit. The bond between these brothers would have allowed Guard to keep Cornelius Elliott close and compliant, for he could always send Aaron into the pit.

How Elliott had the heart and the courage to hope in the face of all of this remains a mystery. But the deed books, massive and water-stained, smelling of old leather and mud, still sit in the county courthouse, telling the story of what he did. They show that Elliott must have worked very hard indeed, for in just two years he purchased his freedom for $1,000. The clerk was slow to record this fact, not entering it until 1829, but the words clearly read, "Timothy GUARD of Gallatin

County, Illinois, having purchased CORNELIUS, age about 28 years of John ELLIOTT of Maury County, Tennessee for $1,000 in March 1819." They go on to explain what Cornelius Elliott paid Timothy Guard for his freedom, Timothy Guard speaking the words to the clerk, confirming that "for the sum of $1,000 paid me I declare said CORNELIUS having lived from March 1819 to August 4, 1821 in Illinois and in consideration of same payment do free CORNELIUS."[23]

Cornelius Elliott was free.

But there was a problem. In 1821, Timothy Guard's pit was not yet finished. He wanted it deeper, more productive. He intended to get more money out of his salt works. So Guard kept Cornelius's brother, Aaron Elliott, enslaved, promising Cornelius Elliott that he would sell him for $550 when Elliott came up with the cash. But where could Elliott earn that kind of money? He lived in a company town, and the company was owned by Timothy Guard. Whether Guard paid Elliott too little or just refused to sell Aaron, Elliott was not able buy his brother's freedom for another six years. He finally did in 1827, a couple of years after the completion of Guard's deepest pit.[24]

Now, finally, Cornelius Elliott was truly free.

Technically, Aaron was not. By law, upon purchasing his brother, Cornelius Elliott became a slave owner. He may not have been able to afford both the $550 and the $1,000 bond he knew that Gallatin County would charge him. He and Aaron also knew that Aaron had to pay Cornelius back. They were almost certainly in agreement on this, for their mother was still held in bondage, and they desperately wanted her free. She could not make the kind of money Aaron could, with his brother almost certainly training him up in the lucrative coopering business. So Aaron worked for five years, technically in bondage to his brother, before they could finally go to the courthouse and get his free papers. The purchase of a healthy, strong family member such as Aaron could provide valuable aid on the frontier, where land was more plentiful than labor. But Elliott, like most freedom entrepreneurs, bought not only the healthiest and youngest members of his family but also his elderly mother and others besides. For this was not the economics of greed; this was the ascendency of love.

So while the salt mine owners kept to their math of misery and slave owners in the South turned a profit on the sale of their own children, Cornelius Elliott and the thousands of other freedom entrepreneurs like him in antebellum America honored their families. Of course there were a few free African American slave owners in the South. Some could not resist the profits to be made through enslaved labor, no matter their skin color.[25]

However, Elliott and many other freedom entrepreneurs turned their backs on the financial temptations of owning human chattel. Some of these freedom entrepreneurs had experienced the ultimate betrayal: sale by their own white fathers. These African-descended freedom entrepreneurs rebelled against that culture. Instead of turning a profit from the sale of their own blood—or even just abandoning kin to focus on their own prosperity—they valued their families, protecting and preserving them by purchasing them, often at enormous expense and self-sacrifice.

Not every African-descended person around the Northwest Territory states made this decision, of course. Armistead Lawless did not. He had been freed in Saint Louis in the 1830s when he was still a fairly young man. By the late 1840s he had amassed a fortune there, part of it in enslaved people whom he forced to work for him. After years in Saint Louis he ended up living in Illinois on a large piece of land he owned, proudly proclaiming his immense wealth when the census taker came calling in 1850.[26]

Still, many recently enslaved people decided to build their families rather than their businesses. Just a few years after Elliott bought his brother, another freedom entrepreneur moved into Illinois, about 250 miles northwest of the salt works. His name was Frank McWorter, although many called him Free Frank. Frank's mother may well have been born in Africa, giving birth to her son while enslaved in South Carolina. Frank's white father almost certainly owned both him and his mother. Frank labored for years under his father's ownership, including in the saltpeter mines of Kentucky. When he fell in love with Lucy, also enslaved, he married her, then worked to buy her freedom. Her owner, knowing of Frank's interest, charged the atrocious sum of $800. But in 1817, Frank paid it before he himself was free.[27]

Frank was now owned by the men who were possibly his half brothers, and they were not enthusiastic about the idea of their property being free, even if that property may have been family. Did they mock Frank with the amount he paid for his wife, Lucy? We may never know, but the records show that it took Frank two more years to earn another eight hundred dollars, and that eight hundred dollars finally convinced the white McWorter brothers to sell Frank to himself.[28]

In the early 1830s, Frank and Lucy moved to Illinois, where he became the first African American in Illinois to legally found and plat a town, the community of New Philadelphia. Free Frank was brilliant at real estate transactions, and as he sold the land in New Philadelphia, often to whites, he bought another member of his family, bringing a whole new meaning to the term "property flipping."[29]

Such freedom entrepreneurs were by no means unique. Cornelius Elliott's home county of Gallatin, Illinois, was full of them. County deed books from the earliest days before statehood record one freedom entrepreneur after another, some of them women. There was Susan, who earned $150 to buy her freedom in 1816, and Lilly who paid her enslaver, Samuel Givens, $300 for her freedom in 1819. Over and over again these enslaved people used their strength, their intelligence, and their lives to invest in their freedom, their future, and their families.[30]

While many freedom entrepreneurs in the South came to the Northwest Territorial frontier by choice, some had the decision forced upon them. To discourage a free black population in the slave South, and fearful of any actions that might weaken slavery's grip, some whites in those states created laws making the freeing of enslaved people more difficult. By the 1820s all the states of the upper South had passed legislation requiring any freed people to leave their territory within a year's time or risk reenslavement. This was a hardship for many who had family members still held captive, and southern archives are full of heart-rending court petitions from recently freed people begging to stay close to kin.[31]

But Cornelius Elliott could stay in Illinois, and he wanted to, despite the fact that the salt works were not the only danger on the frontier.

Away from the horrors of the salt works, the wilderness started, and people with every right to call that land their own still lived there—the Native Americans. The First Nations of the Northwest Territory states had been dealing with people from across the Atlantic for over 150 years by the time Cornelius Elliott arrived in Illinois. They had seen it all: trade and betrayal, cooperation and conflict, war and genocide.[32]

And pioneers coming to the northwest frontier to clear lands and farm were not a welcome presence, no matter what the color of their skin. And as the territory was opened for sale, free African American pioneers were as vulnerable to Native American attack as whites, for they were a part of the same settlement movement that was destroying these First Nations' homes and livelihoods. The slave registry book in Elliott's own Gallatin County, shows that a free African American by the name of Alfred J. Jones, who had lived in the region through the War of 1812, requested his free papers in 1819. He was intent upon leaving because he had "suffered considerably from Indians."[33]

But then, the American frontier has always been infamous for its lawlessness, brutality, and violence. So maybe the horrors of the salt works and the attacks and counterattacks between pioneers and Native Americans are not all that surprising. The surprise is Cornelius Elliott and his family and all the other freedom entrepreneurs in the Northwest.

Now, Cornelius Elliott was not just a freedom entrepreneur; he was also a brilliant entrepreneur on many fronts, with a sharp understanding of how he could succeed out there in that mess of a place. As he walked those miles of wooden pipes, doing his work for Timothy Guard, checking for leaks and repairing them, he must have noticed the soil under his feet. For while Elliott was a cooper, he also wanted to be a farmer. He did not want to own just himself; he wanted to own land—a piece of his nation. The burning of acres of woodland, while appalling, was clearing the trees. And he must have heard the rumors that the territorial government was planning on selling some of that land.

Elliott had been saving up for just this opportunity, and in July 1829, when the government put up the first, best lots for sale, he walked into the land office to buy eighty good acres at a dollar an acre, cash on the barrel. The deed officer handed him his slip of paper noting that this was Federal Land Deed Number 1 for that region. Elliott was the first, and he knew his land was the best.[34]

By the end of his long life, Elliott had worked to buy the freedom of four family members, including his mother. His brother named his son Cornelius in honor of the brother who freed him. Cornelius Elliott and his wife, Sarah, on the other hand, named one of their sons Amistad, almost certainly for the ship of enslaved people who had rebelled and won their freedom.[35]

Meanwhile, more African American pioneers were coming onto the northwestern frontier, seeking the same freedom and success that Cornelius had dreamed of. But these pioneers had not been born into bondage; they were long free and wealthy. And by coming to the Great West they were risking the loss of much, including their liberty.

5

"To secure these rights, Governments are instituted among Men, deriving their just powers from the consent of the governed"

Robertson County, Tennessee, Winter 1838

The rooster was crowing, and the sharp smell of wood smoke was filling the air as they all worked together to get the morning chores done. January is a quiet time on a farm in Tennessee. But the animals still need tending, never an easy task when every water bucket fills with ice by morning, so Nancy Lyles would have done her morning chores with her youngest ones tagging along.

Getting water meant walking the ice-slicked path down to the stream a little way off. Once there, they had to break a hole in the ice. Sometimes this took an axe and some hard hitting, but on milder mornings it could be a game, whacking at the thin skim of ice, which would crack and shatter in a most satisfying way. Then the buckets could be filled and hauled home.

Everyone was busy, with even the smaller children ducking into the henhouse to gather eggs. Gathering eggs was always a particular delight on those winter mornings, being able to put their cold hands under the feathered bellies of the hens to find the warm eggs there. Eggs were scarce now that the days were so short, but still they would have hoped. At least there would be cream—Nancy made sure of that, milking their cow every morning.

Even with the cold fogging their breath, if it was a clear morning surely they must have stopped for a minute to look at the sunrise. With acres now cleared around their home and barn, they could see for some distance across their land, their lovely land.

How could they leave it?

This region of Tennessee had been home to them since the early pioneer days. Nancy's parents and siblings were all here, most of her sisters now married and living nearby. Nancy had married Daniel Lyles, and all of the Lyles family also lived close. But they were not supposed to be here anymore. Whites wanted them gone—even if they had helped to settle the state, as the Lyles family had, arriving right here in Robertson County, Tennessee, before the War of 1812.[1]

And they had all come in such hope.

Daniel's parents, John and Patsy Lyles, had left their home in Henry County, Virginia, for the Tennessee frontier around 1810. Leaving would have been hard, for Virginia had been home to generations of the free Lyles family, since before the Revolutionary War. But they were eager to settle on this new frontier, with good land and low taxes. Better yet, if John could purchase some of that good land, Tennessee's constitution clearly stated that he had the same right as any man to vote. Tennessee had become a state in 1796, during an unusual time when many American whites were still dedicating themselves to the ideals of liberty and equality. This meant that if a man could rise to the position of property holder, then he was a citizen in Tennessee, regardless of his color.[2]

And John Lyles, with his son's help, intended to do just that.

Nancy's husband, Daniel, would have remembered that journey well. Leaving their home and everything he had known to go out with his parents and his three brothers. They were already getting big enough to help settle a frontier farm. There was James, the eldest at almost twenty, then there were the three younger ones, all spaced about three years apart, Daniel, John Junior, and Joshua.

Their parents, John and Patsy Lyles, were not the only long-free and propertied African American pioneers choosing to settle the southern frontier in those early days. Free African Americans had long been coming out to protect the borders of the newest portions of the nation, even in the slave South.

Peter Caulder, like Nancy and Daniel Lyles, had been freeborn, although his home state was South Carolina. He had fought in the War of 1812 as a patriot and then gone out with an integrated group of eight soldiers to the Arkansas Territorial frontier as part of the first guard at the newly built Fort Smith. After serving as an active soldier and ranger at Fort Smith for fourteen years, he fell in love with Eliza Hall, the daughter of a free black pioneering family who had traveled together to the Arkansas frontier in 1819. Peter and Eliza married and settled on good land to start their farm in what is now Marion County, Arkansas.[3]

It may seem odd that long-free African Americans settled the frontiers of slave states and territories. But at the time they came, their decision would have seemed sound. They could buy good land for little money and pay low taxes. They were also farmers, familiar with working in the climate of that region of the United States. And most people in the early 1810s assumed that slavery in the United States was dying, especially in the frontier regions, north or south. They would have seen all that had happened in their country to abolish slavery, and then in 1808 the international slave trade had been officially shut down. Everyone could see that at various ports, from Rhode Island to South Carolina, corruption was making the ending of this trade incomplete, but people were no longer supposed to be imported into enslavement, so how could slavery grow?

Nancy's and Daniel's parents must have talked of those early pioneer days. And there was more time in the winter to talk, to gather. There were no crops to harvest, no fields to plow. Instead, there were well-built homes, warm fires, good food, and family.

When they gathered together there were so many of them—three generations all calling Tennessee home. Most remembered their pioneer days and would have told the young ones the stories of that long trek from Virginia, their wagons loaded, their children so little. Although, as everyone must have laughed, it was hard to believe Daniel's younger brother Joshua was ever very little, now topping out at six feet, two inches of lean strength.[4]

Yes, John and Patsy could look at their babies now grown men, and fine, able to work the land their parents had settled around twenty-five years ago. And it was such good land, finally free of roots and rocks, a day of plowing pure pleasure. The younger ones may have shrugged and met each other's eyes as the old ones talked of those frontier days. They knew the stories all too well, for they had lived them. They had also cleared the rocks, led the ox teams, wielded the axes that split rails for fences, hammered together the beams that built the barns. They had labored with their parents and now, now when they should all be reaping their reward, now this, the loss of their rights, which was now being followed by harassment.

In 1834 the whites of Tennessee had spoken—whites, Grandfather Lyles must have reminded them, who had arrived long after their own family had. No longer would their freedom and their land give them the right to vote, as it had for almost forty years. No longer could they encourage more family and friends to come join them from Virginia, for the borders of Tennessee had now been officially closed to free African Americans. And they could no longer bear arms.[5]

They could not hunt the deer or turkey they had always relied on. They could not keep the coyotes from the hens or the rabbits from the kitchen garden. Worse yet, they could not protect themselves. Then, in 1836 the Lyles men started being ill-used by white ruffians—with no discouragement from Robertson County's justice of the peace.[6]

The attacks had happened before, but this was worse. Daniel and his brothers had been hauled up on charges of disturbing the peace. The charges were dismissed, but they all knew it could happen again.

Nancy and the other women, generations of them, must have talked together quietly in the evening, trying not to wake or worry the children.

The older women must have talked of that first leaving from Virginia. They knew the pain of departure, the difficulty of starting over, and now they faced that prospect again—of arriving on another frontier and making a new home in rough conditions. Nancy's kin would have known her heart and all the reasons she delayed going to that county office to get the free papers she needed to travel. Daniel had gone in December, before Christmas, but Nancy had waited until January. Standing in front of that clerk as he measured her height to within a quarter inch, eyeing her as he wrote down the color of her skin, the shape of her body, must have been so hard.[7]

And maybe she hoped they wouldn't have to leave after all. Maybe things would die down as they had in 1823.

They would have reminded each other of the troubles they had seen before. They had survived hard times. Life here had never been exactly easy, but they had still made a way.

Daniel's parents, John and Patsy, had been expecting things to be hard on the Tennessee frontier when they arrived around 1810, but they could not have known there would be war. The War of 1812 did not trouble Tennessee too much, although it must have made this pioneering family's life uncertain, for their new nation did not seem guaranteed to survive the conflict.[8]

In those troubled years Patsy must have surprised them all, including herself, by having Tabitha in 1812 and Sanford in 1813. When Sanford was born he became the fifth living son in the Lyles family, his older brothers ranging in age from twenty-one to thirteen. In 1816, when Tabitha was four and Sanford only three, that terrible freeze hit. Seeing the ice lying thick over their crops in June must have been terrifying. Who knew if things would ever get better.[9]

Luckily, there were still the woods and the animals to hunt there. Daniel's parents made sure their family had food, even though the oldest boys were growing so fast they must have been hungry all the time. But they did not starve. Instead they thrived, and more family and friends came to join them from Virginia.

Then in 1823, the local justice of the peace threatened the Lyles family. He demanded that they prove their freedom. It was purely harassment: everyone knew they had arrived years before, free and with the money and resources to give them a good start. But evidently this success did not sit well with the justice of the peace.[10]

He may have been new, may indeed have arrived in Tennessee after them, for he seemed unaware that the Lyles family had a powerful and loyal friend.

Colonel Hopson was a white Revolutionary War veteran who had also come west from the Lyles family's home county in Virginia. He stood with them before the justice of the peace and affirmed that the entire Lyles family was free and had been free for generations back in Virginia.[11]

Roughly a dozen years had passed since then, but a great deal had changed.

Back in 1823, the colonel was not the only white man in Tennessee interested in the old revolutionary ideals. At that time there were still those in that state who had grown up believing slavery a sin and that the nation should do everything possible to extinguish it. Indeed, Tennessee had once had a thriving homegrown abolitionist society that started publishing its own newspaper in 1819. In the late 1810s and early 1820s, over 4,500 white Tennessee residents petitioned their government to end slavery. They reminded their political leaders of the Declaration of Independence's words and ideals and spoke openly of the cruelties inflicted on enslaved people in their state.[12]

Now, in 1838, their ally Colonel Hopson was dead, as were most Revolutionary War veterans like him. Few abolitionist petitions were sent anymore. And slavery—far from dying—had grown monstrously large in many of the newest slave states. In Tennessee alone, the number of people enslaved had grown from roughly 80,000 in 1820 to over 141,000 in 1830.[13]

The Lyles family and their neighbors would have seen people chained in coffles coming from the east, bound together and made to march until the metal bands around their ankles bit deep. These were death marches, for only the strong made a good product and got a good price for the "drivers." If a child or grandmother died, there was one less mouth to feed on the long trail to Tennessee.[14]

If they survived the march, they were forced to clear land, dig up roots, build mansions, and make wealthy the people who felt entitled to call themselves pioneers and the founders of the state of Tennessee.

How could Nancy explain it all to her children? True, she had been raised in the slave state of Virginia. But now whites in Virginia were breaking up families and selling people about as fast as they could to the traders who were marching those people into Tennessee and the other slave state frontiers.

For Nancy and the other free people around her, freedom meant family. They had come out of Virginia together, and now three generations of parents, brothers, sisters, aunts, uncles, nieces, nephews, and cousins were living together in Tennessee.

But their children were seeing terrors—other children in chains, brutalized and bleeding. And alone. Did her own children ever ask Nancy if they would be taken away from her? How could she reassure them when their father and uncles were taken by a white lawman whose job was to enforce slavery in that county?

Yes, this miserable monster of slavery was growing very large, perhaps too big to kill.

But the Reverend Nat Turner had tried. Enslaved people had waged battles against bondage before, but there was a sense that Nat Turner's revolution was different. Turner was a preacher, a man of God, and enslaved. And he lived near Richmond, Virginia, close to where Daniel Lyles's grandfather had grown up free. In August 1831, he had mounted one of the deadliest slave revolts in the United States. It was quickly put down. When Nat was found a couple of months later, he was put on trial, hanged, flayed, and his body torn apart.[15]

In the weeks before Turner was found, whites were hungry for vengeance, hungry for blood, and it seemed that no one with a dark complexion in Virginia was safe from retaliation. Soon there were rumors of revolts rising in almost every slave state. The whites in Tennessee were far from immune to such rumors, which grew all through the winter and early spring of 1832. It could not have been an easy time for Nancy Lyles and her family.[16]

The news had spread all the way up to Boston, where the white abolitionist William Lloyd Garrison wrote a piece favorably comparing Nat Turner and the rumored rebel leaders in Tennessee to the struggle for independence occurring across the Atlantic in Poland.[17]

Garrison may have been hated by every enslaver in the United States, but the enslavers may have been thinking very similar thoughts to Garrison. They knew all about revolutions, having kept a close eye on the successful slave rebellion in the Caribbean island of Saint-Domingue that had been controlled by the French and was now a free nation known as Haiti. Indeed, enslavers would have made it their business to know of every revolution, by blacks or whites at that time, anywhere in the western world.[18]

They knew that no one could take away people's freedom without some kind of revolt, whether it was a large armed militia marching toward New Orleans or poison in the Sunday soup. And the only way to be really safe from the threat of slave revolution was to get rid of slavery. So both Virginia and Tennessee considered doing just that.[19]

Had the Lyles family heard rumors in 1831 that the Virginia General Assembly was shaken enough to consider abolishing slavery? When the rumors turned out to be true, they must have been encouraged by the sentiments coming out of Virginia, with even Governor John Floyd admitting that he would do everything in his power to "have a law passed gradually abolishing slavery in this state."[20]

In an odd twist, while white lawmakers in Virginia and Tennessee seriously contemplated ending slavery in their states, many white lawmakers in the North excused their creation of prejudiced laws against free African Americans as mere friendly support for slaveholding southern whites who could never be expected to abolish slavery.[21]

Virginia brought a bill abolishing slavery to a vote, where it was hotly debated but ultimately rejected. Instead, the opposing side won, forcing through laws that not only strengthened the system of slavery but also resulted in terrible losses for free African Americans in the state. They lost their right to assemble, to worship with an African American preacher, and to teach their children to read and write. Whites in Virginia and throughout the South had made their decision—the Bill of Rights was less important than prejudice and bondage.[22]

Soon afterward, it was Tennessee's turn, where whites were working on a new state constitution. Constitutional delegates and lawmakers seriously debated ending slavery, but in almost all cases their abolitionism was tied to massive prejudice, with most desiring to rid Tennessee of all people of African descent, enslaved or free. These were almost all colonizationists, as were most of the politicians in Virginia.[23]

But those who supported enslaving people quickly killed the notion of ending bondage, even if it could result in the deportation of every African American in Tennessee.

One of the men working on the new constitution was William Blount, who was a supporter of growing slavery and reversing rights for free African Americans in Tennessee. Blount was a man the Lyles family would have known. Daniel's brother Joshua was now married and living in Montgomery County, the same county as Blount, who would certainly have noticed the six-foot-two Joshua on his fine farm surrounded by all those other free African American farmers.[24]

So now the slavery debate was settled in Tennessee. Slavery would continue; it would be protected, and it would be grown. Now the white constitutional convention attendees turned their attention to the free African American population, which was, as convention delegate

Edward B. Littlefield put it, "a curse to society" and "a degraded, debased race." Another convention delegate, Leonard H. Sims, said Nat Turner's rebellion had been the result of allowing "the free black and the slave to associate together." He concluded that if laws were loosened to make it easier for more people to be freed, "the country would soon be filled with a race of free negroes . . . who will be a pest and a degradation on society."[25]

And before long the Lyles family and all free people with Africa in their blood had lost almost everything except their freedom. It was not exactly Nat Turner's fault. Whites had been chipping away at equality ever since the Revolution.

Since those heady early days just after the Revolution, when almost all state constitutions had inclusive language where suffrage was concerned, whites had been working hard to separate free African Americans from their right to vote. Delaware had denied African Americans the vote in 1792, but soon more states took the same action to strengthen exclusion and prejudice: Kentucky in 1799, Maryland in 1801, Washington, DC, in 1802, New Jersey in 1807, Connecticut in 1818. And now there were so many new states, with new constitutions, all of them with white residents who were working to create exclusion. Whites in each one of the Northwest Territory states had added in exclusion clauses barring African Americans from voting, from Ohio in 1803 to Illinois in 1818. As the free African American population grew and started to rise, whites in states across the new nation fought to exclude their fellow Americans from the vote. Whites in Mississippi did so in 1817, Alabama in 1819, and Missouri in 1820. Whites in Michigan, which was not even a state yet, decided to exclude African Americans from voting in 1835, possibly because African Americans had already started to settle and vote in that territory under the guidelines of the Northwest Territorial Ordinance.[26]

Indeed, whites in the Northwest Territory states helped to lead this attack on African American voting rights. When these territories became states, none of them kept the voting rights of the original 1787 ordinance, an ordinance that never mentioned color, only gender and property ownership as the definition of a citizen. All of the whites who created their state constitutions in the Northwest territories discussed and agreed that they should add in the words "white" when describing who could vote. And these decisions did not happen without a debate. There was always a dissenting voice arguing for equality. This meant that whites were very thoughtfully and deliberately withdrawing the right of citizenship from African Americans.[27]

These prejudiced actions in the Northwest Territory states had national significance. In fact, the Northwest Territory states and their exclusion laws were cited by Tennessee lawmakers in the 1830s to strengthen their arguments for prejudiced laws against free African Americans in Tennessee.[28]

This exclusion was a terrible injustice, and it was known and resisted. As African Americans in Ohio demanded of the white politicians and voters of their state, "We ask that the word 'white' in the State Constitution be stricken out at once and forever, and of course that the privileges growing out of such a striking out be restored to us."[29]

And these losses hit the South. Whites in Tennessee had excluded the Lyles men and any other men with African blood in their veins from the right to vote in 1834; similar measures followed quickly in North Carolina in 1835. And whites in the Arkansas Territory, which bordered the Lyles family's home state of Tennessee, were working on doing the same.[30]

This was about more than a few white men in a back room arguing over a new constitution. True, they did argue. They often debated fiercely about the removal of equal rights and the creation of exclusion in these documents. But in the end it was about the whites in these states going to the polling stations to cast votes approving the destruction of the rights of their neighbors just because of skin color or blood.

During the revolutionary era and the few decades that followed, the nation seemed poised to embrace liberty and equality, but it was being replaced with a darker vision.

The loss of voting rights was especially bitter in North Carolina. While only about 4,500 free African American men, women, and children lived within Tennessee's borders in 1830, North Carolina had almost 20,000, most of them rural and farming families like the Lyles family. And they had been voting.[31]

Indeed, John Chavis, a free African American school founder and teacher in Raleigh, North Carolina, not only voted but often wrote to Willie P. Mangum, one of his white former students, who was now a federal congressman, giving him advice and even criticizing some votes and decisions Mangum was making. In July 1832 Chavis wrote to Mangum, "I disapprove of three of your votes . . . but my greatest grief is that you should be in favor of the reelection of General Jackson for the Presidency. . . . Let G.J. be elected and our government is gone and even in its present situation it would require a Hamilton, a Jay, and an old Adams bottomed upon G. Washington to repair its ruins." He could not know just how ruinous things would get when "G.J." was reelected.[32]

Leory Pitford knew firsthand the sorrow of losing civil rights. He and his daughter Mary Anne had left for Indiana from their home in Wake County, North Carolina, in 1838, just after whites in that state had stolen his right to vote. He had made careful plans, ensuring that both he and Mary Anne had their free papers. He had told the official in North Carolina of his plans, and the man had duly written on the free papers that the Pitford family planned on "removing to Indiana or some other northwestern state." Sure enough, soon after he and Mary Anne arrived in Jefferson County, Indiana, they were forced to file their free papers and their bond. Whether it was actually $500 in cash, or just the promise of it, the amount was a terrible sum. And Leory Pitford knew that at any point that bond could be used against him. Any white person in the county who decided his land was a bit too good or he was doing just a bit too well could levy some false accusation, and the justice of the peace—whom Leory would have no say in electing—could make sure that that bond came due.[33]

As the white clerk registered them, he wrote a description of Pitford. In front of his daughter, Mary Anne, the clerk wrote that Pitford was "stout and well made." The clerk may have thought he was complimenting Pitford, for the term "stout" was the description given to the strongest and healthiest men of the day, men who were filled out with muscle. But it was also how enslaved people were described at the auction block to bring up their value, and this was written—and possibly said aloud—in front of Pitford's daughter. Before the clerk finished up, Pitford informed that clerk that he had been a property owner and a citizen back in North Carolina, insisting that the clerk add the words, "He has voted for members of Assemblys."[34]

This information may have surprised the clerk—after all, no African American had voted in Indiana since it had become a state, no matter how much property he had. But those words stayed in that deed book, preserving Leory Pitford's pride in the civil right he had once had and the pain of his loss.

Back in 1791, Abraham Bishop, an advocate of equal rights in America, had warned of the ways in which white men like himself could try to force their way into a position of privilege, writing, "We glory in the equal rights of men, provided that we white men can enjoy the whole of them." Now, forty-five years later, whites across the South were finally enjoying "the whole of them," and they were being joined by whites in the North, eager to strip African Americans of their right to equality.[35]

No, this was not going to get better. This was not 1823; this was 1838, and the Lyles family and their extended kin could see that it was only going to get worse.

And there were the children to consider, the next generation. Maybe it was not just the loss of rights but the growing horrors of slavery that their children were now witnessing that decided them.

They knew that they had to leave, but they would not flee. They would go with dignity, with their wealth intact. And they were determined to go somewhere where this would never happen again.[36]

They could take the strong encouragement and funding of Tennessee whites and be "colonized" to Liberia or some other foreign shore. But terrible reports of disease, death, and general chaos were coming back from Liberia, and being exiled from their own land had never been a popular notion with these successful property-owning farmers. They already had good land, and it was as American as they were.

Some had gone to Canada, which was now finally free of slavery. But the short growing season, the different crops, and the cold presented a real challenge. Free African Americans knew it was a haven for refugees from slavery, but they were free, with free papers, and they still had a legal right to settle in many northern states.[37]

And certainly not a city. Free African Americans in the cities of the North were being constrained, forced to live in certain neighborhoods, and were now being targeted for horrific violence. And what would they do in a city? They were farmers, and good ones.[38]

They knew they could get ahead in the country, even the frontier. They had done it before; they would do it again.

They were not alone in their hope in the rural and frontier spaces of the United States. As African American farmers urged their urban brethren, "Agriculture is the bone and sinew of our country: Therefore be it resolved, that we recommend it to our people as best calculated to promote their rise and progress." Their urgings were not based on a dream, they were based on their experience.[39]

The Lyles family and their kin must have hoped that there were still places where a family who was experienced at living on their own land and farming it well could still garner some respect. For a while this could win a man much more than respect, it could gain him citizenship. Maybe in their new home they could work to regain that right.

They might have to leave their land, even their state, but they were not going to leave their nation.

Quite a few of the families moving out of the slave states had roots that went so deep into the American past that their ancestors included all the people living in the New World in the seventeenth century.

Some could just as easily call themselves Dutch as Igbo, or could claim the Native American people who were their ancestors as much as they could the Scottish. But it all depended on who was looking at them, and with what sympathies, or lack thereof. And for many of these people, the backlash of the 1830s caught them up and labeled them "colored," which was enough to bar them from citizenship in the land they had lived in for so long.[40]

The Lyles family, their kin, and their friends were deeply rooted in their nation and wanted to stay there. They could see that things were going wrong, but Daniel's and Nancy's grandparents and parents had seen, however briefly, just how right their nation could be—how, when inspired, Americans of all colors and backgrounds could uphold and work for the ideals of freedom and equality.

They wanted to stay in the United States, in a new place where they could put down roots and work to return their country to its better nature.

And right now they needed to be safe, they needed their children to be safe, and they needed to be able to thrive.

They were not the only dark-skinned Americans leaving Tennessee at this time. The Cherokee were being forced to leave their land, some with enslaved people in tow. No matter how "civilized" the Cherokee had become, with their big homes, fine farms, and slaves, President Andrew Jackson wanted them gone to make room for more whites and their enslaved people.[41]

In the end the Lyles family and many of the free families around them decided on the state of Indiana, due north. It offered less than they would have liked but more than they had now.

They knew they were not the only southerners to leave for the Northwest Territory states. Many were leaving the South, regardless of their ancestry, because they were southerners who stood for freedom.[42]

And now their South was dividing. Not along state lines, but within the states, dividing within counties, within churches, even within families.

And many had been leaving for the frontier of the Northwest territories and states, to try to root their southern vision of freedom in a new land.

This pioneering movement was integrated. Some, like the white Reverend James Grier from Virginia, came with people they wanted to see free. In other cases long-free African-descended people and whites moved together, bonded by a common belief in freedom. They chose to support each other, traveling together as they made the difficult journey to the frontier.[43]

Upon arrival in the new land, they sometimes divided, creating separate settlements and communities. Sometimes white prejudice lay at the heart of this separation—a common belief in freedom did not always come with a common belief in equality. But while some black and white pioneers separated once they reached the Northwest Territory states, some continued on together, forging a common bond in the causes of liberty and equality, a bond shared with others whether they were from Connecticut or the Carolinas.[44]

As free African American pioneer Thomas Hedgebeth said when explaining his choice to move from North Carolina to Indiana around this time, "The white people did not seem so hostile altogether, nor want the colored people to knuckle quite so low. There were more white people who were friendly than in North Carolina. There were more who wished colored people to have their rights than in North Carolina."[45]

Despite the fact that the lands of the Northwest Territory and states were filling up with millions of whites, despite the fact that in the cities and some rural areas prejudiced whites were attacking their African American neighbors, there were still rural regions with decent neighbors and good land to be had.

As an abolitionist newspaper reported in 1837, in a farming community in Ohio, "there are several families of colored people, most of them doing very well, and they are highly esteemed by their white neighbors. . . . [F]rom conversations with several gentlemen, I did not learn that colored people were looked on any differently from white people of the same character." The author does add, however, "This is the only village that I know of [in Ohio] where the colored children are admitted without opposition in the district schools."[46]

No, the Northwest Territory was far from perfect, but the Lyles family, like many southerners at this time, were deciding that it would do.

But before risking their children and families on the journey, they would have sent someone to find the best place to settle. They were not going to move to just any place. The Lyles family, and those who came with them, could afford to be picky. Their scouts—brothers, sons, and husbands—would have had a lot of questions, and good ones, when they came to Indiana.

They were looking for good land, with a growing season not too far off from what they were used to. They would have wanted to be close to a river or waterway for ease of transportation and a good source of water. And if there were whites nearby, the pioneers needed to know those settlers would not burn them out. They were going to move in a large group, so they did not need a lot of help; they just needed to not be hindered.

They knew how to find the land, and they wanted the best, that desirable good land near the Wabash River and the Ohio, in Indiana. But for much of the information and advice they needed, they had to talk to the African Americans who were already there. Somehow they found Charles and Keziah Grier. As a founding family, the Griers could help new families settle in, locate the best land that someone might consider selling, introduce them to the neighbors, and show them how to get their goods to the lucrative markets of Louisville, Saint Louis, and Cincinnati. This was the kind of home place the Lyles family was looking for.

Of course, the Griers would have warned them that while Indiana was a free state, it had its troubles, and the Lyles family would probably not get the right to vote again any time soon. But they would have the right to own a gun, to worship freely, and to educate their children without the terrors of slavery closely surrounding them.

And thousands like them were making the same decision. Long-free people from Virginia, North Carolina, Tennessee, Kentucky, and so many other southern states where whites were stripping away rights.[47]

But all of them knew that both coming into and settling on the northwestern frontier constituted a formidable challenge to free people of African descent. Not the least of their challenges was the cost.

There were the wagons, and often an ox team to invest in. Many of these pioneers were coming from well-cleared land that a horse could plow, but they would need oxen to clear the frontier land they were going to.

Then, once they got there, they had to buy the land and start a farm. Estimates vary, but in the late 1830s, establishing a 160-acre farm in frontier Illinois—enough land to allow its owner to become a successful commercial farmer—cost close to $1,000. Of course, the Lyles family and their group may have planned to buy improved land that was already cleared or even purchase settled farms. And that would make their move even more expensive.[48]

But it was an expense some free African Americans were prepared to pay in order to start from a good position in the Northwest. And not a few were leaving large and thriving farms and could afford the best land that money could buy.

Arthur Allen had decided to leave North Carolina even before it turned its back on voting rights, drawn by word of the good farming land available in Illinois. He and his wife were in their forties with eight children when they moved from Northampton County, North Carolina, to Illinois in the late 1820s. They were free and came with enough money to pay cash for a settled farm of eighty acres including a house and a barn that a white family was selling. At his death in 1840, Arthur Allen owned 320 acres and had loaned over $700 to local farmers. In addition, four of his sons and a son-in-law owned over 1,000 acres of farmland combined, making the Allen family the equivalent of landed gentry in that county.[49]

Another group of wealthy free African American families fled the area around Richmond, Virginia, just after Nat Turner's rebellion.

While they traveled together, once they arrived in Ohio they scattered across the countryside, finding the farmland that suited them best. Abraham and Mary Goode-Depp choose Concord Township, in Delaware County, where they bought around six hundred acres worth $7,500 by 1850.[50]

Their fellow pioneers, Pleasant and Catherine Litchford, bought a similar massive estate in the township of Perry in Franklin County. Pleasant Litchford had been born around 1789, and like Arthur Allen and many of his fellow travelers, he was approaching middle age when he and his family arrived in the Old Northwest. In 1850, his land was worth $8,000, making him one of the four wealthiest landowners of any color in his Ohio township.[51]

Of course, the very act of buying land could put African Americans at risk of further costs, for those whites responsible for selling government land could decide to enforce Black Code bonds, adding perhaps $500 or $1,000 to their financial burden.[52]

While the costs and legal challenges were daunting, the journey to the frontier held its own dangers unique to free people of African descent. Nancy, Daniel, and all the Lyles family knew that in leaving they were risking what little freedom they already had.

They had their families, their funds, and their freedom, but all that could be lost, for they were walking wealth. They were traveling through a nation that valued them more as chattel than as citizens, and once they left their home they became rich pickings. Even though they were sure to have their free papers with them, those were just pieces of paper. But their bodies, their bodies were ready cash to any white man who could overpower them. And it was not a little amount. By 1837, with the international slave trade now officially shut down and whites on the slave frontier in America demanding more forced labor to clear their land, the market value of a healthy man of African descent was $1,300.[53]

And Daniel and his brothers were such healthy men.

There could be attempts to kidnap them before they ever left the South. Thomas Weaver had only been traveling for a few days through

North Carolina on the way to Indiana when his family stopped in a village. He was young, but he was playing with another boy who was traveling with them, and his mother must have only looked away for a minute. But by the time she looked round the two boys had been lured away by some white men in a shop with promises of a shiny new tin cup. A missing child is every mother's nightmare, but Thomas's mother, Elizabeth, would have known of the horrors of slavery and what could happen to her child if he were taken. The men who had offered Thomas the tin cup saw him only in terms of pounds, inches, and cash, but he was his mother's heart, her life. Even with the help of a sympathetic witness who had seen what had happened, it took Elizabeth hours to find her son.[54]

Then there were the Waldens and their group, who were also trying to get to Indiana, but from North Carolina. Like the Lyles family, they had sent ahead a few men to scout out and buy land before the wagon train left. But even after they crossed the Ohio River, they were not safe. As they traveled through Indiana a gang of white men stopped them, seeking to make a fortune from the Waldens' flesh and blood.[55]

The gang was highly organized, shoving thick poles through the wagon wheels to bring them to a deadly halt. They had obviously been preying on the African Americans flooding into Indiana, and now they were putting an end to every hope these pioneers had for the future.

One of those pioneers was Martha Walden. Her father, Drewry Walden, was born free in Virginia in the 1760s and had fought as a patriot in the Revolutionary War. Martha had been born on the Walden estate, three hundred acres her parents had settled in Northampton, North Carolina. Her father would have been able to vote, worship freely, and educate his children in that state, but now he—and all of them—had lost those rights.

Martha had given up so much to make this move, and now she faced the loss of her family and freedom. Did she look down at her hands, their skin almost as pale as the men who now surrounded her? No matter how light her skin, it could not protect her from prejudice and the loss of rights in North Carolina, but it could be a possible protection here in Indiana. Gathering all the courage she had, this daughter of a Revolutionary War hero must have stood up to scold her attackers, telling them that she was the white owner of the people they were trying to steal. She may have even threatened them with legal action. Whatever she said, she was so confident that the attackers became confused, withdrawing and taking the wooden poles from the wagon wheels so the pioneers could move again, and Martha and all her beloved kin and community continued northward toward their new home.[56]

Not everyone was as lucky as the Waldens and the Weavers. There can be no knowing how many pioneers lost their freedom on the journey to the Northwest, but the Conner family never forgot the one they lost on the way. William Bright Conner and his wife, Elizabeth, traveled to the frontier with their family in the 1840s. They left behind not only a lucrative turpentine plantation in Greene County, North Carolina, but free roots in that state reaching back to the seventeenth century. On their trek they were stopped many times by whites demanding to see their free papers. Along the way, however, an aunt lost her papers and was stolen from them by white "patrollers." This devastating event so terrified them that, despite their free status, they decided to travel only at night until they reached the free states. Their caution was not misguided, for on the southern banks of the Ohio River, they barely escaped capture by whites scouring the area for African Americans to sell into slavery.[57]

No, the journey would not be easy for the Lyles family. But they finally made the hard decision to be pioneers again. They loaded the wagons, then lifted their elderly parents onto the high seats, the same way those parents must have once lifted them onto wagons all those years ago in Virginia.

Everyone who had the strength to walk would be walking, even Nancy, keeping watch over her children. Did she promise herself that she would make Indiana feel like home, a place of shelter and comfort to the family she and Daniel were growing?

Daniel gave the call and the oxen would have started walking, moving them to the Great West as the cities of the North burned.

> We inform our opposers that we are coming—coming for our rights—coming through the Constitution of our common country—coming through the law—and relying upon God and the justice of our cause, pledge ourselves *never* to cease our resistance to tyranny, whether it be in the iron manacles of the slave, or in the unjust written manacles for the free.

"To the Citizens of Ohio"
Convention of Colored Citizens, Ohio, 1849[58]

6

"Burnt our towns, and destroyed the lives of our people"

Cincinnati,
Late August 1841

They were barely breathing, all of them quiet as they lay on rooftops and stood in alleys that bled into darkness. The night seemed to be holding its breath with them. It was so hot. The clouds were a lid holding in the stink of Cincinnati, that Queen City of 46,000 souls on the banks of the Ohio River.[1]

The ghosts of millions of hogs slaughtered every winter in the city rose from the ground in a stinking steam. The pork business had given their city the nickname "Porkopolis." In the winter many of the streams that drained the city couldn't freeze, warmed by the blood running into them. They ran a mucky red, emptying into the Ohio River, staining the ice so that the entire city was rimmed with rankness.[2]

Now it was summer, and the hog-slaughtering season was over. But James Wilkerson and his men knew that summer was the season for another kind of slaughter. For summer in Cincinnati was the time for war.

The first battle had broken out in the heat of August 1829. A thriving community of over 2,000 African Americans reduced to 1,000. But the numbers only told part of the story. This was a peaceful entrepreneurial community of African Americans, trying to work and raise their families in one of the largest cities of the Great West, attacked because of their success.[3]

They were supposed to be lazy, ignorant, and brutal failures. Many whites argued that African-descended people were born that way. Others had a shiftier argument—that while they were fully human, enslavement had ruined them, and that if liberated, they would fail at freedom. If they could be redeemed (which some whites thought doubtful), then it was only whites who could show them what hard work, a love of learning, and true faith really looked like.[4]

The only problem was that African Americans were not failing as they were supposed to. They were starting successful businesses, founding churches, and building schools. They were organizing to change politics and the law in favor of liberty and equality. They were even outstripping white men in finance, with Jeremiah Hamilton becoming a famous and successful broker on New York City's Wall Street by 1836. In the late 1820s a series of bigoted cartoons released in Philadelphia mocked the African Americans in that city, who, some whites thought, were becoming too successful. One shows a finely dressed African American couple with grotesquely drawn faces. The man asks the woman how she is handling the hot summer weather. She replies, "Pretty well I tank you, Mr. Cesar, only I aspire too much!"[5]

All over the nation, whites were turning in violence toward African Americans they considered to be aspiring too much. And Cincinnati, with its thriving African American community and active abolitionists—both black and white—saw one of the earliest and worst of these attacks.

In 1829 there had been some warning, and many of Cincinnati's African Americans had managed to escape to Canada, creating thriving communities north of the border. But some stayed, and there would have been men on the rooftops around Wilkerson who would have remembered 1829. The attack started at night and lasted for days. White men mobbing the streets, their hands filled with fire as their burning torches set African American homes and businesses alight.[6]

But Wilkerson, the militia's chosen leader, was not there. In 1829 he had still been enslaved in Virginia. Now, in 1841, he had only been free for six years, but he knew much of what the men around him had suffered, and they trusted him.

Wilkerson had come up with the idea of arranging them on the rooftops and in the alleys of their neighborhood. It was he who was leading them this night. He was only a young man, but all the men he led called him Major. They knew he was the grandson of a Revolutionary War leader, and so they honored him, even though that grandfather may not have even known—or cared—about the existence of an enslaved grandson.[7]

But Wilkerson and his men claimed that revolutionary blood, and now they were leading their own revolution. They understood Thomas Paine's famous words better than most: "These are the times that try men's souls." They may have been summer soldiers, but they would not shrink from the service of their cause.

But more than his ancestry made these men choose Wilkerson to lead them. Some African American men in the city had seen their homes burned, rebuilt, and burned again. There were men there who had invested in this community. But then there was Wilkerson, a preacher, literate and well traveled, a survivor of slavery, a man of deep courage and faith. And they trusted that he would lead them well in the defense of their community.[8]

According to the laws, the courts, and the market, Wilkerson's life was worth a great deal of money. And he had earned every penny of that worth, buying his own freedom. Now, finally, he owned his own body. His life belonged to no one but himself, and he was willing to give up that life for his new brethren in Cincinnati.

Wilkerson had been born into bondage in Little York, Virginia, and like most enslaved people he was denied the knowledge of his birth day. But it must have been around 1810, when the United States was less than twenty-five years old. His mother labored to bring him into the world even as she must have dreamed of her own freedom. And she kept alive that dream in her son.[9]

Her owners, and Wilkerson's, were kin. All of them descendants of their common ancestor, James Wilkinson. That James, James's grandfather, was widely known as a self-serving scoundrel. The foreman of the grand jury that investigated his treasonous activities during the Revolutionary War could hardly find words strong enough to describe his loathing for the man.[10]

But even if his grandfather had done little to uphold the values of the American Revolution, his grandson had the true spirit of liberty in his heart. As soon as Wilkerson could escape, he ran. He ran, and then he ran again. But every time he was caught. Finally, in 1826 his owners, his own flesh and blood, decided to let him rot in prison after one of his escapes. They must have hoped it would teach him a lesson.

It did, but not in the way they expected.

Wilkerson would later admit that what happened to him in that Richmond prison was "the most Providential circumstance probably on record," for he met Lucy Harris there. Harris was a white Quaker woman whose home was Virginia but who had been educated at the Weston School in Pennsylvania—an unusual occurrence for a young woman at that time. In 1826 she was imprisoned in the Richmond jail for a debt she refused to pay. Instead, for four months she cared for the young Wilkerson, teaching him to read. Wilkerson would later point out that in doing so, Harris was technically breaking the laws of Virginia, which made it illegal to teach an enslaved person to read. But as the two of them reasoned, they were already in prison for breaking the law, so what did it matter if they broke one more?[11]

So Lucy Harris taught Wilkerson to read, going through the Bible together. Harris must have pointed out the stories favored by abolitionists of that time, the stories of a blessed people struggling to be free of bondage in Egypt, their God parting the Red Sea in front of them so they could gain their liberty. But Wilkerson would be forever taken by the story of a young man called Joseph, sold into bondage by jealous brothers.[12]

Later, when Wilkerson was taken out of that prison in chains and once again forced to labor in bondage, it may have seemed that little about him had changed. But Wilkerson had been heartened, his yearning for liberty strengthened. In later years, he would describe Harris's help as a "most righteous and praiseworthy act," and because of their work together, "the children were free."[13]

Wilkerson did not give up on freedom. Nor did other enslaved young men in Virginia, with the Bible in their hand and a love of liberty in their heart.

Nat Turner lived not far from James Wilkerson, and when he led his revolution, it became very dangerous to be an enslaved man with the ability to read, a deep knowledge of the Bible, and a belief in a God who was "the author of all love and liberty."[14]

Wilkerson's white kin—his owners—must have come to see Wilkerson less as an asset than as a liability, a risk, an impossible young man. So they sent Wilkerson down river to New Orleans. This was not unusual. It was happening to more and more people in Virginia, whose bodies were now worth more than the overfarmed soil they worked. So they were being taken away to markets, often sold to those who had an eye on the slave frontier. Wilkerson's enslavers were not alone. Greed seemed to be hardening the hearts of many, who disregarded the cries of their enslaved kin as they severed them from their homes and families.

It may have been hot that night in Cincinnati in 1841, but Wilkerson knew heat. He had already survived New Orleans in bondage, and that was its own kind of battle. He had seen the slave market of New Orleans, where a strong body could lead to death in the rice ponds of the Carolinas, and a beautiful body could lead to death in a brothel.

Richard Clague was one of the men busy in that market, buying and selling. He was wealthy, with interests in various enterprises in the city from slave trading to banking. Somehow Clague discovered that Wilkerson was literate, and he purchased him. Indeed, Clague may have had first pick of a shipment of people from Virginia and selected Wilkerson before anyone else had a chance. Soon, like Joseph in the Old Testament, James Wilkerson was put in a position of trust by this American Pharaoh, for Richard Clague decided to put the literate young man to work in the City Bank, giving him the keys to all of its treasures.[15]

Then a miracle happened: Richard Clague fell in love.

Now Clague was already married to Marie-Delphine-Justine, a member of one of the most elite French Creole families in New Orleans. By the time Wilkerson arrived in chains in New Orleans, Richard and Marie had been married at least a decade, splitting their time between Paris and New Orleans, living in wealth and comfort with their three young sons.[16]

Elite white men in New Orleans commonly took mistresses of African descent, some of them even free women. And Richard Clague was in a relationship with the free woman Adele Wiltz, and by the early 1830s they had a son together. Of course, Richard's wife, Marie, would have been deeply familiar with this tradition. But there must have been something different about Richard Clague and Adele Wiltz, because in 1832, the Catholic Marie-Delphine-Justine did something that broke with tradition in that city: she sued for a legal separation from her husband—and won.[17]

Many whites in both the South and the North hated mixed-race unions. Some abolitionists even argued that a white person could never love a person of African descent, because their differences were so great that repugnance could be the only emotion that arose. But the reality—and the laws created to stop that reality in both the North and the South—proved this was nonsense. What was considered a solid color line was not a line at all, for there was already kinship. Many nations ran through the veins of people in the United States, whether they were perceived as white or as "colored."

Soon after their separation, Marie Clague left with their three sons for Paris, and Richard Clague left for England with Adele Wiltz and their son. But before he left, he gathered together the people he owned in New Orleans, James Wilkerson included, and gave them the astonishing news that he was offering them their liberty.[18]

To be fair, Clague was granting that liberty on his own terms. While he was gone, he gave those he enslaved leave to work for themselves, and if at the end of his time away they had raised the money he demanded as their purchase price, they could buy themselves. These were not easy terms or certain ones, but they offered a chance.

Was it Adele Wiltz who influenced Richard Clague, or could it have been their young son? Did Clague hold his son's hand in his as they walked together, that hand the same color as many of the young men Clague owned?

And Clague was not alone. This was a fact that slavery supporters did not want in the public eye: there were other southern enslavers like him who were continuing to free the people they enslaved.[19]

So when Richard Clague, Adele Wiltz, and their son boarded the *Talmur* for England, James Wilkerson went to work for his freedom.[20]

Wilkerson took as many jobs as he could, working punishing hours in the New Orleans heat. His literacy allowed him to find employment in the city's booming printing presses. Newspapers were the new medium of the period, and their popularity was rising. Wilkerson worked for many of them, receiving "the most liberal wages in particular of the editor J.G. Esq." Wilkerson would never forget him.[21]

Working in those presses, Wilkerson was at the forefront of the news coming in from around the nation and the world. He would have read reports of the riots wracking the cities to the north of him. But he would have also heard of the revolutions in the New World and in Europe as people rose up against tyrannical governments. And he would have heard of freedom.

The news that in 1833 Great Britain had officially ended slavery not only in England but in all her colonies was so important that Wilkerson probably did not have to read a newspaper to learn about it, for free African Americans across the United States rejoiced. Here, finally, was renewed hope that the West had not given up on the dream of freedom.

Was there talk of Mexico, Bolivia, and Uruguay as well? Those nations had begun rejecting slavery earlier, between 1830 and 1831. And New Orleans, that city once held by the Spanish, would have been hearing talk that Spain was considering abolishing slavery as well.

The supporters of slavery in the United States must have been furious—and frightened. Now freedom flanked them—with Canada and Mexico taking a stand for liberty. Maybe they became so fierce in their defense of their cause because they felt its popularity was weakening.

There was certainly a new abolitionist movement growing in the United States, and James Wilkerson would have been able to read much about its actions as he helped to print the news in New Orleans.

For years, African Americans and whites had petitioned their local, state, and territorial governments over issues of equality—from voting rights to due process under the law. Even in frontier Michigan in the mid-1830s, over two hundred white people sent such a petition from their homesteads on the territorial frontier. Many were barely surviving, living in small cabins while unseasonably cold summers destroyed their crops. But still, in their outrage over how their territory was sowing inequality and injustice for African Americans through its legislation, these pioneers traveled door to door, across miles of wilderness, to collect signatures.[22]

They were not alone. While some whites rose up in organized violence to strengthen white supremacy, others worked hard against prejudice and slavery. Across the nation, from Massachusetts to Indiana, white and African American abolitionists petitioned their state and federal politicians. The petitions and proposals to abolish slavery and strike down laws that unfairly targeted African Americans grew so numerous that discussions of slavery, freedom, and equality dominated the Congress by 1835. This was not about some fringe group of wild-eyed abolitionists pushing a radical vision; this was about Americans demanding that their elected officials remember the core values their nation was founded on.[23]

So in the early 1830s, the federal government decided it had to do something. Instead of even considering the petitions, they tried to figure out the best way to silence them. Rather than throw them out, the Congress would "table" them indefinitely. This "gag bill" passed with a majority of the vote from both southern and northern politicians. Its defenders claimed the bill was preventing the United States from breaking apart; its critics asked just how far the United States should go—how many of its most basic principles it should ignore—to keep the nation together. What kind of a nation would be left?[24]

James Wilkerson and the other African Americans in New Orleans would have been paying close attention as the federal government all but shut down over the subject of slavery. And still Wilkerson worked to gain his liberty.

But first he had to survive, and that was not the easiest task in New Orleans in the 1830s. The population of the city was growing—it would double in that decade alone—while at the same time it was wracked with yellow fever epidemics. But Wilkerson continued to work, and Richard Clague finally returned in 1835.

Wilkerson never knew his birthday, but he would always remember the day he got his freedom. Clague was gone for roughly eighteen months, and when he returned, Wilkerson met him with cash in hand, as he later wrote, "not like a poor slave, with an aching heart and a head bowed down, but as an heir to inherit the promise of a father—even his liberty—yea that pearl of great price—the next gift to heaven itself."[25]

And so, on June 10, 1835, Wilkerson met with Richard Clague and his trusted attorney, Mr. Carlile Pollock, who drew up the emancipation papers that officially made James Wilkerson a free man.[26]

And the first thing Wilkerson did was to leave New Orleans, moving as fast as he could to Virginia. He had to find his mother. He prayed she was still alive. He may have lived in a culture where people would sell their own kin for a profit, but Wilkerson rejected this. He wanted to find his mother, not just to embrace her, not just to rejoice with her at his liberty, but to make her free.

But freedom was an expensive business. It would have made better economic sense to use his money to start his own printing press or to keep working, purchase a house, and find a wife in New Orleans. Instead Wilkerson met with the people who owned his mother, who could charge him anything they pleased, for they knew he was desperate and in no position to bargain.

Still, Wilkerson met with lawyers, he paid the money, and in the same year that he gained his liberty, he created a family—his mother and himself, finally free.[27]

Wilkerson decided to become a preacher and missionary. He sought out some of the top men of the African Methodist Episcopal (AME) Church, who educated him, and for six years he traveled all over the United States, from Virginia to Kentucky, from Maryland to Indiana, and almost everywhere in between. He became a familiar figure to some of the most renowned abolitionist and human rights activists in America at that time. And in 1841 he came to Ohio.[28]

As he traveled around that state Wilkerson would have seen numerous African American farms and farming settlements. Many of them would have looked like the small settlement of Lexington, in Columbiana County. By 1837, a Quaker visiting the community reported that since its founding in 1821 it had grown to a "settlement of 51 families, numbering 264 individuals . . . altogether 1860 acres of land, valued at $29,200." The community had funded and built two schools "taught by abolition females" and had also built a meeting house. The meeting house was central to that community of far-flung farmers. It was where they worshipped and their Sunday school met. And it housed their library. Community leaders proudly showed their visitor the library of over 120 books they had purchased. And there were, of course, freedom entrepreneurs like James Wilkerson. One of the fathers in Lexington earned $1,700 in order to purchase his entire family.[29]

But James Wilkerson also went to the cities of Ohio. And in Cincinnati Wilkerson was quickly made that city's African American militia leader. As an African American resident of that city would later recall, the militia "had full confidence in his ability, sincerity, courage and devotion, and were ready to follow him even unto death."[30]

Wilkerson had a way with words. He could give a speech or sing a hymn that could move men to action. And action was needed. After all, as he must have reminded the men of his militia, "dreaming, talking, singing and shouting about God and Liberty, all avails nothing." So they would pray. They would dream. But they would also defend their community.[31]

So here they were in Cincinnati in late August 1841, all of them dressed in darkness, all of them armed, all of them waiting for the storm to break.

August 1829. July 1836. Each of those years had seen a riot. Well, some called it a riot, but it was really more of a war where whites attacked the African Americans in the city with the intent of killing their community. And now in late August 1841 it looked to be happening again.[32]

When that first attack had come in 1829, the outrage of their being driven from their city, their state, their nation was reported nationally, and the injustice of it was felt by many people, both white and black.

What these advocates of justice did not realize was that the riot in Cincinnati was just a start, that there was a newer and fiercer opponent. For the 1830s would see the explosive growth of a movement that was fueled by prejudice, driven by hate, and deeply destructive. The violence of this movement reached the level of warfare in the 1830s. As a contemporary witness later recalled, "The days of thick darkness to the colored people were approaching." This movement against equality and freedom had its own funders, its own organizers, its own meetings, and its own newspapers. And its supporters held some of the most powerful positions in government at that time.[33]

Of course, it was not some monolithic movement, any more than the abolitionists were. It was not terribly cohesive. It had local chapters and organizers, and many of these were at odds and disagreed about their goals. Some wanted to abolish slavery, just as long as the United States was rid of anyone with African blood. Others wanted nothing more than to grow slavery and reopen the ports at Charleston and all along the coasts to shiploads of chained people from Africa. But all of them supported inequality and prejudice. And they were quick to turn to violence to achieve their goals.

And this powerful movement loved nothing better than to blame the very people who were trying to resist them—resist the growing violence and division—for creating it.

But still the abolitionist movement grew. African Americans had long been writing, organizing, and working to end slavery and advance equality, but this was a new time and there was a need for something new. The devastation in Cincinnati was one of many catalysts. For years now, whites in every state had been holding conventions to create—or re-create—their state constitutions. These conventions excluded African Americans and increasingly enacted state constitutions that barred African Americans from some of the most basic civil rights. So African Americans started their own convention movement: hundreds of African Americans gathering from all over the United States, organizing, meeting, and making known to all that they would fight injustice, bondage, and inequality. They held their first convention in Philadelphia in 1830.[34]

Philadelphia made sense, for that city was home to the nation's first national gathering of abolitionists in 1794, as well as the birthplace of the first African American denomination, the African Methodist Episcopal Church. By 1830 the AME's founder, Bishop Richard Allen, was close to death, but his extraordinary leadership had given life to a church that had spread across the entire nation, north and south. But those churches had been under attack for a while now, and it was getting worse.[35]

In early June 1834, people had gathered for their fourth annual convention, this time in New York City. The African American human rights advocate William Hamilton had been invited to give the opening speech. There was much to grieve for. Bishop Allen had died in 1831, and the movement to grow prejudice and slavery was gaining strength.[36]

Speaking in a powerful voice strong enough for those seated at the farthest ends of the large hall to hear, Hamilton began speaking the truth and grieving: "How lamentable, how very lamentable, it is that there should be, any where on earth, a community of castes, with separate interests! . . . The society must be the most happy, where the good of one is the common good of the whole. . . . But alas for the people of colour in this community! . . . [F]rom them white men stand aloof. . . . Long, long, long has the demon of prejudice and persecution beset their path." The opposition to equality was spreading. This was no longer just about Cincinnati.[37]

In 1831 whites attacked the free African American community in Providence, Rhode Island, for so many days that the militia had to be brought in. African Americans in Providence had already been hit by smaller riots almost ten years earlier—some of the earliest known prejudice-driven riots in a northern city after the Revolution. But this mob action in 1831 was larger and became an all-out battle. When the guns finally ceased firing and the white mob was finally dispersed, an entire African American neighborhood had been destroyed.[38]

Two years later Detroit was hit. There may not have been very many free African Americans in that territorial town, but they were brave, willing to risk living on the rough edge of the nation. When two of their longtime neighbors were captured and imprisoned for the crime of being refugees from enslavement, the free African Americans of that city decided to take action. The African American refugees—a married couple—were imprisoned as they awaited their return to bondage, even though they had been living profitable and peaceful lives in Detroit for years. But when a few of their friends tried to rescue them, a local white lawman was injured.[39]

The repercussions were terrible. Almost every free African American man and woman in Detroit was rounded up and imprisoned, held hostage until they paid their $500 Black Code bonds. African Americans were blamed for a few fires set in buildings around the prison, and in retaliation whites burned over forty African American homes. Finally, after weeks of violence, with white gangs attacking any African Americans who dared walk the streets, the mayor ordered the final act of violence—that the militia banish all African Americans who could not pay the $500 bond. By early August almost all African Americans in Detroit had been forced out of the city.[40]

Then it was Philadelphia's turn. In 1834 whites attacked African Americans in their homes, breaking, burning, and looting the places that gave shelter and comfort to equality.[41]

And still the dreadful list grew. In 1834 it was New York City and New Haven, Connecticut. In 1835 it was Boston, Utica, and Washington, DC. Then in 1836 it was Cincinnati's turn again.[42]

The violence in Cincinnati, as in most of the cities, was well orchestrated. Powerful, sophisticated businessmen had been organizing antiabolition and pro-prejudice meetings since January, attended by hundreds of whites. It wasn't just bank president Robert Buchanan and Methodist minister William Burke; it was the mayor, the postmaster, a former US senator, and military men like colonels Charles Hale and Robert Lytle.[43]

Both Hale and Lytle were northerners, Hale from Pennsylvania and Lytle—who, as a congressman, had firmly supported President Andrew Jackson—was from Massachusetts. Their prejudice was native to the North and virulent.[44]

It was an old story. They claimed that everything was fine in Cincinnati, that the only problem was those outsiders—those abolitionists—riling things up by spreading harmful ideas about freedom and equality. They argued that their city was perfectly content, no one of any color needing or desiring equality. Conveniently forgetting that it was prejudiced whites in Cincinnati who had been trying to violently destroy equality and social harmony since 1829, and that many in the hall that day were outsiders—newly arrived white men enraged by the successful African Americans they saw all around them in Ohio.

These prejudiced whites were the radicals, for some of the oldest, most powerful white curmudgeons in the state cherished the old ideals of equality. Senator Thomas Morris of Ohio continued to hold to the old values of the Revolution he was raised up in. In 1838, while a senator for Ohio in the federal government, Morris made clear to the Ohio press that the Declaration of Independence was still his guiding light. He wrote, "I have contended that all men were born equally free and independent, and have an indisputable right to life, liberty and the pursuit of happiness."[45]

The pro-prejudice organizers may have been respected and powerful men, but they were using language so threatening and disturbing that local newspapers would not print the words. This indecency was surprisingly common among leaders of this movement. The language used by prejudiced white politicians in the Northwest Territory states was viciously violent against African Americans. These men and these words had very real power. They were encouraging hatred and violence, encouraging whites not only to turn their backs on equality but to hate, to torture, and to even kill African-descended people.[46]

No other group—women, Native Americans, Jews, Catholics, or any other ethnic group—was targeted with this level of violent hatred in the speeches of powerful white men in the Northwest Territory states. This language was a tool to strengthen division and prejudice and encourage violence. And it worked.[47]

As Colonel Lytle from Massachusetts wryly put it, he was all for the mixing of the races. If anything could improve the "bestiality" of people from Africa, it might be forcing them to "mingle their blood with foreign currents." To do this, he advocated castrating all the men and raping all the women. Of course the nineteenth-century press would not print his brutal language in full, even if newspapers had no problem advocating the most obscene violence against African Americans and their allies. Instead, they delicately reported that Lytle had thundered out to hundreds of angry and prejudiced whites in Cincinnati, "You must castrate the men and _____ the women!"[48]

In April 1836 the attack started. The repeated attacks mostly followed the same pattern: target the white abolitionist editors and presses, then move on to attack African Americans and destroy their homes and businesses.[49]

But Cincinnati was not the only city to harbor prejudiced leaders and suffer repeated assaults. That same year whites in New Haven, Connecticut, again went to battle, burning churches and wounding African American citizens. As a Connecticut gentleman wrote to a friend around this time, "The colored people can never rise from their menial condition in our country; they ought not to be permitted to rise here. They are an inferior race of beings, and never can or ought to be recognized as the equals of whites."[50]

So much energy, so much organization, so much destruction, just to reject the ideals of their forefathers. And so the murders and oppression continued. Conservative estimates put the number of these battles waged against African Americans in the cities of the North at roughly forty-six, in just a three-year period between 1834 and 1837. So many whites going to war against equality, and some even fighting other whites.[51]

In 1837, the murder of a handsome young white abolitionist in Alton, Illinois, by radical antiabolitionists, brought much sympathy. Elijah Lovejoy had died trying to prevent the destruction of his newspaper press from a battalion organized by some of the most powerful men in the state of Illinois.

Elijah Lovejoy had recently left his home in Saint Louis, Missouri, horrified by the murder of a free African American man there. That African American man in the city had been captured and tied to a stake where he was slowly burned to death on a bonfire as hundreds of whites looked on. This incident had made Lovejoy more than a little anti-Catholic, blaming the murder on Catholics in the city. But Lovejoy was about to find out just how murderously prejudiced Protestants in a free state could be.[52]

As in so many of these battles, those organizing the attack against equality and freedom in Alton were high-ranking officials. Among the Alton group that opposed Elijah Lovejoy was the new attorney general of Illinois, Usher F. Linder, and Dr. Thomas Hope, soon to become mayor of Alton. They were joined by men of great rank and education: the Harvard-educated Dr. William Emerson, Dr. Horace Beal from Maryland, and Dr. James Jennings from Virginia.

These men met to discuss whether to murder Lovejoy or just torture him. In the end they decided to destroy Lovejoy's press, then capture him, strip him naked, pour hot tar over his body, and force him to straddle a thin splintered log as they carried him out of town. This, they all agreed, would be the most humane option. But in the end, Lovejoy died defending his press, as the gentlemen of Alton tried to wrest from him his right to free speech.[53]

What is rarely mentioned is that Alton lies in Madison County, which was already home to a large settlement of African American farmers by the time Lovejoy arrived. Nor was Lovejoy the first equal rights advocate to live in Madison County. George Churchill had been its earliest state representative and by 1822 (when the state of Illinois was only four years old) had presented a petition put together by the large and established free African American population in Madison County. In it, they asked for the right to vote as well as protection from kidnappers. Historians have not noted what happened to the African Americans who signed the petition, but George Churchill was soon burned in effigy by some of the whites living in his county at the time for his willingness to represent the African American taxpaying members of his county.[54]

The attack on Elijah Lovejoy's press was not just an attack on abolition; it was an attack on racial equality of all kinds. As a white farmer who was part of the mob that killed Lovejoy shouted, "How would you like a damned nigger going home with your daughter?"[55]

Historians have so far not unburied what happened to the African Americans of Madison County during the attack on Elijah Lovejoy. But if whites murdered this respected and well-connected white man, there is little telling what they did—or had been doing—to the landed African American farmers in the county.

One year later, in 1838, Philadelphia was hit again. But this time it was worse. Schools, orphanages, churches, meeting halls, and printing presses were all destroyed as whites attacked the engines of equality, try- ing to break hearts and hope. They seemed intent upon making a nation divisible, all to empower inequality and privilege.

By 1841, many of the cities and towns of the northern United States had glass from the windows of African American businesses, homes, and churches ground into the mud of their streets, shards of crystal pressed into the cracks between their paving stones, glittering—sharp reminders of violence and loss.

This violence had a powerful and circular logic. Bigoted whites vi- olently attacked anyone or anything that might represent a productive or peaceful coexistence between Americans that these prejudiced people were labeling "black" and "white." These prejudiced whites then pointed to the growing division as proof that whites and blacks could never live together in harmony.

Worse yet, if their circular argument was convincing—that whites could not possibly tolerate free and successful blacks—then the abo- litionist movement to end slavery was cut off at the root. Why would northern whites support the ending of slavery if they believed that equality for all was impossible—if they thought freeing enslaved people in the United States would only lead to division and violence?

Pro-slavery advocates rejoiced in the violence against African Amer- icans and the destruction of examples of successful equality or integra- tion. They must have hoped that this destructiveness would convince more whites to support the forced removal of free African Americans through the work of the American Colonization Society. And even con- vince African Americans themselves that the hearts and minds of whites in their nation had changed so drastically that they had to leave. The goals of this warfare were not secret; nor did they go unnoticed. After one of these many attacks, the Boston-based abolitionist newspaper the *Liberator* decried the fact that prejudiced whites were using these battles as "proof . . . of the inveterate antipathy between the two races."[56]

No wonder John Forsyth, President Andrew Jackson's secretary of state, urged Vice President Martin Van Buren in 1836 to encourage even more attacks against African Americans and their white allies in the North. Forsyth and many he worked with knew that there was still too much sympathy for the old ideals of liberty and equality in the North, so he asked the vice president, a New York native, to organize "a little more mob discipline." Forsyth, understanding that any mob actions must look like the work of rabble-rousers, not gentlemen, cautioned that "a portion of the magician's skill is required in the matter." He wanted Van Buren to do some deft misdirection and some fancy hocus-pocus but urged him to be quick about it, adding, "The sooner you set the imps to work the better." But misdirection couldn't disguise the fact that the people of the nation were being sawn in half, not just between North and South, but along a violent color line.[57]

But prejudice did not move every white person, and most African Americans could see right through to the truth—that these were choices being made to destroy equality and strengthen slavery. And together advocates for equality and freedom continued to fight injustice through their petitions, their organizations, their sermons, their schools, their newspapers, and their pamphlets.

And prejudiced whites could not destroy all of the newspapers that were rising, that were bearing witness. Editors, writers, reporters, and newspaper owners were making sure that this movement against equality did not go unreported. They tried to print the truth—that these forces rising to strengthen prejudice and the color line should not be defended as regional or a local spat. While some tried to explain away a particular mob action as sparked by an influx of Irish immigrants or a dried-up river, a brothel or an insult, these newspapers reminded their readers that this violence was a national problem, a national wounding. In addition to abolitionist presses, many presses that were not actively bigoted were bearing witness.[58]

And the prejudiced whites of the United States, whether secretaries of state, city mayors, or farmers, despised not just the words of these torchbearers for liberty but any instance in which whites were not trying to destroy blacks. They condemned any example of toleration, peace, or cooperation between people of different skin color—because each example revealed that prejudice was a choice and inequality a violent invention.

No wonder so many whites hated James Birney, for he was a white man willing to stand with African Americans for the causes of equality and freedom. He was editor of the *Philanthropist*, one of the oldest abolitionist newspapers in the United States, first started in Ohio then abandoned. But James Birney had restarted it in Cincinnati in 1836, hiring some of the most ardent equal rights activists in the nation to write for him. And he paid dearly for it.[59]

James Birney's press was attacked and destroyed in 1836, and if he had not been out of town that night, Elijah Lovejoy may not have been the only white abolitionist killed in the Northwest Territory states.[60]

James Birney was an interesting one. Born into a wealthy slave-owning family in Kentucky and educated at Princeton University, he enslaved people from a young age. His first enslaved people were received as a gift, so that he and his young wife could start their life together in luxury. Much about Birney's youth must have pained him later. There was the weakness for gambling that led his young family perilously close to ruin and did ruin the lives of many enslaved people when he sold entire families in order to pay off his debts. Then there were his years as the owner of a cotton plantation in Alabama, where he became an ardent supporter of the colonization movement and its mission to remove all free African Americans from the United States. But in the mid-1830s something in him changed.[61]

It could not have been easy to turn his back on wealth, on social standing, on respectability. But by 1836 James Birney had done all of this. No longer part of the southern slaveholding elite, he was now a despised abolitionist in Cincinnati, trying to change the nation.[62]

Birney was gripped with a fervor for the immediate end of slavery. He published the work of equal rights advocates intent not just on the plight of the enslaved south of the Ohio River but on the evils of prejudice rising in the North, even in Ohio itself. But how strange it must have been to find himself transforming backward, embracing the old-fashioned ideals of the Revolution now more than a generation past, while he watched both his church and his nation shift away from them.

But he was not alone. He was joined by a new generation of people, black and white, who were arguing for equal rights and freedom in America. He worked with William Lloyd Garrison, another abolitionist newspaper editor based in Boston, although the two men could not have been more different, for Garrison was raised close to poverty in the North.

Garrison's parents had signed him on to an apprenticeship in the rapidly booming newspaper printing business. In 1831, this idealistic twenty-six-year-old decided to start a newspaper called the *Liberator*, in which he advocated for the immediate end of slavery and resistance to inequality. He could not have done it without the financial support of African Americans, who became his first subscribers and spread word of his paper.

While Garrison had never supported slavery, Birney was a convert, and he had a convert's zeal. This zeal sometimes blinded him to the trouble his passion might bring to those around him, whether it was his family or his African American neighbors in Cincinnati. But he was trying. And he had a new project he was excited about.

James Birney was immersed in a project that gripped his lawyer's mind. He was planning a trip to England to give a series of lectures in London and around that country to raise money and interest in the abolitionist cause. He had decided to talk about the churches of the United States and the ways in which they supported slavery. He particularly focused on the Methodist Church, a church he had once helped lead back in the South.

So he started digging around in church records, appalled to see just how much churches had changed in just fifty years and how much they had forgotten. He discovered so many facts that he had not known. His own Methodist Church had once required all its members to free their slaves or be "barred from our Society or to the Lord's Supper" till they had complied.[63]

And in 1794 the Presbyterian Church had written strong words acknowledging that African-descended people were fellow human beings and that enslaving them was a grave injustice. Yet by the late 1830s that same denomination had reversed itself, not just staying neutral but actually encouraging slavery and inequality. Even Birney, who knew that church well, was astounded by the terrible transformation, as he found example after example of churches siding with enslavers and growing in monstrous prejudice.[64]

As he read through church records, Birney could see the various denominations going from their original stance of seeing slavery as "a mournful evil" and a "gross violation of the most precious and sacred rights of human nature" to reversing their course and choosing to uphold slavery, rejecting the concept that people of African descent were fully human. Indeed, many were now arguing that slavery was a necessary good rather than a necessary evil. Birney was well aware of this troubling turn and published the resolution of a group of enslavers in Clinton, Mississippi, who wrote, "Slavery through the south and the west is not felt as an evil, moral or political, but it is recognized . . . as a blessing to both master and slave." This was a reversal of the revolutionary ideals of the nation, the ideals that had propelled its actions toward freedom and equality for decades. Instead, these supporters of slavery were clearly basing their arguments on the belief that all men were not created equal.[65]

Were the enslavers surprised by how rapidly whites in the non-slave states and territories took to their argument? Maybe they had not realized just how strong the backlash against freedom and equality had become in the states to the north of them. Did they imagine that Harvard-educated men from Maine would support their cause in Illinois? That the former abolitionist Reverend Joel Parker, who now held the powerful position of president of the Presbyterian Theological

Seminary in New York, would preach a sermon titled "Abolition might be pronounced a sin as slavery"?[66]

And now supporters of prejudice and inequality in the North were using swords, guns, cudgels, torches, and words. Because for this evil to rise, it took more than words; it took destruction—and intent.

In Pennsylvania, there was careful planning to advance inequality. Most white lawmakers did not respond with outrage or sympathy at the terrible losses the African Americans and their white allies suffered in Philadelphia at the hands of mobs. Instead, these white leaders took a stand for increasing prejudice and supporting slavery—using as their excuse that it was the only way to keep friendly with the slave states and thus keep the nation from dividing. True, the white politicians defended their actions by arguing that slavery and prejudice were realities they could not change. But it was not a reality they were facing; it was a reality they were making.

Of course, as these prejudiced white politicians and their supporters in the North were already making violently clear, they were not happy with the population of free and successful people of African descent that had grown out of the first wave of abolition in America. Maybe they thought it was better to passionately uphold an argument that no white enslaver in the South could possibly wish to end slavery than to face the possibility of more free African Americans.

Whatever their reasons, white lawmakers in Pennsylvania worked hard in 1837 and 1838 to draft a new state constitution that would steal the vote from anyone of African descent. It went to the polls for ratification in October 1838. Despite the riot that May that destroyed Pennsylvania Hall—the city's newest and grandest meeting hall built to host meetings supporting the cause of liberty and equality for all—whites turned their hatred into political action and voted for the new constitution that denied the vote to African Americans. Their votes outnumbered, African Americans could not block its passage.[67]

Pennsylvania, that state that had hosted the nation's first national gathering of abolitionists, that state of brotherly love that was supposed to lead the nation toward its best ideals, not follow other states down a path of injustice, now had a majority of white people who had decided to turn their backs on those ideals. This was a particular sorrow.

But that state was far from alone in doing this. It was merely joining other states in both the North and the South that were working to destroy equality by destroying African Americans' rights. Whites in Indiana had finally joined most of the other Northwest Territory states in passing an anti-immigration Black Code bond law. Now any African American entering that state had to register with a local white official and the Black Code bond was $500.[68]

Of course, these injustices were not going unnoticed. Each one of these attacks were reported in sympathetic newspapers. They were discussed at conventions. They were spoken of in churches and by traveling preachers. And as the news spread, it must have seemed to African Americans, and to all who fought with them against this rising prejudice, that equality was not just dying; it was being murdered.

Now it was 1841, and the men on the roof around James Wilkerson were convinced that violence was about to rise again. After all, they knew this city better than he did. They were "Freesies," the name given to free people of color in that city. This city was their home, their base, and many of them were rivermen working on the Ohio and Mississippi. And they had seen much in their travels. Some owned their own boats—flat boats, cargo boats, passenger ferries—carrying anything that needed moving. Others worked those floating palaces, the steam-driven paddle wheel ships.[69]

These Cincinnati men went farther than the Ohio River, for good money could be made taking loads south down the Mississippi River. And those travels put them deep into the new slave states, where the brutal work of cotton production was leading to horrors. These new plantations were large, set in a vast freshly settled land whose entire legal and social system rested on forcing large groups of people to labor. But the rivermen would have witnessed.

There are few accounts from them of what they saw, but they were likely similar to what the African American Isaac Griffin saw. He first made the trip down the Ohio and then the Mississippi as a young man sometime in the 1840s, still enslaved. Later he would try to tell what he witnessed: "Just before day, the first time I went down, as I was floating down the Grand Gulf, I heard the whip cracking and a man crying, 'Oh Lord! Oh Lord! Oh Lord!' I was afraid somebody was murdering: I called my master—he said, 'Somebody is whipping his slave.' We had to put in there. I saw the man. He was put over a log, his feet tied, his hands tied, and a rail between. They would whip him, then rest upon it. They flogged him off and on until daylight. His back . . . " Here Isaac Griffin stopped, unable to continue.[70]

And many on the rooftops of Cincinnati that night in 1841 knew these horrors more intimately, for they had survived them.

They had run hundreds of miles to be here; others had come already free. But all of them were agreed: they were not going to run anymore. Here they were free. Here they could do something. They could keep their families together, and they could protect them.

Their life here in this city might be hard, but it was better than what others suffered in bondage. Here they possessed their own bodies, their own lives, and their families, their friends, their community. Now they were prepared to lay down their lives to preserve all that they held dear.

So they waited, waited as hundreds of men began to organize and move with violent intent toward their neighborhood.

Wilkerson was on the roof of one of the handsome row houses that lined the boulevard of his neighborhood. He must have been lying down to stay hidden, the heat from the day's sun still rising up from the roof, burning his stomach and legs. Sweat would have run into his eyes as his grip became slippery on his gun.

They all would have been there for a while, guns in hand. The militia were everywhere, lining the flat roofs on either side of him. He would have barely been able to see them, but once in a while the flicker of a far-off torch must have illuminated the eyes watching him, glittering in the faint light. Was Wilkerson ever tempted to slowly inch toward the edge of the building that dropped into darkness, to glance down into the alley to check on the men waiting there? Even if he had, he would probably have seen little. But he would have known the other men were there; he would have been able to hear them breathing.

It was so hot.

They could see the lightning flickering off to the west and hear the low rumble of thunder. Otherwise it was quiet. A city in 1841 could be a very quiet place at night. There was no hum of machinery, no tires on pavement, no sirens, no airplanes. Usually there would be the thrum of a paddle wheel ship passing by on the river, its bell jangling. But not this year. This year it was so dry there were record low waters on the Ohio River. So the steamships were stuck in port, the river they were supposed to travel mostly silt and slag.[71]

For months now they had been praying for rain. That thunderstorm building in the distance, blocking out the stars, was something they had all been hoping for.

But Wilkerson was listening for something else—he was listening for the sounds of violence. There were always noises along the docks and from the brothels and saloons that edged the waters, the places where the foulness of the city washed up late on a summer night. There always seemed to be violence there, a knifing, a rape, a brawl. But his ears were trained on the sounds of a mob: songs shouted, marching feet, the clamor of angry men in motion. And shattering glass. Glass was valuable out here in the Great West, and the breaking of a window could well be a higher offense than the breaking of a body.

Everything seemed ripe for war. All it took was a spark.

Maybe that spark was the Brough brothers. They had certainly been working hard to start something. The Brough brothers had been passionate supporters of President Jackson, and even after his presidency was over, they continued to support the darkest of his ideals, starting a newspaper in Cincinnati in 1841 to incite ire. It was full of divisive reporting, panicked stories of the evils of equality and the terrors that free African Americans supposedly inflicted on whites. It was also full of misspellings and errors, such as "Southrons" for "Southerners." But their prejudiced white readers didn't care. The Brough brothers were not only telling them what they wanted to hear but encouraging them in their sense of outrage and prejudice. And it seemed that every city and town across America had at least one such newspaper.[72]

And all of those newspapers, those editors, were skilled at manipulation, finding the right words to spark flames of violence and fan them into firestorms. They would find something, anything, or nothing at all. Sometimes the mere number of African Americans in a county or a city was blamed for the rise in white violence, as if numbers were an excuse. As if it were utterly natural for white folks to start turning murderous if African Americans rose above a certain percentage in a local population. But if numbers were the answer, then whites would have long ago slaughtered every single enslaved African American in South Carolina or any other region in the nation where enslaved African Americans outnumbered whites.

And no matter what their numbers, African Americans in the North were blamed for every imaginable ill: economic hard times; taking jobs from more deserving immigrants with lighter skin; brothels, robberies, murders, and rape. Whether the stories were true or not, these prejudiced papers were now blaming free African Americans for almost every single problem in American society.[73]

So African Americans, especially the many who had elevated themselves, who were successful, educated, and outspoken, tried to be perfect. But even perfection was no protection. Some abolitionist and human rights leaders, both black and white, pointed out that many prejudiced whites openly hated black success. And when whites rose in violence, their targets were invariably the most noble, powerful, admirable, and sacred products of the African American community: its schools, shelters for the poor, meeting halls, printing presses, and churches.[74]

The Reverend Hosea Easton—a great New England equal rights advocate—knew that there was no simple recipe for overcoming white people's belief in their supremacy or their growing prejudice, whether it was uplift or integration. The Reverend Easton could claim the deepest roots in New England, with African, European, and Narragansett ancestors. He had come from a prosperous family. His father, James Easton, had been a patriot soldier, fighting in the American Revolution. And James Easton had worked hard to become a successful entrepreneur in Massachusetts. By the late eighteenth century he owned a thriving ironworks. The Easton family had seen the tide turning in the Northeast, watching the fervor for freedom and the commitment to equality weakening in many whites around them.[75]

By the 1830s his son the Reverend Easton had seen much, and he knew that if integration could solve the problem of prejudice—if every white person could just live near people of African descent and see how human they were—then every white enslaver would already be an ardent equal rights advocate. And if free black success was enough to convince white people that prejudice was wrong, then his plans for a school to educate African Americans in Connecticut would not have met with violent opposition in 1836.

Soon after a brutal attack on African Americans in his home community of New Haven, Connecticut, in 1836, Easton asked William Lloyd Garrison to publish a pamphlet he had written. Garrison agreed, certainly impressed by Easton's thoughtful brilliance as he explored the illogic of prejudice and the damage it was causing to the nation. Easton pointed out that prejudiced whites could see people of African descent as "most odious at one moment, and the next beautiful," depending on whether those African Americans were enslaved or free or even just downtrodden or successful.[76]

Like a tour guide in some strange land that Gulliver might have visited, Easton pointed out that the bodies of African-descended people could magically become massive and deformed or tiny and beautiful in the eyes of whites, depending on their context. He explained that if an African American man should chance to be found in any other sphere of action than that of a slave, he magnifies to a monster of wonderful dimensions, so large that they [whites] cannot be made to believe that he is a man and a brother. Neither can they be made to believe that it would be safe to admit him into stage coaches, steam-boat cabins, and tavern dining rooms. . . . Mechanical shops, stores and school rooms are all too small for his entrance as a man; [but] if he be a slave, corporeality becomes so diminished as to admit him into ladies' parlors, and into small private carriages, and elsewhere without being disgraceful on account of his deformity, or without producing any discomfiture.[77]

But the men on the rooftops of their homes in Cincinnati were not enslaved; they were free and part of a community that was refusing to be destroyed. No wonder the Brough brothers, those newspaper men in Cincinnati, were on the warpath. Their recent pet cause had been the city's decision to support a school for African American children near Cincinnati that might possibly be integrated. The idea of the school had certainly been a cooperative and integrated effort. It had been requested by a petition signed by 105 African Americans in the area and ultimately supported by local white politicians. The Brough brothers worked hard to raise the wrath of their white readers against every form of equality for African Americans, writing that the idea of schools for African Americans was a waste and would give African American children "pretensions and privileges that they neither deserved nor could appreciate."[78]

James Wilkerson and the rest of the men on the rooftops of Cincinnati in 1841 knew that a change in their behavior or a reduction in their numbers would not quell whites' wrath. And more uplift or harder work would not prove their equality. They had already proven that they could be successful enough to make many whites in Cincinnati uncomfortable.

And now they were laying their bodies across the tops of their homes and businesses and down dark alleys, a human shield against the evil that was rising.

Who saw it first? The light growing as torches were lit. Someone was funding this, someone always did.

Wilkerson could hear them coming now, the sound of breaking glass, the screams, and finally the fire as the mob came closer, carrying torches high.

It was so much bigger than they had expected—hundreds of men.

But Wilkerson's men knew to wait. They had been planning for a long time.

There were people running ahead of the mob, being chased. Everyone was supposed to be in hiding; who was still out? Who had been caught? As soon as news of the mob spread, everyone would have tried to find safety. This was no time to be out of any building. Wilkerson must have hoped everyone would be safe.

But he was wrong.

The mob was smashing its way into places where people with dark skin might be hiding, armed men breaking into white abolitionists' homes to find any African Americans sheltering there. And now they were driving terrified people ahead of them, gathering everyone they found for their fire, their knives, their violent desires.[79]

The mob was moving faster. Still Wilkerson and his men held their places. If Wilkerson's plan was going to work, most of the mob had to be in their sights. But those being chased would have been screaming for help.

The mob was closer. Did the men on the roof throw their arms over each other to keep themselves still—to keep themselves from jumping down three stories to the ground to help? "Hold," Wilkerson must have thought, "just hold."

They were holding.

Soon they would be able to help. Soon they would be able to rescue. And they knew what was at stake. Their families, their children, their babies were hiding in the buildings they were lying atop of and surrounding.

The mob was further in, running hard now, almost there.

One more breath, one more prayer, and Wilkerson would have made the signal his men were waiting for.

Now!

It was just about the midnight hour
When Jesus displayed his Heavenly power
And with his chariot drove along
While angels chanted a morning song.

His lightning played and thunders roll,
It shook the earth from pole to pole
At this the devils took affright
And left before the morning light.

As Zion's sons marched in and took the field,
Old Molock of hell was the last devil to yield.
And with a most tremendous yell,
He leapt from thence down to hell.

And here with Job I was called to stand,
And show myself a worthy man:
Thus born of God, I know I am
And thou deny it if thee can. Selah.

—Major James Wilkerson, c. 1850

Aftermath

Young John Langston had never run so fast in his life. Then he heard the yells of white men behind him. They had guns, and they were telling him to stop, to be punished for being a twelve-year-old black boy in Cincinnati. But he kept running. He managed to make it to his brother's, but he had asked more of his young heart than it could give, collapsing as he fell through the door. When his brother managed to revive him, John gasped out the news: the battle had turned worse.[80]

They all knew that it had started in the night—a mob forming itself into a fighting force and marching on the African American neighborhood where the young Langston lived. Anyone out on the streets, man, woman, or child, was murderously attacked.

But then came the surprise, a defense by an armed black militia that had been secretly organizing under the leadership of Major James Wilkerson. The white attackers were repulsed as soon as they came into the African American neighborhood, and they retreated, pursued by the Major's forces. Then the storm that had been building all night broke, the rain washing away the blood on the streets.

But the mob would not give up. While Major Wilkerson's militia had courage, good tactics, and guns, the mob got into the city's arsenal and hauled out a cannon. The sound of thunder was soon joined by cannon fire. Wilkerson and his men kept the mob at bay so the cannon could not hit them at close range, but they could not destroy it, and the mob loaded it with hot pitch—over and over again—breaking and burning.

The terrible sounds of gun and cannon fire lasted most of the night until the military finally marched in to end the conflict.

Then the real terror started. Having successfully defended themselves, the African Americans citizens of Cincinnati were being punished. The white mob had come limping into the town hall claiming they had been terrorized by the black militia and demanding that African Americans be punished for refusing to submit to their violence.

And the mayor agreed.

Little Langston had taken shelter in a friend's home when they were warned that the military was out, rounding up every dark-skinned man it could find. The men were being imprisoned, the city leaders insisting that they pay a Black Code bond of $500 or rot. Langston's friends hid themselves in specially created bolt-holes and must have urged Langston to join them. But Langston refused, running out the back door toward his brother Gideon's home. His brothers were the only family he had left, and he had to warn them.

After all, his brothers had taken him out of Virginia after their white father died, leaving them much of his vast fortune. They wanted their youngest brother, John, to have some schooling. This was no longer possible in Virginia since laws had been passed making it illegal for African Americans to even learn to read. Education for African Americans was not popular among many whites in Cincinnati but it was possible. Now his brothers' lives were in danger.

So Langston ran.

And his warning worked. But that war left its mark on John Langston. Cities were not safe. But he was hearing of hope growing outside cities, of thriving farming communities, of rich frontiers full of promise. He must have met some of those wealthy farmers building schools and churches, building their lives. As soon as Langston could, he left Cincinnati and moved to the country, determined to join the others there who were fighting against injustice, prejudice, and oppression from their farms.

7

"The right of the people peaceably to assemble"

Randolph County, Indiana, Summer 1847

Someone had been setting off fireworks at the school again.

Well, it was really gun powder, but lighting it in the right kind of container made a similar ruckus. It must have delighted the students who set it off, but it was upsetting the livestock, causing fear of fire, and shaking the nerves of the school staff, who were already on edge.

The Union Literary Institute was only about a year old. It was a boarding and day school for precollegiate students in Randolph County in eastern Indiana, on the Ohio border. The school was also a labor institute, meaning that students who could not afford tuition could pay for their education, and support the school, by working for the school. But the board members did not intend for this to be a poor school. After all, they were planning on sending their children there, and they were not poor at all.[1]

The board had been planning the institute's creation for a few years now. It had finally opened in 1846 and was proving popular. But the school board was realizing that they might need an update to their original constitution. They needed a clear ban on burning gun powder for one.

Then there were the students who were refusing to get up at 5:00 a.m. to do the labor required of them before classes started. And at least one of the board members had been unhappy to learn that some of the students had been caught playing checkers, chess, and other games of "chance or skill." And there were some troubling reports of students using slurs and offenses, language that they knew could cut deep and cause hurt and division among the students.[2]

And clearer guidelines on courting were needed as well. Most of the students were aged fourteen to seventeen and getting distracted from their normal farmwork. Some were "walking out," strolling together on the school grounds, surrounded by a haze of delight and affection.[3]

So on June 14, 1847, the board met to talk about how best to deal with these and other issues that had arisen at the school. Almost all of the board members made it. They were black and white, male and female, Quaker and not, southerners and a few northerners. While there were Quakers in the Northwest Territory states who did not feel warmly toward people of African descent, it did not include these Quakers. And while there were southerners who were pushing a movement for slavery and inequality, these southerners were not. Did these board members, most of whom were southern born, ever joke about this? Here they sat, black and white, with their differing regional accents, most from Virginia and North Carolina.[4]

Powerful whites from the slave states kept describing the ideals that this school board was acting on as northern, despite the fact that the nation had been witnessing just how violently antiabolitionist and prejudiced northern-born whites could be.

Doubtless the board members had their disputes, but they agreed that the safety and well-being of their students was important and that equality was essential to their project.

The board had written the original school constitution in 1846, a year after they had first started working to create the school. The preamble started, "Whereas a number of benevolent Men and Women, have given land and contributed money and goods for the purpose of building up and sustaining a Manual Labor School, principally for the benefit of that class of the population whom the laws of Indiana at present preclude from all participation in the benefits of our public school system." There were a number of guidelines and rules that followed, which they titled articles. Article 7 stated that the board would hold a general meeting once a year at which "all interested as Teachers, Benefactors, contributors, whether male or female, shall have equal privileges in discussing and voting on all matters and questions that may come before them." This was a startling governing statement. When it was written most African American men did not have the vote in the United States, and not a single woman did. It would be two years before the first convention on women's rights would be held at Seneca Falls, New York.[5]

But the board was not finished. Its members wanted their school to reflect who they were. They were trying to live a reality that they dreamed of for their nation—one in which all were truly equal. So Article 8 stated, "There shall never be tolerated or allowed in the Union Literary Institution, its government, discipline or privileges, any distinction on account of Color, Rank or Wealth." This was revolutionary in the truest sense of the word. Article 8 was based on the first, best ideals of the United States, moving justice forward at a time when it seemed to be moving backward.[6]

This provision was sure to enrage many prejudiced whites. But the board knew that those whites had been enraged long before the Union Literary Institute's founding. This prejudice that was sweeping the nation, this passion for injustice that they were trying to defend children against, was indeed moving things backward. If African Americans being educated was enough to cause this ire, schools would have been burning for decades.

The board probably did not know of all the schools that had been started and successfully run by African Americans and whites to teach children of all colors during those early years of the republic. They rose so quickly.

The earliest even predated the Revolution. One of the earliest known was the Bray School in Williamsburg, Virginia. Between 1760 and 1774, Ann Wager, a white woman, educated roughly three hundred to four hundred free and enslaved African American children.[7]

And then there was Anthony Benezet's school. Anthony had been born in France, and his family had been refugees from their government's persecution of the religious group they belonged to. They had moved to various countries in Europe when he was a child, trying to find a home. In the end they settled in Philadelphia around 1731, when Benezet was eighteen years old. By that time he had already converted to Quakerism and developed a passion for equality and justice.[8]

When he arrived, Philadelphia was a rapidly growing town of about 10,000 people in the colony of Pennsylvania. Benezet would become a transforming force within that city, teaching in and founding schools that reflected his vision of equality. By 1750 he was teaching classes to people of African descent, many of them enslaved. In 1754 he founded a school for girls, and in 1770 he founded a school for people of African descent.[9]

Of course, in the colonies and the early republic, educated families most commonly taught their children themselves, with wealthier families hiring tutors. After the United States was formed, there was not automatically a system of public schools put into place and policies to go with them. The commitment to educate children differed hugely from region to region, sometimes even between cities in the same state. But there was a movement to create schools, and African Americans were often at the forefront of that movement, attending, teaching in, and founding schools.[10]

After the Revolution, the colonial belief that children of African descent should be educated separately—segregated—proved difficult to shake. Often, white parents did not want their children educated alongside children with a different skin color. Responding to such discriminations, African Americans in Boston founded a school to educate their children in the late eighteenth century.[11]

And in 1794 the white leaders of the New York Manumission Society invested their time, energy, and money in the goal of educating African American children in New York City when New York was still a slave state.[12]

Advances were being made in other slave states as well. In 1807, when the White House was only fifteen years old, two African American men in Washington, DC, who had purchased their own freedom, invested their resources in founding a school for African American children.[13]

Just a year later John Chavis founded his popular and well-respected school in Raleigh, North Carolina, in 1808. The African American Chavis was highly educated at a time when few whites were even literate. Although blocked from fully integrating his school, he refused to compromise his vision of education for all Americans, teaching his white students during the day and his African American students (or "children of Color," as he called them in 1808) in the evening. His school thrived for decades, educating some of the most elite and powerful whites in the state.[14]

Then, around 1812, the African American pastor Daniel Coker started a school in Baltimore, which taught both boys and girls. Meanwhile, Ann Marie Becraft started the first school for African American girls in Washington, DC, in 1820, when she was about fifteen years old. It quickly became a thriving girls' seminary school supported by the local Catholic Church. And by 1819 African Americans, some aided by the African Methodist Episcopal (AME) Church, had started schools in and around Charleston, South Carolina.[15]

While their true numbers may never be known, during this period right after the Revolution there was a blossoming of educational opportunities for people of African descent, as newly freed people worked to give themselves and their children all of the opportunities liberty could offer in their new nation, from New Orleans to Boston.[16]

But then schools started being shut down, started being attacked, started being burned.

By the early 1830s it was not just the largest cities of the North that bore the scourges of the mobocrats intent upon asserting the rule of prejudice through violence. Education was about citizenship. People of the early republic believed that it was the root of a democratic government, a place to prepare people for citizenship, a place to train them how to listen and speak, how to read and write, how to reason and discern. But prejudiced whites were attacking those roots so that no new fruit could ripen.[17]

So Prudence Crandall knew that her decision would cause a fuss. She lived in the quiet village of Canterbury in rural Connecticut, and she was considering educating African American students. Some of the wealthiest local white families had hired her to teach and manage a white girls' school in the early 1830s. Prudence Crandall was a well-educated woman of means, and she was able to purchase the almost 4,000-square-foot house on the central green of Canterbury. It was a beautiful building, its large windows gleaming, its chimneys rising high as smoke from all the cozy fireplaces inside drifted into the air above the crossroads. Everyone passing by could see what a fine school the white citizens of Canterbury had to educate their girls in.

In 1832, Sarah Harris, a young African American woman, asked Prudence Crandall if she could also attend the school. It had only been open about a year, and Harris suspected that her attendance could cause problems, so she was cautious, telling Crandall, "If you think it will be the means of injuring you, I will not insist on the favor." But Crandall decided to take the risk and open her school not just to Harris but to any African American girls who could afford to attend.[18]

In some ways her plan was not that radical, for she would still be doing what she did best, educating and caring for young women in her boarding school. The girls would come from homes and families with a good income—families who could pay her for her teaching. The only difference would be the color of their skin.

Crandall knew she would need help to resist the coming backlash, so she contacted William Lloyd Garrison. She explained that in order to make a quick conversion of her school, she would need African

American families and students willing to sign up and pay before it even reopened.

Crandall could not have started her school alone. The feat required the courageous involvement of young women and their families, willing to risk much to be educated. And the daughters of some of the wealthiest African American families in Connecticut and the Northeast came to join Crandall's school, their families willing to make this stand for equality with her.

And they came, carrying their lovely clothes and fine bedding, their candle holders and shoes, their best bonnets and their books, all carefully packed into well-made trunks, ready to live with Crandall and get the best education that money could buy. But many of these girls, most in their teens, understood that they were coming as activists. Some came from well-off and well-connected families in New York and Philadelphia, where there were still schools for them, but they were committed to getting an excellent education from Crandall.

The school reopened on April 1, but the resistance was worse than expected. First, the most powerful white men of the town began to demand to see Crandall. Dr. Andrew Harris told Prudence that her school was a danger because "the blacks of the town . . . would begin to look up and claim an equality with whites."[19]

By May 6, over nine hundred white people in the region had signed a petition asking that the Connecticut government pass a law to shut down Prudence Crandall's school. And working with extraordinary efficiency, the politicians of Connecticut did just as they were asked. On May 24, less than two months after Crandall started teaching her students, the governor signed off on the law. The law not only shut down the school but ensured that no other Connecticut school could accept African American children from out of state and that opening a school for Connecticut African Americans would require the written "consent" of basically every powerful white man in a town.[20]

But Crandall and her students stood strong. She refused to stop teaching them, and her students refused to stop learning, despite rising violence. Soon Crandall was arrested and jailed, charged with breaking the law written just for her, her county's newspaper proclaiming, "She has stepped out of the hallowed precincts of female propriety and now stands on common ground, and must expect common treatment."[21]

Her case went all the way to the Connecticut Supreme Court. Some of the top lawyers of the time, including US senator William Ellsworth, defended Crandall. The son of a framer of the Constitution, Ellsworth still believed in his father's vision of an America where all men had an equal right to "life, liberty and the pursuit of happiness."

Many people—both black and white—across the Northwest Territory states must have anxiously awaited news of that state supreme court trial, for if Crandall succeeded the suit would establish a precedent for overturning anti-immigration Black Laws throughout the region.

Still, the local forces against equality were strong. The judges of the Connecticut Supreme Court let Prudence Crandall go on a technicality but refused to rule on the new Black Code, having neither the heart nor the inclination to make a just decision in favor of children. And those children, bravely making a stand for their rights in the village of Canterbury, were almost murdered by locals who tried to burn down the school while they were asleep inside of it.[22]

To this day, broken glass from the lovely windows shattered during those attacks still lies in the earth all around the school, a sharp reminder of the battle against equality being waged against these northern girls trying to be educated in New England.

Those who were willing to burn children for the cause of prejudice won their battle, forcing Crandall to close her school little over a year after she opened her doors to African American students.[23]

Even while Prudence Crandall was fighting for her school's survival, African Americans and their white allies were working with supporters in New Hampshire to create a school back in the hills of that region. They planned a manual labor institute that would be open to all.[24]

A local white lawyer by the name of George Kimball encouraged Garrison and his supporters to build the school in his town of Canaan, New Hampshire. But none of the local residents knew just how radical this school would be, for in addition to being a labor institute, it would also be integrated—accepting both blacks and whites. It was to be called the Noyes Academy, and hopes ran high for its success as it neared its opening date in February 1835.[25]

The Noyes Academy had an opening class of forty-five students, seventeen of them African American. All of them were men, except for Julia Williams, an African American student from Crandall's school who had survived its attack and was still set on getting an education. Many of her fellow students had to make the long, slow journey through the mountains exposed to the weather, forced to ride on the outside of the stagecoach because of the color of their skin. When they finally arrived, Julia Williams and her fellow African American students were met with a warm welcome from Kimball and the other white abolitionists who welcomed them into their homes to board there until living quarters could be built for all of the students.

Most of the town residents, however, were not so warm to the idea of an integrated precollegiate school in their community. There were months of protests and violence, the students and their teachers hanging on despite the growing danger. But in August it all ended. The school was attacked. A large group of whites brought in dozens of ox teams and, attaching chains to the school building, pulled it off its foundations and dragged it away.[26]

The board members of the Union Literary Institute knew that while these attacks were growing against African American schools in the Northeast, there was a chance that the Northwest Territory states offered more space for such schools. They were all inspired by Oberlin College in Ohio, which had decided to integrate soon after Crandall's school was shut down. Of course, there had long been a few African Americans educated at colleges around the United States, but that was in an earlier, less polarized time. When Oberlin made its move, it was in the face of a national backlash against equality, but by 1847 the college was still thriving and was now accepting female students as well. Members of the board of the Union Literary Institute had visited Oberlin and hired an Oberlin graduate, Ebenezer Tucker, as the institute's first teacher.[27]

But the board knew that this was a time when whites were making it dangerous to teach African Americans, even in some areas of rural Ohio. After all, they would have heard of what happened to Clarissa Wright and the African American farmers working with her.[28]

It was just a few years before, in 1839, over in Portage County, Ohio, roughly thirty miles south of Cleveland and on the opposite side of the state from the Union Literary Institute. The settled and successful African American farmers in that county had organized and financed a lovely grammar school for their youngest children. Finding a teacher had been a challenge, but they finally found Clarissa Wright, a young white woman willing to come on her own to live with these farmers and teach their children.[29]

Clarissa Wright knew exactly what she was getting into. She had been born and raised in Portage County, Ohio. Her father had been educated at Yale and come from Connecticut to Ohio in around 1810, founding a school called the Tallmadge Academy. Clarissa Wright and her siblings were educated there by their firmly antislavery father, who also was a proponent of equal education for boys and girls. One of those boys was the young John Brown, the fierce white abolitionist who would later lead the attack at Harper's Ferry.[30]

She and her brother, Elizur Wright, were committed advocates of freedom and equality. They had personally witnessed the war that had arisen in the cities of the North in the 1830s, from Cincinnati to New York. In 1833 Elizur Wright helped to create the national American Anti-slavery Society on the East Coast. But unlike some of his fellow white abolitionists, he was a staunch anticolonizationist, believing that African-descended people had a right to freedom and full American citizenship.[31]

While the school was in Portage County, it may have been far enough from her home that she needed a place to live nearby. In those days, teachers usually "boarded" with a family involved in the management of the school. In this case, it would have been an African American family.

There should have been nothing upsetting about this. Education was supposed to be the firm foundation of the American republic, a pillar of a healthy democracy. Indeed, the men who wrote the founding document of the Northwest Territory—the Territorial Ordinance of 1787—considered education so important that they included specific mention of schools, noting in Article 3, "Religion, morality, and knowledge, being necessary to good government and the happiness of mankind, schools and the means of education shall forever be encouraged." And just as in the voting clauses in the ordinance, none of those instructions mentioned race or the exclusion of any group.[32]

In this case African Americans and whites were merely working together on a common goal of education. But the intimacy of this situation alone was appalling to the prejudiced—people with different-color skin sharing meals together, using the same outhouse, and socializing with each other in the evening after the work was done. These prejudiced whites had an easily offended sense of their own identity, and they were quick to come to wrath when a case arose where the order they wished to impose on America—white men at the top and everyone else below—was challenged. The idea that a white woman would not only be equal to but dependent on wealthy African American farmers for her livelihood was not to be tolerated. And the fact that she was also helping the children of those farmers be educated, to have an equal opportunity for life, liberty, and the pursuit of happiness, was not just an insult, it was a killing offense.

First, a threatening letter was sent to the African American farmers who were running the school, informing them that if they did not fire Wright (whom they referred to as "your straggling stranger") immediately, they would gather together the "citizens" of the area for a meeting to "consider the situation." This was a threat, for everyone knew in those troubled times that when powerful white men gathered other white people for a "meeting," they were planning violence.[33]

When the African Americans who had hired Wright refused to respond to the letter, another letter was sent a few days later, filled with obscene slander and threat.[34]

There was an intimacy to this hatred. Rural communities were small and scattered, but that did not mean that people did not know each other, or know each other's business. It was not just letters sent, it was people walking out of the general store to avoid seeing a neighbor. It was a rider galloping by on a horse cursing a family as he passed. It was two men inside a home, sitting on chairs while someone brought them something hot to drink.

A visiting white abolitionist, Amzi D. Barber, was invited to the home of a Mr. McMullen (whom the abolitionist described as "an influential white man"). Barber almost certainly knew Clarissa Wright and had come to her aid. He was secretary of the Cincinnati Anti-slavery Society and had briefly run a school for African Americans in that city in 1836. During their conversation McMullen was more explicit about the threat to Wright, stating that a mob would burn the schoolhouse if Wright did not stop teaching there. McMullen kept assuring Barber that he would not hurt Wright or personally burn down the school. But Barber called his bluff, replying, "I have no fear of violence unless some influential men encourage it. And the very way to get up a mob is for every [white] man to prophesy that there will be one." This so upset McMullen that he called Barber the worst thing he could think of— an abolitionist—and accused him of preaching abolition to the African Americans in the township. Barber replied, "I have *never* given an abolition lecture to the colored people. There is no occasion for it; if they were in favor of slavery they would go to the south, and put their necks under the yoke."[35]

Barber probably took courage from the fact that many whites in Ohio had arisen to combat the growing prejudice in their state, which was now home to over two hundred antislavery societies that would be reading and repeating his words. He may have been pleased with his wit in his argument with McMullen, but no argument between a young abolitionist and a powerful white man in an Ohio farming community would stop the threats to Wright and the families and children she was teaching. A few days later Wright wrote that she was now receiving the threats personally and that they included plans to tar and feather her and ride her out on a rail.[36]

Elijah Lovejoy, the white abolitionist, had endured threats of similar abuse, but the fact that the threat targeted Clarissa Wright was significant. Everyone knew that if a person survived the coating of hot tar, their being forced to straddle a thin splintered rail was a form of sexual assault.

But Wright would not give up; she stood with the African American farmers, and they stood with her, at the risk of terrible violence and loss. Her brother, Elizur, had almost been stabbed to death by two attackers during the 1834 race war in New York City because of his support of equality for all Americans. She knew that threats of violence could have very real consequences. She was not naive; nor were the African Americans who had hired her. As she wrote, "Should I fall victim to the fury of these wicked men, it is but little that they can do. The thought of departing from Christ is more dreadful than death."[37]

While Wright seems to have escaped alive, there is little record of what happened to the school or the children she was trying to teach.[38]

The board of the Union Literary Institute knew that what they were doing was a rebuke to prejudiced whites, for the school Wright was teaching at was segregated, but the Union Literary Institute was most definitely not. But they also knew that they were not alone, for other African Americans and their white allies were working in the Northwest Territory states to found manual labor schools offering advanced education to African Americans.

In Michigan two labor institutes were up and running, even though that state was less than ten years old. One was founded by the African American equal rights leader Prior Foster in Lenawee County. He had been joined in Michigan by James Birney, the previous editor of the *Philanthropist*, who had left Cincinnati and now sat on the board of trustees of Foster's school. This was a family project, for Prior Foster's brother was making the long journey from his farm in Wisconsin to bring wagonloads of corn for the school's supplies.[39]

As the Union Literary Institute's board met in 1847 in Indiana they would have heard that the Union Seminary, just outside Columbus, had just been opened as a Manual Labor Institute by the AME Church. And there was talk that abolitionist-minded whites were planning a school they intended to call the Eleutherian Institute, down in southern Indiana in Jefferson County. But the nearest labor institute was the Emlen Institute in Mercer County, just forty miles north of them.[40]

Mercer County had long been home to a thriving community of African American farmers. By 1840 the African American farmers there owned thousands of acres. And Charles Moore was one of their most successful residents. A freedom entrepreneur, he not only bought his own liberty but paid $2,200 to purchase his entire family's freedom. By 1840 he had platted a village in the middle of this farming settlement that he named Carthagena, in honor of the North African city of Carthage.[41]

It was no surprise that Augustus Wattles would want to try to work with these African Americans to found a manual labor institute in Mercer County. He was a white abolitionist and equal rights activist who was well aware of many of the African American farming settlements across rural Ohio.

In 1839, Wattles had begun to work on creating a manual labor institute in the county, and in 1842 he managed to get good funding for the school. He traveled to Philadelphia to talk with the trustees of the estate of Samuel Emlen. Samuel Emlen had been a wealthy equal rights–minded native of New Jersey, and his trustees were now trying to figure out how to best spend his money. Having seen their city wracked by the war against African American equality, they must have been relieved to hear of a place where black success was not being violently destroyed and gave Wattles the money he was asking for.[42]

But by 1847 the board of the Union Literary Institute would have been hearing troubling reports from Mercer County. There had been a bad incident in 1846 when a large group of people recently freed by the will of John Randolph had come to Mercer County, looking to settle there. Whites in Mercer County made clear that they did not want the population of African Americans in their area growing any larger. Violence had broken out not just against the recently freed people but against long-established African American farmers.[43]

In August 1846 some of the most powerful white men of Mercer County, including Congressman William Sawyer, met to write up their stance on the free and successful African Americans of Mercer County. Mocking the black conventions now meeting in their state that were publishing beautifully worded resolutions calling for liberty and equality for all, these white men of Mercer County published their resolutions as well, which clearly stated their values: "Whereas the Supreme Ruler of the Universe has fixed immutable laws for the government of the world, and marked his lines and boundaries, and made undeniable distinction every where perceivable, between the different races of men." They then made many formal resolutions, including that "we will not live among negroes. . . . [W]e have fully determined that we will resist the settlement of blacks and mulattos in this county, to the full extent of our means, the bayonet not excepted."[44]

And the board of the Union Literary Institute was trying to run a revolutionary school roughly forty miles south of this violence. But it was not without defenses. The board alone was a formidable group. And the Clemens and Alexander families could offer some support as well. They had already given money and land, but they had more—they had their standing.

The Alexander and Clemens families were well represented both on the donor lists and on the board. The two families were neighbors, although the Alexanders were in Indiana, and the Clemenses were just across the border in Ohio. They had arrived in that region in the early 1820s, Thornton Alexander from North Carolina and James Clemens from Virginia. As soon as Clemens arrived, he bought over three hundred acres from the federal government, and it was some of the best land on the western Ohio frontier. These two farming families were now the closest their two counties had to landed gentry, black or white, though they happened to be black. Between them, the two families owned almost 1,000 acres of land. These pioneers were community founders and deeply committed to freedom, equality, and education.[45]

In some ways their large farms protected them. When harvest time came there would not have been enough African Americans in the region to harvest all the crops grown by these two wealthy families. Harvesting any grain involved intensive labor. A strong man, well trained with a scythe, could only harvest a quarter acre of grain a day. Many whites in the area would have relied on the Clemens and Alexander families for extra income at harvest time and at other times as well.[46]

Of course, not all the money the Alexander and Clemens families made went to farm labor. All those acres of good land they owned were taxed to pay for the local public schools, but those schools were for white children only. The Alexanders and Clemenses had long lived with the injustice of taxation without representation, but they also had to suffer taxation without education. It must have stung.

But they were not going to let prejudiced laws or people stop them.

Founding an integrated school for both African American and white children was not the only path open to them. The extraordinary success of African American farmers across the Northwest Territory states meant that some African Americans were taking different paths to educating their children. In Illinois, for instance, the wealthy African American farmer Arthur Allen hired a local white teacher (who was also a justice of the peace) to tutor his children.[47]

But the Alexander and Clemens families chose to work with local whites to create a more revolutionary educational opportunity for their children. They were joined by other wealthy activists, including the white Underground Railroad conductor Levi Coffin, another North Carolina man, elected to their board in 1846. As they gathered together, led by their African American board president, William R. J. Clemens, they knew that their board's integration alone would be reason enough

THE BONE AND SINEW OF THE LAND 149

for prejudiced whites to bring guns and torches to end them and their school.

But wealth and standing were not the only defenses the board had, for the black convention movement was rising in the Great West, and it was gaining strength. After starting in Philadelphia in 1830 and struggling in the cities of the East Coast, this movement had spread through the Northwest Territory states, starting in Indiana in 1842 and quickly followed by Michigan and Ohio in 1843.[48]

African Americans from the farms to the cities of the Great West were gathering to organize, to petition, to criticize, and to encourage. They called upon whites to remember the early ideals and actions of the period just after the Revolution, reminding them just how far they had moved away from those founding beliefs and actions.[49]

This new generation of equality activists knew exactly what had been stolen from them—the equality promised in the Northwest Ordinance of 1787 and then denied when whites created prejudiced state constitutions. This new generation of activists may have been strongly rooted in the nation's old ideals, but they used every modern technology available to publicize their words and agendas, printing the proceedings of their conventions in newspapers and broadsides so that they could influence as large an audience as possible.[50]

As was spoken (and later broadly published) during the main address at the 1844 Ohio convention, "The Declaration of Independence, the American Bill of Rights, the Ordinance of 1787, as well as the political Creed of every intelligent, generous and patriotic freeman, are clearly violated, nay shamefully desecrated, by that feature of our constitution that renders the color of the skin a qualification for electors and suffrages. . . . We shall urge our second plea upon the ground of justice. . . . '[D]o to others as you would have them do to you.'"[51]

African American farmers from this region were attending and helping to lead these conventions. For there were many places in the Northwest Territory states where African-descended farmers could still safely leave their farms in the hands of family or friends for a few days so that they could lead a committee at the convention. And these brave and outspoken leaders knew all about the Union Literary Institute.[52]

At the Ohio convention in Columbus in January 1849, a number of resolutions were voted on, including Resolution 15, which stated, "That the attempt to establish . . . schools for the benefit of colored persons EXCLUSIVELY . . . is in our humble opinion reprehensible." Attendees also stressed that segregated education had a profoundly damaging effect on children of any skin color and that "in children thus divided by law, the most Satanic hate is likely to be engendered. This, no one who has studied human nature will deny."[53]

The daughter of Frederick Douglass, the great African American abolitionist whom they all knew and worked with, had just been expelled from a school in her hometown of Rochester, New York. The act, as they reminded their audience, had caused international outrage, "rebuked" by the "ladies of England, Scotland, Ireland and France." No wonder one of the first articles about the Union Literary Institute was written up in Frederick Douglass's newspaper, the *North Star*. The article praises the fact that the school "is intended especially for colored youth of both sexes; and the greater number of pupils have been such, though persons of all complexions are freely admitted, and about one-fourth of the whole number were whites. Two of the five trustees and four of the thirteen managers are colored men."[54]

The Union Literary Institute was standing by the old revolutionary ideas that division and prejudice hurt children and the nation. It could do this, in part, because African American farms were now established and thriving around them. And more were being established, with many successful African American farms now scattered across the Northwest Territory states.[55]

It took roughly twenty years for frontier farmers to clear their land so that they could plow with horses instead of oxen. Twenty years of felling trees, chopping roots, pulling rocks. But many African American pioneers were now established farmers, and like the Clemenses and Alexanders, they were in a position to support organizations that supported equality.

That did not mean there was no prejudice in much of the Northwest Territory states. Whites in some Ohio townships were burning barns. Whites in rural Illinois were creating vigilante groups to force African Americans out of Cornelius Elliott's own Gallatin County. Whites in an Indiana county had risen to violently drive out the African American owner of the county's most successful mill. While Frederick Douglass was speaking in nearby Madison County, Indiana, people tried to murder him. A crowd set upon him and the other abolitionists, screaming, "Kill the nigger, kill the damn nigger." He only escaped with his life after one of his fellow abolitionists threw himself over Douglass's body to shield him from the blows meant to finish him off.[56]

The majority of whites in Madison County, Indiana, did not want freedom for all, for they had seen what the first wave of freedom had brought to that state—thousands of African-descended pioneers settling on thriving farms. So they had made sure that not one black landowning farmer lived within the county's bounds in 1840.[57]

But the blanket of prejudice had not smothered most of the rural and frontier spaces of the Northwest the way it had in the Northeast. Many of the African American farms in the region covered large spaces that required a level of trust in neighbors to survive. There could not have been constant attacks—the sheer number of African American farming homesteads settled by this time spoke to this reality.

And in the areas where they were not run out, African American farmers were rising. And what a rising it was, growing out of the farms now scattered across those five states of Ohio, Indiana, Illinois, Michigan, and Wisconsin—farms that were now improving, with vast acreage under cultivation, giving those farmers the means to resist injustice and advance equality.

The young people now attending the Union Literary Institute knew all about that rising. They had been a part of it.

Not all of them would have been fond of farmwork, but they were used to it. They would have helped their parents clear land or heard their parents and grandparents talking of those early days. Even now, as many of those farms were more settled, they could have listened to the old ones talking about their land with love, praising it and fondly complaining about its many moods and foibles—the pasture that had a tendency to flood every spring, the few acres that still spat up rocks to blunt the plow, the high point that was always windy—gesturing with strong hands, cracked and worn.

These students were the fruit of that land—good harvest of those farms and those families. And maybe their parents hoped more for them than farming. Maybe they dreamed of their becoming doctors, teachers, pastors, and engineers. Their dreams may have seemed fabulous, impossible. But they, and that school, had hope.

So, as the board met that June day in 1847, its members knew they had some hard work to do.

First, there were those fireworks.

Soon they had added to their constitution this amendment: "No student shall burn gun powder in or near any of the Institution buildings."[58]

Next there were those upsetting games. So it was resolved that "No members of the Institution shall play at cards, checkers, chess, or any similar games of chance or skill."[59]

Then came the harder issues, such as courting. Had they heard that before the Noyes Academy was pulled off its foundations in New Hampshire, the local newspaper published terrible articles warning that the black students might start courting white women? That school had been all male except for the African American young woman Julia Williams, but those articles intentionally and successfully fueled the prejudice of whites in New Hampshire. The board members could not take this issue lightly.[60]

At the same time, this racially integrated board, composed of women and men from the North and the South, seems to have wanted something its members knew was almost impossible for their students. They wanted normality, even if that meant that they had to do extraordinary things to make that possible. So instead of banning the courtship, they formalized it, writing an amendment that read, "The sexes shall refrain from spending time with each other—provided that the public sitting room shall be free for such as choose to occupy it on first day (Sunday) from one to three P.M. and from half past six to half past seven on Thursday evening." They originally wrote until "half past eight on Thursday evenings," but someone must have remembered that they were having a hard enough time getting students to rise at the required time of 5:00 a.m., and letting them stay up that late might make things worse.[61]

But more than one board member must have remembered the giddy times of their own courtship. How they had wanted nothing but the company of the person they had lost their heart to. Some of these board members were also parents of young people attending that school, and they knew that having only two chances to meet in a week would be very hard indeed. So the next resolution added, "Males and females may walk out in company only by permission of the Principal or male or female Superintendent."[62]

Finally there was the issue of the language.

This was a difficult decision. But it was also tied to this board's ideals and the ways in which they were trying to model a better way of being than currently existed in much of the nation. So they wrote the resolution, "No distinction shall be allowed on account of complexion and especially every member of the Institution shall carefully avoid all unkind, reproachful, or opprobrious names, or language."[63]

Adding this resolution to their school constitution may have seemed frivolous, given the reality of race relations in much of the nation. After all, millions of people were being held enslaved just south of their state, and Cincinnati had been wracked by open warfare fueled by prejudice. But this decision was essential for this integrated board, for they were intent upon moving America forward into a place of fairness, justice, and kindness toward all. They not only wanted to abolish slavery, they wanted a better nation, a nation free of prejudice, a nation where all were equal. And so they started with themselves and their school, hoping that they could lead their nation by example, showing the way forward on the frontier.

8

"For taking away our Charters, abolishing our most valuable Laws, and altering fundamentally the Forms of our Governments"

Gibson County, Indiana,
March 1851

The women of the house would have been up and moving before their friend at the door finished talking, one of them calling out the back window for the children, her voice rising urgent and sharp. As their friend rode away to warn their other neighbors, one of the men would have taken the gun off its hooks. Once everyone was safely inside, he would have stood guard, gun in hand. The wolves were on the loose.

These were not the creatures that used to howl around their cabins—the last of the four-legged kind had been shot years before. No, these wolves were the two-legged kind—slave hunters—and they were hunting for prey.

These wolves moved in packs and were quick to kill—not their prey, for those bodies were worth something to them alive, but anyone who aided the hunted. And while the slavers may have been despised, they were not without allies, for they had the general backing of the law and some very wealthy clients besides. As those allies and laws gained strength, more wolves appeared—some of them dressed as marshals, justices of the peace, and other local officials.[1]

The Lyles family must have breathed a prayer of thanks for friends and the law that allowed them to have their gun but cursed the new law that now endangered their family. For it was March 1851, and the 1850 Fugitive Slave Law was now in full effect. The federal government, all the way back east in Washington, DC, had made a decision that changed everything for the Lyles family, for the family of Charles and Keziah Grier, and for all people of African descent in the Northwest Territory states—or anywhere in the free states for that matter. It had passed the harshest fugitive law the nation had ever seen. It allowed the federal government to reach its long, sticky fingers into every state, ignoring states' rights and habeas corpus.[2]

The Fugitive Slave Law meant that any white man who had a mind to could grab a person off the street or even enter a family's home and take their children—as long as that person or family had a dark complexion. Once that person was chained up, there was little they could do to ever be free again. According to that new federal law, a white man could chain up a person of African descent and take them to the nearest federal agent, usually the local justice of the peace, whom the federal government paid double for ruling that the seized person was an escaped slave rather than a free citizen.[3]

In Indiana, the consequences of the law were felt almost as soon as it was passed. John Freeman, one of the wealthiest and most powerful black businessmen in Indianapolis, was targeted. A white man came from Missouri to Indianapolis and seized John Freeman, claiming Freeman had escaped from bondage. To make matters worse, whites in the state had just ratified a new constitution that took many rights away from African Americans and strengthened the old laws that banned them from testifying against white people. Combined with the 1850 Fugitive Slave Law, it made freedom very fragile in Indiana. Even for John Freeman. Everyone who could testify to his being legally free was of African descent, so they could not defend him. It took a year and most of his substantial wealth, as well as the financial support of many others, to prove he was free.[4]

The act shook even the bravest of freedom's defenders in the United States. As Frederick Douglass stated just after its passage, "The night is a dark and stormy one. . . . We have lost some of our strong men. . . . [M]en who were our pride and hope, we have heard have signified their unwillingness to return again to their National field of labors in this country."[5]

H. Ford Douglass was an equal rights advocate who, like Frederick Douglass, had freed himself in the 1830s and come north. He knew that his lack of free papers and very public speaking on the fact that he had freed himself endangered his liberty. Yet even after the Fugitive Slave Act had become law, he stood up to speak at the Ohio convention being held in the Second Baptist Church in Columbus, Ohio. He had to respond to another speaker, a Mr. Day, who was calling on all of them to remember that as Americans who had fought and defended the nation since the Revolutionary War, they should be protected by the constitution. H. Ford Douglass argued that "the gentleman may wrap the stars and stripes of his country around him forty times, if possible, and with the Declaration of Independence in one hand, and the Constitution of our common country in the other, may seat himself under the shadow of the frowning monument of Bunker Hill, and if the slaveholder, under the Constitution, and with the 'Fugitive Bill,' don't find you, then there don't exist a Constitution." This would be one of the last speeches made by H. Ford Douglass before he left for Canada.[6]

And the threat was worse in the rural areas like the Lyles family's home county of Gibson. This was their home now and had been for almost twenty years. They had purchased good land near the village of Princeton and close to the Patoka River, and many others had joined them there.[7]

And now, how could a young son be sent to the far field to hoe weeds around the corn without fear? He was so strong and firm, his muscles just coming in. Did their nightmares see him on an auction block? How could their daughter walk to a friend's house? She was so lovely, she could be captured and on a fast steamer for those terrible houses in New Orleans before she was even missed. They must have tried to keep the terror from ruling them, but it would have had its effect, for their fears were not just imagined.

They would have all heard the terrible story of the pioneering African American couple kidnapped in Gibson County in the 1840s, despite having lived in the area for twenty years. If it had not been for the Knowles family leaving late from a church camp meeting with the Reverend Hiram Hunter, all would have been lost. But luckily they met the kidnappers in the darkness. It took some hard knocks from the reverend's fists and all the other men in the party to overpower the abductors, but it was a good thing they did, for the couple had been bound and gagged and tied to the bottom of their own wagon, unable to even cry for help.[8]

Was it Keziah Grier or her friend Mary Stormont who first thought of keeping a kettle of water simmering over the fire, no matter what the weather? If the wolves got in, they could throw the hot water in their faces to protect themselves.[9]

But this was March 1851, and the wolves were gathering for an attack. Word was now circulating that a man named Seth Concklin, and the refugee family he had brought out of Alabama, had been captured a few miles north of Vincennes. Seth Concklin had been thrown in jail and fearing for his life had appealed to the Stormonts for aid, for as Underground Railroad agents they had secretly sheltered him just days earlier. Until that day no one had suspected that the white Stormonts, who had lived in Gibson County for so long, were Underground Railroad agents. And the Griers were next to them on the line, conveying Concklin and the fleeing family to safety. Now the wolves were swarming over three counties, from Evansville to New Harmony, hungry for blood.[10]

Did Keziah and Charles regret their decision to help? Few would have known that they were continuing to do their work, despite all the changes. The fewer who knew the better.

But the Stormonts knew. Like the Griers, they were early settlers in the area. They and the Griers were alike in some interesting ways, for both David Stormont and Keziah Grier had been born in South Carolina. Somehow the two couples—one black, one white—discovered that they shared a deep sympathy for refugees fleeing bondage. Both families were willing to put their lives in each other's hands, trusting and hoping that their dangerous secrets would be safe.[11]

The Griers were part of a secret and organized network that stretched into Canada, managing one of the riskiest links of their branch of the Underground Railroad, a section close to the Wabash River down there in southwestern Indiana in a region that was crawling with "Christian wolves."[12]

It must have been the Stormonts who told them about the request all those months ago, a request that was coming all the way from Philadelphia. A request so risky and dangerous that no one else along the Ohio River, no matter how fiercely abolitionist, would support it.[13]

A young man called Seth Concklin had come from Philadelphia, contacting every Underground Railroad agent he could find close to the Ohio River in both Ohio and Indiana with a crazy story about an attempted rescue of Peter Still's family. Everyone knew Peter Still, the long-lost older brother of William Still, one of the most famous African American abolitionists in the nation. Closely connected to Frederick Douglass, William Lloyd Garrison, and many others, William Still had long been running a well-respected center in Philadelphia to help refugees from enslavement. No one could have been more surprised than he was to find his own brother, Peter, entering his office. It took them a while to figure out that they were kin, but when they did, their joy was great, and the entire abolitionist community on the East Coast knew of it.[14]

Peter had not run away but had managed to raise a large sum to purchase himself. But he had been separated from his enslaved wife and children, who were still in Alabama. There were few worse places. Just fifty years before, even southern states had legally encouraged freedom, but whites in Alabama had turned their backs on those ideals and made freeing enslaved African Americans all but illegal. In Alabama, a white man could donate a cow to an orphanage, or a white woman could donate her books to a church, but should they wish to emancipate the people they owned or even to allow those people to purchase themselves, Alabama law all but forbade it.[15]

It seemed hopeless, but Concklin approached the Still brothers and offered to go into Alabama and rescue Peter's wife, Vina, and their three children, all now almost grown, "without pay or reward." As William Still later wrote, "The magnitude of this offer can hardly be appreciated. It was literally laying his life on the altar of freedom for the despised and oppressed whom he had never seen." Peter Still was deeply moved, but at first "the very idea of such an undertaking seemed perfectly appalling." The Still brothers knew exactly what terrors the slave South could hold and the damage it could inflict on a young, idealistic abolitionist such as Concklin. And then there was the safety of Peter's wife and children if he entrusted them to Concklin's care.[16]

Concklin's offer did seem a kind of madness. He intended go into Alabama, get Peter's family, and then, posing as their owner, immediately catch a steamboat that would take them up the rivers of the South all the way to the Ohio River and safety.

Seth Concklin had two sisters who loved him dearly, but otherwise he was unconnected to anyone, with no wife or family of his own. And he had a trade, having worked as a miller for a few years now. Indeed, he planned to go to Alabama in the guise of a miller looking for work in the region where Vina Still and her children were enslaved. While full of courage and heart, Concklin could also offer strength. Millers were massively strong, for all day they hauled large bags of wheat and flour. Both Peter and William knew that strength would be needed. But they also knew that no amount of strength could stand alone against the powers of the slave states.

The Stills did everything they could to dissuade Concklin, telling him of all the friends they had lost trying to do exactly what he was offering to do. Those allies had been killed or were still rotting in prisons.

As William Still later recounted, "In short, he was plainly told that, without a very great chance, the undertaking would cost him his life."[17]

But Concklin would not give up. He kept his offer open even when Peter Still refused him outright.

The situation seemed hopeless. Peter Still tried to distract himself from his terror for his family. He reunited with his mother and brothers, whom he had been separated from when he was just a child. But he was clearly miserable. Finally, one of his brothers asked if he could survive without his wife and children, and Peter said that he would rather die. So he decided to go back into the slave states to visit them and see what he could do.

The danger of this journey was great, but greater still was his family's joy on seeing him again. He had thought to risk an offer to purchase their freedom, but with his color and the law both against him, as well as the immense cruelty he saw on all the plantations around him, he became sure that such a plan would result in his disappearance and death. He talked with his wife about Concklin's offer, and then he and Vina talked it over with their children, who were now all in their teens. They finally agreed to try Concklin's plan, for "they were ready to assent to any proposition that looked like deliverance." Vina Still, ever wise, gave her cape to her husband just before he left, telling him that if Concklin managed to make it to them, he should show the cape to her so that she would know he was indeed their rescuer.[18]

Finally, Concklin was able to go to work to rescue one of the most famous enslaved families in America. But he could not find much help among the abolitionists along the Ohio River. All they could see was a well-built young white man talking of Vina Still and her children in Alabama and a plan that seemed one step away from insanity.[19]

And Concklin's timing could not have been worse. In the time that had elapsed since his original offer, not only had the federal 1850 Fugitive Slave Law gone into effect, but Indiana had just approved a new constitution so prejudiced that it looked to all but destroy the lives of the free people of African descent in that state.

That constitution included the infamous Resolution 13. As the white men at the Indiana constitutional convention worked on it, they considered various ideas for waging political warfare against the people who had pioneered that state before statehood. One was to close Indiana's borders to any free people of African descent who planned to stay for any length of time. And anyone, white or black, who hired those free African Americans who dared to enter Indiana would face heavy fines. And then there was the clause that would make it illegal for African Americans to purchase property in the state.[20]

Of course, next door Illinois had put in place an immigration ban on free African Americans in 1813 before it was even a state. And by 1847 it had decided to draft its own new constitution, which—yet again—closed its borders to free African Americans when ratified in 1848.[21]

But some in Indiana desired to take a more brutal route. James Rariden argued during the 1851 convention that they should wage "a war of extermination" to kill off all African-descended people. To strengthen his argument, he added that whites in Indiana would merely be following in the footsteps of the Puritans, who killed the "Indians who were infinitely more magnanimous and less impudent than this colored race." While other delegates were more cautious about expressing such views, the majority made their prejudice clear by drafting and approving Resolution 13 to the Indiana state constitution, which was blatantly hostile to people of African descent.[22]

It was plainly a reaction to protests for racial equality and the gains made by African Americans like the Griers and the Lyles family in that state. In Ohio some Black Laws had just been weakened after years of struggle, and in Indiana the black convention movement was now strong—known nationally for its fervor, rooted in the wealth of the African American farmers and other African American entrepreneurs now rising across the state.[23]

On the eve of the election that they were all certain would pass the terrible new 1851 state constitution, Indiana's great equal rights organizer and orator John Britton stood before hundreds of black Hoosiers at their annual convention, urging them not to give up. While Britton was from Indianapolis, many there that day were landowning farmers in Indiana, some of them very wealthy indeed. And they reflected the reality that in Indiana and the Northwest Territory states, the vast majority of African Americans still lived in rural areas. Britton urged them all to stand firm, knowing they had truth and justice on their side. He reminded them, "As Americans we are entitled to all the rights, privileges and immunities of citizenship as other citizens, according to the letter and spirit of the constitution of the United States. . . . [Yet] we are deprived of these inherent rights, set forth in the declaration of independence, and confirmed by the Constitution of the United States."[24]

Meanwhile, their white allies had been doing their best to prevent or at least weaken the proposed changes to the constitution before it was ratified in an election. When a group of Quakers—some of them with considerable wealth and power—heard of the planned resolution, they held a special meeting out of concern and fear for the people of African descent in their state. They all agreed that if Resolution 13 passed in its current form, it "would lay upon the negro and his descendants a heavy burden . . . strengthening the power in the southern states to hold that class of human beings more securely in Slavery or cause them to leave the American shores and take up their abode in Africa from which land the white man took away their predecessors with force and violence." So they wrote a "remonstrance" to the delegates gathered and working on that new constitution. It was an impassioned plea, calling on the drafters to remember that they all called themselves Christians and thus that they should not "be found making such unjust distinctions on the grounds of color or cast, when He who is Lord over all . . . makes none, in his merciful offer of redeeming love." And hoping that the delegates "minds will yet be brought to see the injustice of such measures and refrain from adopting them."[25]

But the Quakers were not the only whites allying themselves with equality and the cause of African American rights. Others in Indiana and the Northwest Territory states were battling against the forces of prejudice by naming it and making powerful arguments about its danger to the nation. As some white politicians argued at this time, if prejudice could be applied to a group of people to remove them from citizenship because of something as inconsequential as hair texture, then it could be applied to any group, or anyone, at any time. Indeed, it could happen to people who now called themselves white. Thus, prejudice countered the goals of a democratic republic. Prejudice divided people and returned the nation to the concepts of inequality and privilege that held sway before the Revolution—the idea that some were made superior and others inferior, when all should be given an equal chance at life, liberty, and the pursuit of happiness.[26]

This integrated effort seems to have shifted some opinions, for the final draft of the new constitution did not include the terrible proposal that would have destroyed the right of African Americans to purchase land in Indiana. But the other changes looked likely to be approved by the majority of whites voting in Indiana.

And Seth Concklin was walking into this storm of rising prejudice, asking abolitionists in Indiana to help him in harboring the Stills if he got them out of the slave states. No one, not even Levi Coffin, a hero of the Underground Railroad, would take the risk, not with the recent passage of the new Fugitive Slave Law and Indiana's new constitution all but ratified. Some may even have worried that Concklin's plan, if successful, would push whites in Indiana to adopt that terrible new constitution.[27]

Finally, Concklin got a lead. He was staying with Levi Coffin in southern Indiana when an abolitionist preacher named Nathan Johnston visited from Gibson County. Reverend Johnston knew of some abolitionists near Princeton, a town fairly close to both the Wabash and the Ohio Rivers, and he suggested that Concklin investigate his options there.[28]

After traveling hundreds of miles and talking to many people, in the end the only help Concklin could find close to the Ohio River were the Stormonts in Gibson County. But the Stormonts knew they could not do it alone—they needed the Griers' help.

This must have been one of the hardest decisions Keziah and Charles Grier had ever faced. This was not the old days, when there were fewer settlers around their homestead and they could more easily put refugees on the Ohio River to freedom. Surely they had known some of the free blacks working the Ohio River or sympathetic whites on those waters. The right riverboat men would refuse the chance at the large rewards offered for escaping people and instead smuggle people up the Ohio to Pittsburgh.

But so much had changed. The new Fugitive Slave Law meant that the federal government could levy massive fines against anyone helping refugees escaping from bondage—a risk the Griers and the Stormonts shared. Rewards were higher for capturing people trying to escape from bondage, and the law was strengthened by the invention of the telegraph, which could get information out of a plantation in the South to all those newly empowered white lawmen in the North faster than a refugee could run.

The Griers also had to deal with the fact that they were in Indiana, a state that had a growing disrespect for the lives of free African Americans such as themselves. And they were no longer young. Charles was almost seventy now, a rare old age for a man to reach in that region. If they were discovered helping Seth Concklin and the Stills, their age would not save them; nor would the fact that they had been pioneers in the earliest days of the state. They would almost certainly be murdered.

They had worked so hard on those first forty acres of wilderness, always putting something aside, always with an eye to their future and the future of their children. Now they owned 230 acres of rich good land, 80 acres of it cleared. It was cleared so well that they no longer had need of an ox team but could use horses—swift and nimble in front of the plow. It must have been pure pleasure to watch the blade cut through the soil so smoothly. And not all their horses were for plowing. They had five now, for they could afford them for work, for their wagons, and for riding. Keziah and Charles had managed to create a new family from nothing, a farm from nothing, a home from nothing.[29]

And they risked losing all of that if they agreed to Seth Concklin's plan. They would have less than nothing, for they could lose their lives and endanger the lives of all their children still living with them.

But even if Keziah Grier barely knew Seth Concklin, she knew Peter Still's pain. She and Charles would have been wounded just as Peter Still was wounded—his heart hurting with loss and worry for his family. Both Charles and Keziah had almost certainly been torn from family when they were brought north. Did they often wonder what had happened to their kin? Had they wished they could do something? Now they both knew that their parents would be long dead and any family left behind long scattered.

Whatever the reason, Keziah and Charles said yes to Concklin. They would help him, and they would help the Stills.

As Concklin left on his journey deep into slave lands, looking for Peter Still's family, the Griers must have known—as William and Peter Still did—that there was little chance they would ever see him again. But they must have hoped, for in revealing themselves and promising their aid, they were sending their secret with him all the way into the South. And they knew that slavers had many terrible ways to force a suspected abolitionist to give up the names of all the people who were helping him.

To everyone's surprise, Concklin succeeded. He managed to make it down to the Alabama plantation where Vina Still and her children were held. But even after he found her, Vina would not go with him until he had shown her the cape that she had given her husband all those months before. She knew all too well that it was not just free people who could be lured away by kidnappers.[30]

In the end it was too risky to take steamships, so, together, Concklin and the Still family traveled hundreds of miles, rowing in a small skiff for hours every day. Vina's two sons, Levin and Peter, helped, but it must have been exhausting and terrifying work, every moment expecting someone on the river to hail them. And someone did, north of the Ohio River, as they traveled up the Wabash. Just as they neared the point where they were supposed to go ashore, men with guns yelled at Concklin to stop.[31]

At this point Seth was not only rowing against a strong current; he was rowing against the wind and rowing alone. Even though they were now traveling through a free state, it was no longer safe for Peter Still's sons to help him, and he was keeping all of the Stills hidden under a blanket on the bottom of the boat.

Despite the yells of the men on shore, Concklin kept rowing as hard as he could, making his way up the river at a painfully slow pace. He hoped that the noise of the high wind would convince the men that he could not hear them. William Still later wrote of Concklin that he was "a man who seemed wholly insensible to fear." But when the men on the bank started shooting at him, he must have been terrified, even as he refused to stop.[32]

And now, here they were: Seth Concklin and all of Peter Still's family, standing at the Griers' door. The surprise and delight at seeing them must have been immense. But the story Concklin told of being shot at on the river would have been very worrying. It meant that the wolves were watching. Had the telegraph done its job already?

The Griers must have been watched by slave hunters for years. They were too black, too wealthy, too visible. Some refugees had already been lost along the deadly stretch between the river and the Stormonts' house; there were so many wolves. If they could just get this group to the Stormonts', they would be safer, for as Concklin had written William Still, "No one had ever been lost between Stormon's [sic] and Canada. . . . [T]he wolves have never suspected Stormon."[33]

It was sixteen miles from the Griers' house to the Stormonts', sixteen miles of hard walking through a late-winter landscape with little cover to keep them safe. Then again, Charles Grier would have been used to getting people through even in the winter, for people came

seeking freedom when the Ohio River froze, and they could not refuse
to help them just because there were no leaves on the trees or corn high
in the fields to shelter their journey.[34]

At sixty-nine, Charles would have been slowing down, but he was
still strong, and very careful. He had to be.

Finally, it was dark enough to set out. As they walked quietly out,
Keziah must have wished she could do something, something to keep
them safe, to watch over them, to make sure Vina and her children
found their father and that Charles would make it back home to her.

All of them knew that those sixteen miles would take hours to
cover. But once the Still family was safe at the Stormonts', Charles could
walk the sixteen miles home in the light however he pleased, just an old
established farmer out on some business.

She and Malinda and all those still at home would not have slept
much until he returned. But finally he did. And then they waited.

The group now at the Stormonts' would need to rest up a bit before heading north toward Detroit. But they took a significant risk in
remaining there for more than two days, each hour a chance for the
telegraph to spread the alarm and—worse yet—descriptions.

Vina and her group were terrified, but the Stormonts were more
than a bit excited. This was probably the most famous escaping family they had ever helped. They even told their friend, Reverend Nathan
Johnston, who was preaching in Princeton that day, to visit their house
and see who they had there. He was delighted to see Seth Concklin
again. And he was very impressed by Vina Still, whom he later recalled
as "a woman of great natural ability and rare common sense." But he
could also see that the entire group that had just made it out of the slave
state was "anxious about their safety as they knew that though they
were now in a free state they were not free from the danger of being captured and taken back into slavery again."[35]

They were right to be afraid. By the time they finally left and made
their way north, the telegraph had done its deadly work, and every lawman and slave hunter in the region had descriptions of Concklin and

Peter Still's family. Worse yet, a huge reward of $1,000 had been offered for their capture and return to Alabama.[36]

It was cold and raining when they left, and the party was soon chilled. As they walked in the rain, someone saw them. Someone noticed a white man and four African Americans looking very much like a group that was being hunted, and they were captured some miles north of Vincennes, separated from Concklin, and imprisoned. Concklin would not give up, however, and tried to rescue them, coming to the jail with a writ of habeas corpus. Sometimes this could stall proceedings, but not in this case. The Still family's enslaver, Bernard McKiernan, had made it to Indiana and was waiting in Evansville—a town on the Ohio River due south of Princeton—with assurances from the Evansville sheriff that he would get the Stills.[37]

Before Concklin knew what was happening, Vina and her children had been taken away, and he had been thrown into prison with the enthusiastic aid of the sheriff of Evansville, a man by the name of John S. Gavitt. Before long, news of their capture had spread throughout Indiana. Levi Coffin wept, writing, "The hopes of the dear family all blasted by the wretched bloodhounds in human shape. And poor Seth, after all his toil and dangers, shrewd and wise management, and almost unheard of adventures. . . . Then to be given up to Indianians, to these fiendish tyrants, to be sacrificed. O Shame! Shame!!"[38]

The Griers surely wept for Concklin and the Stills as well, but they were also trying to survive. Something had caused Seth Concklin so much suffering and terror that he was willing to reveal the Stormonts, writing to them to beg for help.[39]

And now people of African descent in Gibson County were guarding their doors, gun in hand. There had always been whites in the Northwest Territory states who hated anyone who tried to aid or support the cause of refugees from bondage, but this new federal Fugitive Slave Law emboldened them.

Even in Ohio, which had struck down so many of its Black Laws just two years earlier, white politicians were speaking out against African

American Underground Railroad agents like the Griers. James Loudon spoke to his fellow statesmen, arguing that in order to destroy such African American agents, it "may be necessary to call on the light troops in the vicinity, and even upon the militia."[40]

Concklin was marched in chains through Princeton by Sheriff Gavitt to be put on a boat to Alabama. But first the sheriff kept him and his friends in jail for a little while, separating the family members from each other and—as he later put it—"questioning" them. No one knows what tactics he used, what threats he made, but he later claimed that the young Levin Still finally admitted that Concklin was helping them to freedom. Yet Sheriff Gavitt did not break Levin Still completely, for Levin never gave him the Griers.[41]

Then Sheriff Gavitt put the Stills on a ship back into bondage. They were gone. But the danger was not, and the Lyles family as well as the Griers knew they could not let down their guard. The men must have taken watch in shifts, staying up all night to protect their homes and families. They knew that soon every form of torture would be used on that boat to convince Concklin and the Stills to give up their secrets. As Reverend Johnston wrote to Peter and William back in Philadelphia, "Poor Concklin! I fear for him. When he is dragged back to Alabama I fear that they will go beyond the utmost rigor of the law and vent their savage cruelty upon him."[42]

The Stormonts were targets as well, now that their secret was revealed. But David and Mary Stormont stood firm, refusing to give up the Griers and their secrets even when they heard the terrible news of what had happened to Concklin.

Concklin never made it to Alabama. His body was found bound in chains, washed up on the muddy shore of the Ohio River, his head stove-in.[43]

Seth Concklin had failed to save his own life and rescue the Still family, but he had never broken faith with the Griers. He never gave away their secret, willing to die before he would endanger them and all the African Americans around them.

And the Still family did not give them up either, even though their enslaver, McKiernan, was willing to do just about anything to get information. He knew that once he had names, he could send a telegram, and Sheriff Gavitt would be at the door of those in southwestern Indiana who might have helped the Stills. Vina Still later reported that once they were returned to McKiernan, he had her sons stripped in front of her and whipped, given two hundred lashes until their backs were raw. McKiernan considered this just punishment for their trying to flee, but giving up information about the Griers may have saved the Still sons from such retribution. Yet none of them gave up the Griers.[44]

Still McKiernan questioned them. He was sure that if he did not discover who had helped them, they might try to run again—and succeed. This was war, and McKiernan planned on using all the most inhuman tools of wartime against the Stills.

McKiernan decided to first threaten Vina Still with rape, and then her daughter Catherine. Vina Still knew that this was a deadly threat. Lydia, the young enslaved woman he had been assaulting in his home, was almost beaten to death when McKiernan's wife discovered what he had been doing to her.[45]

Vina Still may have been aware that their fame offered them some sort of a shield, their existence and plight now known by many across the nation. But she must have thought that even this was not enough. So she threatened Bernard McKiernan, telling him that if he tried to take her daughter, she would kill him. Vina knew that her threat could result in her being "killed on the spot," but somehow she got McKiernan to back down. Vina Still had managed to give some protection to her daughter and continued to protect the Griers.[46]

Meanwhile, Peter was doing everything he could to get his family out of danger. When McKiernan offered to sell them for the obscene sum of $5,000, Peter traveled around the country to raise the money, and in 1854 he was finally able to purchase their freedom. At the last minute, McKiernan, who had done so much to keep them in bondage, tortured them one more time, refusing to let Vina and Peter take their beloved little grandchild with them.[47]

Did the Stormonts come running to tell the Griers of the news?

Keziah and Charles Grier were finally safe. They had been in danger every day since the Stills had been taken, knowing that any day something might break one of the Stills as they tried to survive in bondage. And then the wolves would come.

The wolves never came. But some whites in Gibson County decided that the Griers and all of the African Americans in Gibson County should have some hurt. So they inflicted the indignity of registration on them.

The new state constitution required that every free person of African descent be registered starting in November 1851. African Americans had to show proof that they had entered the state before 1851 and submit to bodily inspection by whites. Some counties chose not to enforce the new law; others were slow to start or lax in requiring people to register. But whites in Gibson County started as soon as they could in 1851.[48]

This registry would have been hauntingly familiar to the Lyles family in Gibson County, who had seen such registries in use against free people like them back in Tennessee. Had any of them thought that one day such practices of prejudice might arise in Indiana?

Charles and Keziah Grier and their son John waited awhile before coming to the courthouse to register. When they did, it was not easy. The county clerk wrote down Charles's information: "Negro, dark complexion, stout built, 5′ 8 ½ inches high." But Keziah refused to let the clerk get near her with his measuring stick. In the end he had to content himself with writing down, "Negro, dark complexion, light built."[49]

Their daughter Mary Jane, now twenty-seven, waited even longer—maybe hearing of her parents' experience. And Malinda refused outright. Her parents had seen so many changes for freedom and equality—they had created them, they had lived them, and now they were seeing them destroyed. She would not take part in this.[50]

Despite all of this, or maybe because of it, their friend Jacob Hawkins was going to build a church.

Jacob Hawkins could certainly afford to build a church. He now owned 600 acres of land, at least 180 acres of it cleared and under cultivation. This man, forced onto the frontier as an enslaved child with nothing, not even his own body, to claim as his own, was now one of the most successful farmers of any color in Daviess County.[51]

But his story, his success, had more than symbolic power. Jacob and Ellen Hawkins, Charles and Keziah Grier, and the hundreds of other successful African American farmers in the Northwest Territory states were also managing massive engines of production, creating wheat, wool, corn, meat, and more. They were not merely feeding their families or communities—admittedly a good measure of success for most farming families of any skin color; these farmers were feeding the nation. Whether it was their hogs going to Cincinnati and Chicago or their wheat going to New Orleans and Pittsburgh, free African American farmers were affecting markets and people far outside their own states. And now Jacob Hawkins was going to use some of the wealth he had grown to build a church.

Like the Griers, the Hawkins family had started off attending a church where blacks and whites worshipped together. But something changed. Perhaps their home church started to force segregation or even reject African American members. This was certainly becoming more common. But their involvement with the African Methodist Episcopal (AME) Church probably began with Bishop Paul Quinn.[52]

Richard Allen had founded the denomination in Philadelphia back in the late 1700s, soon after the Revolutionary War. As a very young man, Reverend Quinn had known Bishop Allen, although the elderly bishop and the young pastor had not always seen eye to eye. Quinn was the first AME circuit rider to make it out to the Great West, coming from his training ground in Philadelphia in the early 1830s. He was a man of color, vague about his background, but bold about his calling.[53]

They never knew when he would arrive, but when he did it was wonderful. He was a magnificent sight, beautifully dressed from his fine beaver hat to his supple gloves, riding a huge, half-wild horse. He would gallop into their midst, calling out Bible verses in that big voice of his, bringing his horse to a rearing halt and jumping off before it had even settled.[54]

In many ways, Reverend Quinn was the embodiment of Reverend Hosea Easton's magnified man. For a start, he was large—over six feet—but he was also so very free. And he knew how to found churches.

Whether it was Bible study meetings in log cabins or raising a beautiful clapboard church, he helped African Americans across the Northwest Territory states achieve great things. In eleven years he founded almost fifty churches, from frontier outposts to the slave port of St. Louis—all places of great danger for a finely dressed black man preaching truth, justice, and freedom. Because of his work and the work of hundreds of African Americans across the frontier and rural Northwest Territory states, the AME was able to create a new "conference," the Indiana Conference, its formal founding ceremony held in the Indiana African American farming settlement of Beech in Ripley Township, Rush County.[55]

In 1844 the AME made Quinn a bishop; by the 1850s he was based in the town of Richmond, Indiana, a Quaker stronghold known for its thriving African American community and Underground Railroad activities. Jacob and Ellen Hawkins may well have hosted Bishop Quinn as he rode through, putting him up in their lovely large home, where many could gather for services in the parlor.[56]

The Griers had also been meeting with traveling AME pastors, possibly including Quinn, who came through Gibson County ministering to the African Americans there. For years the Griers had worshipped with the white Elder Wasson, that friend of Reverend James Grier, who had freed Charles back in 1813. But something had changed for them as well.

The Griers, with a large family of grown children and many more African American neighbors, may have freely decided to celebrate on Sundays with a pastor and a congregation that looked more like themselves. But like many of their generation, they were probably comfortable worshipping in a diverse church—just as the Morrises had been over at Fort Allison—for such a congregation reflected the values of equality they would have been familiar with in those heady days of the early republic. But Elder Wasson may have died and his small congregation disbanded. Or whites in his church, like so many others across the North, may have rejected the ideal of integration.

Whatever the reason, both the Griers and the Hawkinses were now members of the AME, connected through ties of faith to African Americans across the Northwest Territory states and the nation. Their traveling preachers would have brought them news from all the other states, updated them on family and friends in other communities, and spoken words of comfort and encouragement. And now, Jacob Hawkins was going to build an AME church.[57]

This took extraordinary courage. Jacob Hawkins's wealth alone could endanger him and his family as more whites used violence to gain the status and power they desired. But a church was worse. It was not safe. Everyone knew that a fine frame church, its windows filled with glass, seemed to be a tempting target for prejudiced whites.

But Jacob Hawkins was going to build that church. The Griers knew that Jacob Hawkins was never one to pick the safest path. And, like the Griers, he was not going to give in to the powers of prejudice that were rising in his state. At least he wasn't starting a newspaper.

And now Keziah Grier hoped the church might be finished in time for the wedding. Malinda, her dear eldest child, was engaged to Jacob's son Charner.[58]

There may have been some surprise about this. Charner was not the Hawkins family's eldest son but the fourth born in a family of eleven children, and he was a good twelve years younger than Malinda. But the Hawkinses and Griers were friends, and they must have been so glad that they would soon be kin.

Malinda had certainly waited long enough, she was almost thirty-five by now. But she was careful, and Keziah must have been grateful to have her at home for so long, working with her and Charles to help the refugees they aided. And Charner, well, Charner was like his father and Charles—a hardworking man who loved to farm. He would not take Malinda away to a city but would stay close and work his father's land as well as his own.

It was a blessing that Malinda had fallen in love with Charner and not some visitor from out of state. Some of the kindly and handsome young preachers pastoring to them could well have caught her eye. But if Malinda had married a man from out of state, she would have been lost to Keziah. The new constitution banned even visiting family from entering Indiana.

And marriage didn't help, as a young couple over on the east side of the state had discovered. When Elizabeth Keith and Arthur Barkshire were married in Indiana in Arthur's hometown close to the Ohio border, white officials in Indiana came after them because Elizabeth had been born in Ohio. Not only did the state force Elizabeth to leave, but it fined her husband $10 for breaking the new law banning anyone in Indiana from entering into contracts with African Americans from outside the state—even the holy contract of marriage.[59]

The Grier and Lyles families must have wondered how their communities could keep growing. Their own Gibson County had seen its population grow with African American pioneers drawn to the good land there. As these pioneers grew their farms, they would have dreamed of the family and friends they hoped would join them. But now that was stopped.

But nothing would stop Jacob Hawkins from building his church. And he was determined it would be done in time for the wedding. And it was—a handsome frame building with its clapboard sides gleaming in the sun, a far cry from the log cabins that many white settlers in the region still lived in.[60]

Then a date was chosen: December 22, 1853, just before Christmas. Keziah would have been baking for days, the house warm and fragrant, her daughter Malinda and many other women helping. But Ellen Hawkins, Charner's mother, must have baked the bread for the first communion in the church. At that first communion celebrated in the new church, they would have eaten bread made from their grain. Each loaf broken for them by their pastor held years of hard work and hope, from the earliest clearing of the land to that fall's harvest.

Harvest, that rich time of bounty, as long as there was no freeze, no storm, no flood, no hail, no swarm of insects or birds landing on the tender crop to consume it. If the conditions were just right, then they would move out with their scythes sharpened, cutting the grain so it could be gathered and bundled up. The harvesters stepped, bent, and swung, scraping their blades low along the ground, the rhythmic song of their scythes rising across the field.

The Hawkins family would have had to hire almost every able-bodied person in the county, and maybe beyond, regardless of the color of their skin, to harvest all of the acres they now had under cultivation. And much of it was in grain—a risky crop but valuable if all went well. In 1850 Hawkins had harvested over one hundred bushels of wheat. He must have hoped for even better in 1853.[61]

Jacob and Ellen Hawkins would always have looked at the sky as they worked with the other harvesters, for rain could ruin everything, rotting the ripe wheat as it lay in the field, waiting to be gathered in. If the rain held off, then the drying stalks could be taken to their big barn, where the floor was cleared for threshing—men and women lifting their flails high in the air to bring them down hard to separate the ripe grains of wheat from the stalks. Then there was the winnowing done out in the wind. The laborers filled large flat baskets with the grain and threw it high in the air, where the breeze blew away the chaff as the grain fell back into the baskets to be caught and tossed up over and over again. Just the right amount of wind was needed: too much and the grain would blow away with the chaff; too little and the chaff would not blow away at all.[62]

Even if the wind was perfect, it often shifted, blowing the chaff into their faces, causing everyone to cough and sneeze as they tried to turn with the wind. Soon chaff was everywhere, in hair and ears, scratchy behind collars and stuck under damp arms. At the end of a long day, the younger laborers must have fairly run for the nearest creek to rinse off, the chaff rising to the surface of the water, specks of gold swirling away downstream as they dunked their heads, gasping with the cold and laughing.

If all went right, the grain could be taken to the mill for grinding. And then, finally, Ellen Hawkins could make her bread.

By 1853 Ellen almost certainly had a fine wood cook stove where she baked her bread, the loaves rising high with the starter she had kept going for years. She would have kept that starter yeasty and alive even in the coldest winter months, wrapping it carefully at night and tucking it close to her body to keep it from freezing.

There might be talk of miracles and the holiness of communion bread, but the African American farmers in the church that day knew that the loaf of bread Ellen Hawkins had baked was a miracle in itself, as wonderfully improbable as they were.

They must have been thankful indeed as they took it into their mouths, chewing it, tasting its rough sweetness against their tongues as they prayed. This day must have felt like an answer to prayer as they knelt in their church celebrating together. Villages forming, churches being built, children getting married. All of it just normal, except in the minds of so many whites, who had decided that the United States should be a nation divisible, with liberty and justice for only a few.

But Ellen and Jacob, Keziah and Charles, Malinda and Charner were still going out to their fields each spring and planting. And they were joined by thousands of others whose names echoed back through the centuries: Lyles, Roundtree, Goins, Nolcox, Allen, and Roberts. They planted even if the future might bring blight, drought, freezes, loss. Still they planted; still they built churches, founded schools, married. Still they walked the long miles forward through their fields behind the plow. Still they hoped, even as the blight of prejudice and injustice infected the land and threatened to spoil everything they had grown.

9

"A history of repeated injuries and usurpations"

Vanderburgh County, Indiana, Summer 1857 to Spring 1861

There was so much blood.

The attackers had finally gone, but there was still so much blood.

The Lyles family knew there would be an attack, but not this, not the children.

That hateful newspaper, the *Evansville Daily Enquirer* and all those other organizers in Evansville had been working for a while now to gather a fighting force against them.[1]

Now it was over, and the outside of the house was pretty much ruined. There were bullet holes everywhere, bullets still stuck deep into the wood. The front door was battered, the log the attackers had used to break into their home still lying on the ground.

Daniel and four others were the only grown men inside, all the rest were women and children. The wounds were terrible.

It was not just their blood either. There had been others wounded as the Lyles family defended themselves. The attackers were gone, taking their dead and wounded with them, but they had left their blood everywhere.

There had been some powerful leaders among them, including Alexander Maddox, the county commissioner. Daniel Lyles was pretty sure he had killed Maddox. But he hadn't been able to protect Nancy, and she was hurt, badly. She had been hit on the head with a gunstock and fallen as the attackers had wielded bowie knives and guns in the close quarters of their home.

This was not about some hogs.

Although by 1857, the Lyles family would have been known for their fine livestock, their hogs included. They were good farmers, that was evident. Evident in their good land that they kept improving and adding to. Evident in their profits, in their success. Evident in all that they had been doing since they had arrived in Vanderburgh County from Tennessee twenty years before. They had worked so hard for their successes and risen far on their new frontier.[2]

Daniel and Nancy and most of the Lyles family had decided to settle in Vanderburgh County on land close to the Ohio River and the village of Evansville. They had picked a two-hundred-acre plot that was practically an island. It was set on a rise and back a bit from the Ohio River to safeguard it from flooding, a creek winding in a loop around three sides of their land, their home on a high point in the middle of that land. The water acted as a natural boundary, a way to keep livestock from wandering out, or those who were unwelcome from easily wandering in. Some said that such land was unhealthy, too close to water, too full of bad vapors that could cause disease and death. But their twelve children were evidence of the goodness of their land and their family. They were thriving.[3]

They were not all living there. Daniel's brother Joshua and his family had found land near his wife's kin in Gibson County, about twenty-five miles north. But they were close enough to visit and did so with some frequency. And Vanderburgh County suited Daniel and Nancy and all the Lyles family scattered around them. Their nearest white neighbors were fairly tolerant, some even working with them, and there was now an AME church nearby where they could worship. Being close to the Evansville docks made it easy to get their hogs to the lucrative markets of Cincinnati on the many boats that traveled the Ohio River.[4]

But then their hogs had started to go missing.

The hogs ran loose in the woods of all of the local farms. Anyone's hogs might wander onto someone else's land, but this was so common that the county kept records of the various "hog marks" the farmers used to keep track of their livestock, including the Lyles family mark. The day of "marking" the hogs would have been a noisy one on the Lyles family farm, as each young pig was held firmly while members of the family did their skilled knife work, putting a smooth crop on the right ear and two slits in each ear.[5]

There would have always been whites interested in those hogs— interested in purchasing them and interested in stealing them. But "hog squeaking," while not uncommon, was a serious offense. And the Lyles family had registered its hog marks with the county, making very clear who owned those fine animals.[6]

Then their hogs must have started going missing in numbers much higher than before. This was more than illness, injury, or some stray dog picking off a pig or two.

Was it the new laws? For years laws in Indiana had made it difficult for African Americans to defend themselves by making it illegal for them to testify against or sue a white person in court. This meant that a white person could walk right into an African American farmer's barn and walk out with a hog, and if the only witnesses were of African descent, then that white person had little to fear, for no one could testify that he or she had stolen it. But the new laws made it worse.

First there was the Fugitive Slave Law of 1850. Then the terrible new state constitution of 1851—ratified in overwhelming numbers by Indiana white men—making perfectly clear that the Lyles family and any others like them were not welcome in that state. But the worst came in March 1857.

There are all kinds of hurt. The Lyles family already knew the pain of having their own home state of Tennessee reject them and their rights. Then they had seen Indiana move in a similar direction. But now their nation—where their families had been free for so long—was rejecting them. They were now officially no longer citizens of the United States. The Supreme Court back in Washington, DC, had just made this brutally clear in its *Dred Scott v. Sandford* ruling.[7]

Dred Scott had worked hard under bondage and finally been able to offer his owner enough money to buy his own freedom and to start purchasing the freedom of his wife, Harriet, and their daughter as well. But his recently widowed owner, Eliza Sanford Emerson, refused. Maybe she relied overmuch on the income she made renting Dred and Harriet to others. Whatever the reason, she would not relent, and so Dred and Harriet took her to court. After all, they had been living in Wisconsin and Illinois for years, and the Missouri court had long understood that an enslaved person who spent time in a free state had a right to a chance at freedom.[8]

But Eliza Sanford Emerson desired to hold others in bondage, just as Eli Hawkins's widow had been unwilling to give Jacob Hawkins his freedom thirty years before. Even when Eliza Sanford Emerson moved to Massachusetts, she was unwilling to give Dred, Harriet, and their family their freedom. Instead, she made sure her brother John Sanford took them so that they would continue to be enslaved. And now, in 1857, Dred and Harriet Scott had finally lost their case, when a majority of justices in the highest court of the land decided that no one of African descent could be considered a citizen.

In his decision, Justice Roger Brooke Taney considered all the rights that families just like the Lyles family had held and then lost over the years—the right to vote, the right to fight for their nation's protection and freedom, even the Tennessee decision denying them the right to bear arms—and used the loss of those rights to justify stripping away even more. Did the Lyles family hear that Taney had even attacked the Northwest Territory states, saying that the Ordinance of 1787 should never have made the region free of slavery?[9]

And the Lyles family? Well, they were not supposed to exist—to have enjoyed freedom, to have voted, to have chosen to become pioneers, to have moved to two frontiers to help settle this nation, south and north. Instead, Justice Taney wrote, since some of their ancestors had been brought to the United States and treated only as "an ordinary article of merchandise," they were not true Americans, further arguing that they had not chosen the United States to be their own nation. This in the face of the fact that African-descended men had fought as patriots in the Revolutionary War to create the country whose highest court had just generated such injustice.[10]

But didn't Taney know of them, of the Lyles family? Of the thousands like them who had chosen to migrate to the Northwest Territory and states? They had chosen to stay in the United States—their "motherland"—despite being urged to leave. The Lyles family and all of their kin had not left the United States in 1838; they had moved to Indiana, refusing to abandon their nation. And Indiana was now their home. They would not leave. Even if many of the whites in Vanderburgh County were determined to force them out.

There were whites in that county who may have long been jealous, may have been covetous, but now they had an excuse to allow their worst passions to overtake them. When Taney and those in power—whether in the Indiana legislature or in the Vanderburgh County government—started practicing and preaching prejudice, they gave energy and focus to hate. And then that hate grew into violence.

The Lyles family knew who was taking their pigs, but those men were white, and the state of Indiana had long said that African Americans could not sue a white man in court. So the Lyles family could not go to the sheriff and have the men of the Edmonds family charged with pig stealing.

So, in July 1857 Daniel and three of his sons—Thomas, John, and Wesley—went to Thomas Edmonds's farm to get their stolen property back.

Politics and prejudice had long bled into the printer's ink in Evansville, and it would have been very difficult for African Americans to have their side of the story told well or truthfully. But what does seem to have happened is that Daniel and his three oldest sons, Wesley, John, and Thomas, went to the Edmonds' farm and found their stolen hog hidden in a shed. As they were trying to get their stolen pig back, there was some kind of altercation between the Lyles and Edmonds men, and in the fray, Thomas Edmonds and his son Mike were both hurt.

Daniel and his sons managed to get back to their farm with their pig, but the Edmonds men went to the papers. Before long, reports were published of six large Lyles men marching with their guns onto the defenseless and innocent Edmonds family's farm with the intent to murder them all. Of course, the Edmonds family gave many excuses to anyone who would listen. One was that they had found the hog lost on their property and were kindly keeping it safe for the Lyles family with every intention of returning it. Another version was that they were merely borrowing the pig. It would have been funny if it had not been so dangerous.[11]

The Lyles family would have known that this was not just about those pigs; it was about them—their good land and home, their thriving.

As soon as Daniel got home with the boys, he and Nancy must have talked, and then started preparing for war.

After all, they knew what had happened to Joseph Spencer.

Joseph Spencer had lived just to the west of them, a few miles down the Ohio. Spencer was a successful entrepreneur, running a lucrative and lovely hotel on his large boat, the *Patrick Henry*, docked at the village of Cairo, Illinois. But he was getting just a bit too successful. As a local report stated, "Some were embittered against him by feelings of envy on account of his prosperity; others because he had been too successful in playing his favorite game of poker with them."[12]

The local reports were greatly biased, but they make clear that a mob of hundreds of white men attacked Spencer on his ship. They arranged themselves around it in sniper positions and started shooting. Spencer was well armed and managed to defend himself, but after a while some whites managed to untie the *Patrick Henry* and push it off into the water where they lit it on fire. Then they surrounded the burning ship in their boats, guns drawn, and waited for Spencer to appear.

Joseph Spencer was soon dead.[13]

So, the Lyles family gathered—all nineteen of them—in Daniel and Nancy's house. It was a lot of people to cook for, but Nancy was used to that. They always had plenty of food; they had worked hard to make sure of that. And there were others to help.

The whole house would have smelled good as they cooked and baked, keeping busy. It was hot work, to be sure, but there were dippers of clear water for their thirst and clean handkerchiefs still smelling of the sun for their warm faces. And there was good company. Normally Nancy would have encouraged the younger ones to take a dip in the stream to cool off, but not today. Today they were staying put. Today they were staying close.

The sheriff arrived to arrest Nancy's husband and sons just as they were all sitting down to breakfast.

There is no word on which sheriff came to their door, but it was likely Sheriff John S. Gavitt, for he had taken a personal interest in this matter. This was the same Sheriff Gavitt who had worked so hard with Bernard McKiernan to capture Seth Concklin and the Still family as they fled north from the Stormonts' home. This was the same Sheriff Gavitt who had put the Still family in the jail in Evansville, separating them and "questioning" the children until they broke. And this was the same Sheriff Gavitt who forced Concklin and the Still family in chains onto the steamboat at Evansville, for a journey that Concklin would not survive. Six years later Gavitt was still boasting of his capture of Seth, whom he called a "slave stealer."[14]

Sheriff Gavitt was still enthusiastically enforcing the 1850 Fugitive Slave Law, along with the other laws that had come after it, all meant to take away the liberty and rights of Americans with Africa in their blood.

And Gavitt, who saw Vina Still and her children only as chattel, now had an excuse from Justice Taney for treating all African Americans as less than human.

When Nancy watched the lawmen walk away with Daniel, with her boys, she would have known that there was a real risk that she would never see them again. There could be a long rope in a tree or a bonfire or worse. There might only be remnants of their remains for her to bury.

They had one hope, and it was the court. Unlike Justice Taney back in Washington, DC, there were some men in the county courthouse who were known to have some fairness in them, their lawyer Horace Plummer included.[15]

First the Lyles men had to stand in chains as they were accused of terrible things. Attempted murder was the worst. The prosecutor urged that they be denied bail and imprisoned in the Evansville jail, where everyone knew there would be little defense against any mob that came to kill them.

But the Lyles men were not without support. They had their lawyer, Horace Plummer, to defend them. Plummer explained the facts of the case and outraged the *Daily Enquirer* editor by expressing his belief in "negro intellect and equality."[16]

Then Daniel, Thomas, Wesley, and John stood before the clerk, Mr. Mills, and told him what had happened. And Mr. Mills believed them.

In the end, Mr. Mills choose to let the Lyles men go on bail, a heavy one of $500 each, and they were each fined $25. But it meant that they could go back home. It meant that they had a chance of surviving.[17]

But when the clerk allowed them to return home, war was declared. The Lyles men were not supposed to go free. They were not supposed to be alive. As the *Daily Enquirer* wrote, "The Lyles are a wealthy tribe of blacks and one thousand dollars can easily be raised by them as we can raise five dollars." Adding that "Judge Lynch could be called," for "it looks to us like Union Township might do herself a credit by ridding herself of the large number of free blacks who now infest it."[18]

Daniel and his sons barely made it back to Nancy. They were attacked trying to cross a bridge, but they made it home. And then the work started. They had to prepare; they knew what was coming. After all, Sheriff Gavitt's colleague, Sheriff-elect John Hall, was organizing an army of county men to attack the Lyles farm.[19]

Once, whites in Tennessee had told the Lyles family that they no longer had the right to bear arms, but they had them now. Their home was well built and sturdy, and the family could guard it well. But they were not expecting so many men to come marching down their long drive to fire on their home.

They ran out of bullets. Then the pounding on the door started, the wood slowly splintering, as the adults inside scrambled to protect the children. In the close combat that followed, one of the boys was wounded, and Nancy was badly hurt. But they had all survived, and the attackers had fled.[20]

Even as they were recovering, binding wounds, and cleaning the blood off the floor, they knew that many of the white men of Vanderburgh County were not done trying. Those men wanted them dead or gone.

But Nancy and Daniel did not want to leave. This was their home.

Of course, they knew others in their state were leaving. Aaron Siddles had. He had been living in a rural area outside Indianapolis. Siddles had settled on his land years earlier, and after years of danger and brutal toil, he and his family now lived on one of the loveliest farms in the region. He had been comfortably situated and on good terms with the other local elites, the doctor being a particular friend.[21]

But the whites who arrived after him were none too happy with his success. Some men had attacked his home, throwing bricks through his expensive glass windows. So, Aaron Siddles had shot at them, using small shot that would have stung their hind parts when it hit them. The doctor may have laughingly recounted to Siddles how the men had limped into his office, but Siddles was furious. He knew his standing in the community made him safe from retaliation, but he wanted to sue the men for the damage to his home, and whites in Indiana had voted to make such action illegal. This right was widely known as one's "oath," and to lose it was to lose one's voice.[22]

Siddles would later bitterly recount, "Living in Indiana I was dissatisfied with the laws of that country. I had a good deal of property there;

it was not safe, for any loafing white might destroy or steal, and unless a white man were by to see it, I could get no redress." So, even with loyal white friends, Siddles knew that Indiana's prejudiced laws, combined with the Fugitive Slave Law, put him and his family in too much danger. So he gave up on the United States and left for Canada.

But the move broke his heart. As he later admitted, "Excepting for the oppressive laws, I would rather have remained in Indiana. I left one of the most beautiful places in that country—everybody who sees it says it is a beautiful place. I had a two-story frame house, with piazza— good stable—and every arrangement about the premises was nice and convenient."[23]

And others were making the same sacrifice that Aaron Siddles had made. Especially farmers who lived along the Ohio River in Ohio, Indiana, and Illinois. For it was all too easy for someone to cross the river from a slave state and grab them, free as they were. Their bodies had not become any less valuable, kidnappers had become bolder, and the local laws were not helping.

Indeed, in 1853 Illinois whites again proved their extraordinary prejudice. Ever since the passing of the new Illinois constitution in 1848, African Americans had been forbidden from settling in the state. But in 1853 it was decided that any who were caught trying to enter the state would be charged a massive fine as well as court costs. And if they could not pay the fine, then the local sheriff could sell them into slavery—effectively turning the state of Illinois into a slave-trading entity. Many Illinois whites were determined to make their state a place where liberty was always at risk and equality endangered.[24]

It was not surprising that African American farmers were deciding to leave. Some chose it freely, others with guns aimed at them. But African Americans in Indiana, Illinois, and Ohio, finding their rights and freedom endangered, knew that they still had an important freedom left, the freedom of movement.[25]

The problem, though, was where to go. Whites in many states to the west had now put exclusion laws on their books to hamper or block

African American immigration, as well as denying African Americans the right to vote. Many whites in these regions wanted no repeat of the successful African American pioneering movement that had settled the Northwest Territory states. At California's first state convention of 1849, the white attendees decided to exclude African Americans from voting, then pushed hard for complete exclusion of any African-descended people from the state. Citing the laws passed in Illinois and arguing for similar ones in California, they warned that otherwise, "You will find the country flooded with a population of free negroes—the greatest calamity that could befall California." Robert Semple of Sonoma added that he considered free African Americans "the worst species of the population."[26]

There was something chilling about these speeches, however, for they were informed by some recent tainted information that these politicians would have known of. In addition to trying to model themselves along the lines of the most prejudiced Northwest Territory states, some of these politicians seem to have been referencing the 1840 census report.

Powerful enslavers had long argued that anyone of African descent was unfit for freedom. Napoléon Bonaparte's colonial minister Denis Decrès had made this argument almost fifty years earlier as he ordered the French military to reenslave freed people.[27]

But the Northwest Territory states were now filled with free African Americans who clearly enjoyed the taste of freedom, a fact that many influential whites did not want reported. After the 1840 census data was tabulated and reported, it was full of so many errors that both experts in the field and politicians were outraged. Their chief complaint was aimed at bizarre data seeming to show that an extraordinary number of free African Americans in the northern states were sick or insane. Representative John Quincy Adams, who had been the nation's sixth president and was now a representative from the state of Massachusetts, pointed out, it "listed insane Negroes where no Negro population existed," and in other regions the numbers were so falsely exaggerated that more were listed as insane than the actual number of "reported Negro residents."[28]

While experts at the time argued that the report was clearly fraudulent, some later argued that the fact that entire aged and infirm populations of white people were transformed into African Americans may have just been a simple transcription mistake. However, these "mistakes" rarely favored people of African descent, with one of the census transcribers converting the entire white population of a hospital for the mentally ill in Massachusetts into African Americans.[29]

These inaccuracies were another attack on freedom and equality; by asserting the frailty of free African Americans, they bolstered the intellectual framework for slavery. Pro-slavery politicians could not conceal their delight. The secretary of state at the time was the notoriously prejudiced John C. Calhoun, who had recently served as the nation's seventh vice president. Calhoun had long praised the virtues of slavery, arguing that it was the best of all possible conditions for anyone of African descent. Despite requests to open an investigation into the 1840 census, Calhoun refused, arguing that the results were to be expected in the northern free black population, for these were a people who could only thrive in bondage.[30]

So African American pioneering farmers worked with what they had: good land, good skills, and, if necessary, the ability to move to a new place. In the current political environment, the frontiers of the Northwest Territory and states must have still seemed their best hope. Many were moving to its edges, mainly Michigan and Wisconsin. Soon the African American population of those two states was growing, and fast. It doubled in Wisconsin from 630 to almost 1,200 between 1850 and 1860; in Michigan in that same decade it grew from around 2,500 to 6,700. Despite these relatively small numbers, the impact of this successful settlement movement must have been immense, for many of these African American pioneers brought enough wealth and resources to become very successful farmers by 1860 (see map).[31]

One of the most popular areas was in southern Michigan in a county called Cass. There were many reasons why successful landowning

African Americans would choose this county. They went far beyond the mere fact that it was farther north and thus further removed from the threats that slave raiders from the southern states could pose. African Americans coming into Cass County in the 1850s would have been well aware that it was already home to successful free African Americans who had founded one of Michigan's first African American Baptist churches in 1838. It was also home to many abolitionist-minded whites, Quakers included, who had been running a successful branch of the Underground Railroad with local African Americans.[32]

There was also still ample good land and a strong network of African American farmers already in place. And there were schools.

Cass County had good integrated public schools, despite state laws forbidding integrated education in publicly funded schools. For years African Americans in the county had petitioned the state for the right to vote in school district meetings, as well as to run for and hold office in the local school district councils. Finally, in 1855, whites in governance in Michigan decided that African Americans should at least have the right to vote in their local school board elections. This fairly minor victory was definitely not a return to the full voting rights of the Northwest Ordinance, but on a national level it had profound importance, for Michigan was one of the rare states in the 1850s moving toward African American equality and citizenship.[33]

The African American population of Cass County practically exploded in the 1850s. By 1860 over six hundred African Americans lived there, making it one of the largest rural African American settlements in the Northwest Territory states. While Michigan was drawing most of this third wave of African American pioneers, Wisconsin also offered some hope. True, it was still a frontier state in the 1850s, but the whites in government there still had not created Black Code bond laws to limit African American immigration. Of course, whites in power had allowed themselves to be ruled by prejudice, changing the Northwest Territory voting guidelines and restricting voting rights to whites only when it became a state in 1848. But just five years later, in 1853, the Wisconsin Supreme Court heard a case involving Joshua Glover, who had freed himself by fleeing to Wisconsin. Aided by those working to overturn the 1850 Fugitive Slave Law, the Court had ruled that law unconstitutional.[34]

However, many of the African Americans settling in that state were not refugees from enslavement but long-free people seeking a new home where they could prosper without so much prejudice. Many came up the Mississippi River from Illinois, moving into the wilds of western Wisconsin, where some were the first settlers to purchase federal land in their chosen townships. And more than African American businesses and farms were rising in the backwoods of Wisconsin. Something else was blossoming in the wilderness: love.[35]

Among the small group of African American landowning farmers in frontier Wisconsin in 1860, four who allowed themselves to be counted in the census were in mixed marriages. Cyrus and Mary Livingston lived in Peshtigo Township, Oconto County. Cyrus was an American of African descent, born in Virginia in 1815, and Mary was a German immigrant. Together they were farming their land with Mary's brother, John Schidt, who lived with them.[36]

Some of these families were astonishing in their blending. In some cases one or both spouses had been widowed and brought children from their previous marriages with them. Mather and Emeline Robinson were farming their land in Plymouth Township, Rock County. Like Cyrus Livingston, Mather Robinson was an African American born in Virginia, while Emeline was white and from Vermont. Together they were raising their eight-year-old daughter, Mary, who was attending the local school, as well as Emeline's son, William Anderson, from her first marriage.[37]

Free people in the North had long intermarried. But as the tide of prejudice grew, it caught love in its current and tried to drown it. A white man raping an African-descended woman was one thing, as Colonel Robert Lytle had made clear back in 1830s Cincinnati. But love between two free people that resulted in marriage was becoming increasingly hated—even among self-professed abolitionists.[38]

And tarring and feathering was increasingly used as a weapon uti-lized in a war trying to enforce hate—a war to destroy any relationship that represented equality—whether it be a white woman teaching Afri-can American children or a couple marrying.

A young man and woman in Indianapolis discovered this fact in 1840 when they wed in that city. Both looked to be of European de-scent, but the young man happened to be of African descent as well. When his ancestry came to light, a mob dragged the young couple from their home; the white wife stripped, tarred, feathered, and ridden out of Indianapolis on a rail.[39]

Pioneer life may have been very difficult indeed, but by the 1850s nothing was as dangerous to these mixed families as other white people.

Nothing about this violence was fated; nothing natural forced whites to rise up in destructive hatred. And some whites in Ohio were proving this fact, despite all the forces rising against equality across the nation.

It began in 1849. The newly elected Free Soil Party in Ohio man-aged to get some of the prejudiced laws in Ohio overturned or softened, including the anti-immigration laws. It was a small victory—African Americans still could not vote and had to pay taxes for public works they couldn't use—but it was something. In a gathering in Columbus at the Second Baptist Church, African Americans made clear that "the re-peal is not an act of grace, but of justice, and right, and evinces a return to the principles of '76, and to the Bill of Rights of this State." Even if many whites in the Northwest Territory states had forgotten the prin-ciples of the early republic, African Americans would remind them and would defend and fight for those rights.[40]

Still, no one had expected John Langston to win them in 1855. Langston had barely survived the Cincinnati riot of 1841, running through that wrecked city to save his brothers. And now, fourteen years later, he was grown and living on his own fine farm in northern Ohio.

He had also become a lawyer. That had not been easy, even af-ter he graduated from Oberlin College with top honors. But his wife would have encouraged him. Langston was lucky to have won Caroline Mathilda Wall's affections. She was an opinionated, strong, and brilliant graduate of Oberlin College. They were quite a couple, committed to the struggle for equality and known to many of the most renowned leaders of that movement across the nation, from Frederick Douglass to William Lloyd Garrison.[41]

Their farm in Brownhelm Township was their home, their base, but with Langston working as a lawyer and both of them busy with their organizing, they had hired the Slaters—a white couple recently immigrated from England. The Slaters managed the daily running of the Langstons' farming estate of a few hundred acres, as well as the cooking and cleaning around the house.[42]

And recently the Langstons had been very busy indeed, working together on John's election. John Langston may not have been allowed to vote in Ohio, but he intended to hold office. John Langston was used to being the first. He was the first African American lawyer in Ohio, and now he intended to be an elected official. He had been speaking all over the township, debating with his white opponent as the white electorate watched. And if elected, he would be placed in a position of power over all the whites in that township.

But more was at stake than just a local township election. Indeed, his race for this position was being closely watched not just in his state but across the nation. For if Langston won he would be the first man of African descent to win an election in the United States—the first, the only, the noticed.[43]

John Langston had managed to survive those bloody days during the Cincinnati race riots, but the memories surely lingered: the screams, the gunfire, the white faces with their eyes glittering in the light of black homes burning. He and Caroline knew all too well the violence and destruction being endured by northern African Americans considered just a bit too successful. Both knew that having a white couple run their fine farm, while John campaigned for an election, would be enough for most whites to coat his body with tar or fill it with bullets.

But on that April day in 1855, John Langston stood in the midst of a crowd of whites closely packed into a hall as the election results were read aloud. He must have looked around at their faces as they all waited there. Did he think of those other white faces fourteen years ago, filled with fury and hate? Now here he was again, surrounded by white men, but this was a different day.

Returning from the election, Langston went to his study to write a letter to his friend Frederick Douglass.

From his seat he would have been able to see out the window to the world blossoming into spring. What a strange place he lived in—a place where politicians spoke of killing all people of African descent and wealthy whites entreated those same politicians to remember that all were equally kin in Christ. A place where whites went to war against successful people with dark skin but whites also voted for black men to lead them. As he penned his letter to Douglass, he filled it with all the irony, humor, and triumph of the day: "They put up a colored man and he was elected clerk of Brownhelm, by a handsome majority indeed. Since I am the only colored man who lives in this township, you can easily guess the name of the man who was so fortunate as to secure this election."[44]

But Vanderburgh County, Indiana, was no Lorain County, Ohio.

Did the Lyles family ever wonder why?

There was no reason why their success should be so hated. There was no reason for the violence now rising against them. The whites around them could just have easily decided to welcome them as neighbors, as equals. No one was hurt that day in Brownhelm, Ohio, when John Langston was elected. Instead, the whites of that township now had a well-qualified lawyer as their township clerk.

As African Americans had asked their white neighbors in Ohio a few years earlier, "What injury could possibly result to you from colored people in your State becoming educated, honest and intelligent, high-minded, useful and wealthy citizens, or rather let it be asked what incalculable advantage might not emanate from such a happy result, to all our fellow citizens?"[45]

But in Vanderburgh County, Indiana, white men were taking up arms and risking their lives to destroy any possibility of the advantage that the white citizens of Lorain County, Ohio, were now peacefully enjoying to their benefit.

Of course, while the whites around the Lyles family were open about their envy and hatred of the African Americans who were outstripping them, some prejudiced white Americans were not. Instead, they spoke of innate African American failure and weakness. These were not new ideas; they were very old, passed down by those who believed in a social order in which a few people ruled over many. Those were the old ideas that so many had fought and worked against during and just after the Revolutionary War. Yet they were regaining popularity with northern whites in the United States in the 1850s.

Some African Americans were trying bravely to use their success to disprove these arguments. Allan Jones from Ohio was one of them. He volunteered to be one of the first speakers at a "Colored National Convention" held in Ohio and attended by supporters from all over the United States. Jones stood up on stage, telling the hundreds of people gathered in the hall that during his time in bondage he had earned about $10,000 for the man who enslaved him, while also working to earn $360 to purchase his freedom. Concluding, "And yet some people would say 'he was not able to take care of himself.'" But the Lyles family and the thousands of other long-free successful settlers of the Northwest Territory states must have wanted to tell Allan Jones that they had long proven that they could succeed when free. Indeed, it was their very success that so often led to attacks against them.[46]

By the 1850s free African Americans were trying to defend themselves on two fronts, for being too successful and for supposedly being doomed to failure. Ultimately, they were not supposed to exist as equals in America, and nothing they did would overcome that belief among many white Americans in the South or the North.

The newspapers were full of news of bleeding Kansas, that state being torn apart as people—many of them white—battled each other over the growth of slavery. But the Lyles family knew that the war over liberty and equality was also being waged in the Northwest Territory states, even though it was not getting much coverage in Washington, DC, or the rest of the nation. It was a war that had killed Elijah Lovejoy, had killed Joseph Spencer, had killed Seth Concklin, had killed and injured so many people fighting for liberty and equality in the Northwest. This was a war that had been dividing and destroying for years.

Even as the Lyles family recovered from the attack against them, another was being planned. Flyers were again being printed to tell white men when and where to organize in order to march on Daniel and Nancy's home. And those flyers were being printed in the sheriff's office.[47]

And then Sheriff Gavitt came calling. He knew of all the African Americans in the area, even up in Gibson County. He also knew of the Stormonts, those white abolitionists who had tried to help Seth Concklin assist the Still family in their escape. After all, Gavitt had participated in their capture. But he hadn't been able to touch the Stormonts, and he could not weaken the bond between them and the African Americans around them. He would have also heard that Peter Still had raised a small fortune to free his wife, Vina, and their children in 1854, and that they had now published a book in which he was mentioned more than once in some rather unflattering ways. All these facts must have rankled.[48]

But he could hurt Daniel and Nancy Lyles. And he knew that would hurt their kin up in Gibson County. And he did hurt them.

While the Evansville newspapers reported Gavitt's actions as kindly intended, his offer to "protect" the Lyles family by housing them in the Evansville jail was actually a threat. At worst, he aimed to bring the Lyles men into a place of bondage where they could be more easily lynched—after all, the Evansville newspapers had been calling for the men to be jailed and lynched for days. Even the newspapers, however, could not mask the threat in the sheriff's actions. He made clear to the Lyles family that they would not be safe, would not be protected, if they stayed in Vanderburgh County. The only other option he offered them—as men printed up those pamphlets calling for war in the sheriff's office—was to leave. They would have to leave their home, their farm, their church, their community. And they would have no choice about where they could go, for Gavitt and his men would march them all the way to Gibson County.[49]

When was the Lyles family told that the men who had attacked them—Alexander Maddox and five others—were now suing them in court for attempted murder? By all rights they should have been able to have those men arrested for trespassing and assault, for the wounding of women and children. Instead they would have to pay a lawyer to defend themselves, and they would have to go back into the Evansville courthouse. This promised peril.[50]

The local newspaper reported on July 29 that whites had lined the roads to watch the Lyles family and other African Americans being forced to leave for Gibson County. It added with evident triumph that whites would finally get their hands on Lyles land, for "arrangements will be made to purchase their property . . . and all occasion for future disturbances will be removed."[51]

In the end, so much of this was about their good land, about their nice home.

But Daniel and Nancy would not sell. They may have been forced to leave, but they would keep their land.

Their lawyer was not their only white ally in Evansville, and they were able to rent out their property even as they lived up in Gibson County. That land helped pay for their defense, the trial dragging through a grand jury, their lawyer asking for a change of venue and being denied. This was a double injustice, for they now knew they could not expect a fair trial, and every trip back into Evansville to attend court endangered their lives. But they survived, making the trek from Patoka Township in Gibson County down to Evansville, their kin all hoping that they would make it back.[52]

In April the court decided. It found all the Lyles men innocent of trying to kill anyone but convicted them of various levels of assault and battery, with fines and jail sentences lasting from one day to sixty. At this obvious miscarriage of justice, they asked their lawyer to request a retrial. The request was denied. They had defended their lives and kept their land, but the injustice must have been hard to take.[53]

Many Evansville whites may have wanted them gone, but Indiana was their home state, even if most whites wanted to claim it for themselves only. Their land in Vanderburgh County had sheltered and supported them when they came from Tennessee, and it was now their home place. Daniel and Nancy must have promised each other that they would return to it someday.

They were not the only ones refusing to leave a Northwest Territory state. Despite many African Americans leaving Illinois after the passage of the dreadful law in 1853, despite the rising tide of violence, African Americans were still staying and organizing in Illinois.

In 1856 they gathered in Alton, Illinois, the very town where twenty years earlier Elijah Lovejoy had been killed. On November 14 they met and read aloud a declaration of sentiment and a plan of action. It was beautifully constructed, connecting the words of the Declaration of Independence and the United States Constitution with their own additions calling on the nation's revolutionary roots. Its first resolution read, "That all men are born free and equal, possessing certain inalienable rights, that can neither be conferred or taken away; they were man's from the beginning, before he could comprehend them, eternal, indestructible."[54]

And they reminded the whites of Illinois and of their nation "that the Constitution of the 'United States' declares in its preamble that it was intended to establish justice, therefore opposed to injustice; to promote domestic tranquility, therefore opposed to domestic turmoil; to promote the general welfare, therefore opposed to the general misery."

While they referenced the founding documents of their nation, they also referenced the writings of Bishop Richard Allen, who decades earlier had witnessed his church—the church he preached in—turn its back on its earlier values to create segregation and support slavery. The attendees wrote, "We the colored citizens of Illinois . . . feel ourselves deeply aggrieved by reasons of the cruel prejudice we are compelled to suffer in this our '*native land*,' as dear to us as it is to white men—as the blood-bought inheritance of our ancestors."[55]

They had indeed bled for the causes of liberty, justice, and equality. And more blood would soon be spilt. There was one more war to fight, one more war to win, for the Civil War was about to start.

African Americans heeded the call yet again, rising up all over the Northwest Territory states to join the fight. They rose up from their farms in Ohio, from the woods of Wisconsin, from the embattled states of Illinois and Indiana. Every single Northwest Territory state organized and sent at least one regiment of African-descended men to the front during the Civil War, and more were recruited to fight in regiments from other states.[56]

They rose up even though they were still fighting the war against equality, the war against them and their families, in their own home states. Those men who had tried to drive them out and destroy them were now being called Copperheads, and they were organizing by the thousands to attack African Americans, whites, and anyone else who stood for freedom and equality for all.[57]

African Americans rose up even though white Union soldiers of the Northwest Territory states might hate their existence and most white lawmakers continued to uphold prejudiced laws in their states. They rose up even though Union soldiers from Indiana aimed their guns at African Americans trying to cross the Ohio River, telling them that they would "fire upon them" if they came ashore, refusing to allow Indiana to become an "asylum" for freedom.[58]

They rose up to trample tyranny and to bring the blessings of liberty and equality along the length and breadth of their land.

> The time has come for us . . . to speak out in our own defense upon the great cause of Human Liberty and Equal Rights. Yes! Yes! Let us assemble—let us come together,

and pledge ourselves in the name of God and bleeding humanity and posterity, to organize, organize and organize, until the green-eyed monster Tyranny, shall be trampled under the feet of the oppressed, and Liberty and Equality shall embrace each other, and shall have scattered their blessings along the length and breadth of our land.

—Black Convention of the State of Michigan, 1843[59]

Conclusion:
"All men are created equal"

The Civil War was over.

There had been terrible losses. Many African American men from the Northwest Territory states had died. Fathers and husbands, sons and uncles, nephews and cousins, all lost to the cause of freedom. But oh, what they had won. Freedom for their fathers and mothers, sons and daughters, grandmothers and grandfathers, uncles and aunts, nephews and nieces, cousins and all—all fought for, all free.[1]

But the violence in the Northwest Territory states against African Americans had not ended just because a war was being fought. Reverend Jackson, the African Methodist Episcopal (AME) pastor back in Daniel and Nancy Lyles's home community of Evansville, was stabbed to death in 1864 as he walked the streets of that town. His white murderers were caught but never charged.[2]

But slavery was finally ended. And in 1870 the Fifteenth Amendment was ratified. Equal voting rights had finally been won—or in many cases regained—for all men, regardless of the color of their skin. Charles Grier was a very old man, eighty-seven years old, when whites in Indiana went to the polls to decide whether to pass the Fifteenth Amendment. Many in Indiana did not want to see it ratified, and its passage was contested, but finally it passed.[3]

Charles was determined to vote before he died. He and Keziah had become free during that first fervor for freedom in their new nation, and he was determined to take advantage of this new wave of rights now sweeping the nation. There was no way to know whether this freedom would last.

Charles Grier died in 1872, just a few months short of his ninetieth birthday, but he had cast his vote. The last words in his obituary were, "It was a great pleasure to him that he enjoyed the privilege of a citizen, and went to the polls and voted."[4]

Meanwhile Daniel and Nancy moved back to their land in Vanderburgh County. By 1870 their land, which they'd nearly been forced to give up, was worth $15,000, and they were working toward building a school for African American children on their property. And members of the Lyles family up in Gibson County worked hard to bring the railroad to their community in 1870, a community that was officially named Lyles Station in 1886.[5]

But while the war had ended slavery, the struggle for equality still continued in the Northwest Territory states. Already there was a backlash against the equality that had been won. Oberlin College, which had defied all the violence arising in the Northeast against African American education by opening its doors to women and men of all colors, started segregating African American students by the early 1900s.[6]

And Darke County, Ohio, home to the wealthy Clemens family who had helped found the Union Literary Institute, was not immune. In 1878 a group of men with white sheets over their heads surrounded the farmhouse of the African American farmer Stephen Wade while he and his three small children slept inside. Stephen was killed, and his children barely escaped. This was not Mississippi or South Carolina; this was Ohio, and even the local Democratic newspaper, infamous for its prejudice, stated, "No community can afford to silently acquiesce in murderous 'Ku-Klux' raids."[7]

But by 1924 the front page of a Darke County newspaper proudly trumpeted the large and popular gathering of the Ku Klux Klan at the county fairgrounds, followed by a grand Klan parade through the streets of the county seat of Greenville, Ohio.[8]

By the 1920s the Klan was claiming hundreds of thousands of members in Indiana. This was a resurgence of an old movement. And one of the first cities to organize a chapter in the northern United States was Evansville, Indiana, that same city that had sent a fighting force to kill Daniel, Nancy, and their children.[9]

This was no mistake. The Klan was rising with great strength, threat, and violence in rural areas where African Americans had been successful pioneers. In 1930, a photo circulated around the nation of two young African American men lynched in a tree, surrounded by whites pointing, cheerful as partygoers. That lynching occurred in Marion, Indiana, in Grant County. And Grant County had been home to African American pioneers who had come there long before the Civil War, founding an AME church by 1849 and continuing to thrive on their farms for generations.[10]

Mobocrats.

Copperheads.

The Klan.

The Whitecaps.

It didn't matter what they were called; they were just new names for old ideas. New names for old actions.

And they were still doing a lot of damage, long after the Civil War. For the Northwest Territory states no longer look like the map in this book. And we have to ask why—why there are so few of these farming settlements left.

We must not assume that the reasons for their disappearance are all benign. Some local historians in this region have been too quick to argue that people just left, gradually and peacefully vanishing from the land that they loved. Some may have, for cities called to young people of African descent just as they called to all young people. But many of these settlements disappeared for reasons that were far from gentle. For some farmers before the Civil War, it was the very real threat of the Fugitive Slave Law, enthusiastically supported by the state or local government. In some cases in the twentieth century, the violence was so terrible and immense that African Americans were driven out of whole counties in Indiana.[11]

And prejudice had many ways to force people out. A church might be burned down, again and again. A county or state might refuse to build levies around rivers that frequently flooded African American farms and homes. Roads might go unrepaired. Farm loans might be denied, not just from local banks but from the US Department of Agriculture. Terrible harm could be done to African American children at a local hospital. And there was exclusion: from seed co-ops, from schools, from libraries, restaurants, and movie theaters.[12]

But that does not mean the accomplishments of these free African American pioneers should be ignored. These hundreds of settlements, these thousands of people, who over generations successfully rose on the land they worked and loved—they all deserve recognition and remembrance. These pioneers helped preserve liberty and equality, defending and growing it on America's first free frontier, and they should never be forgotten.

They were there. Some still are.

Even though the Evansville newspaper triumphantly proclaimed in 1857 that the "obnoxious negroes" had all been removed and their land would now belong to white people, this was not the reality. While the violence in 1857 had a very real effect, the land still belonged to Daniel and Nancy Lyles, and they came back.

As late as the turn of the century, the long-term effects of antebellum black frontier and rural settlements in the Northwest Territory states could still be seen. W. E. B. Du Bois clearly showed their legacy in his 1906 study of African American farmers in America. He was the first to report the startling fact that African American farmers in this region owned more land of higher value than their counterparts in any other region of the country except the frontier West, where a few large single-owner ranches skewed the statistical results. Striking differences appear in the landholdings of black farmers in the South and the Midwest, according to Du Bois's study. In the nineteenth century, the most important land for farmers was improved land, where trees had been cleared and the soil was treated to result in the best crop production. Du Bois found that at the turn of the century, African American landowning farmers in the South owned an average of 51.5 acres, of which 60.4 percent was improved, while African American farmers in the Northwest Territory states owned an average of 64.2 acres, of which 71.9 percent was improved land.[13]

At least two farming settlements in rural Michigan managed to continue to grow equality. Cass County continued to have integrated schools and by the 1890s had elected a wealthy African American farmer as a township supervisor. And Covert, Michigan, where the first African American was voted into political office in the 1860s. Like John Langston in Ohio, whites elected this African American pioneering farmer illegally, before black men had a right to even vote in that state.[14]

One of the secrets of these communities was that most of their residents kept alive the old belief that they lived in a nation that was founded on the ideal—if not the reality—that all men are created equal. And they never allowed themselves to forget that prejudice was a danger to all Americans and must be constantly battled.

These were not color-blind communities; they knew their history. But awareness of any kind of difference, whether hair follicles or faith, does not have to result in prejudice. And these communities proved that, while recognition of difference may be common, prejudice is a choice. They followed the very simple principle that the African American leaders of the 1844 Ohio convention advocated: "Do to others as you would have them do to you."[15]

The famous white college basketball coach John Wooden probably never heard of these early equal rights advocates, but he was raised in the beliefs that African Americans cherished and preserved in his state. He grew up on a small struggling farm in rural Indiana. Taught well from an early age about the ideals of equality and fairness, Wooden went on to fight for integration in basketball. Working with the courageous African American Clarence Walker, their integrated team became champions. And Wooden became the winningest basketball coach of his time, proving—yet again—"what an incalculable advantage" true equality can bring.[16]

But Coach Wooden is well known, while the African Americans who pioneered his home state are not. There were so many more like the Grier, Elliott, Hawkins, Clemens, and Lyles families. They were heroic, but they were not unusual.

And they are not all gone. A few communities still exist despite all the prejudice that rose around them, some now over two hundred years old.

There are still Morrises living in Illinois, in the same region their ancestors came to in order to build and defend Fort Allison. People still gather to worship every Sunday at Jacob Hawkins's church, Beulah AME, in the town of Washington in Daviess County, Indiana—despite the fact that his church was burned down repeatedly. And there are still African-descended residents in Darke County, Ohio, working with others to preserve the Clemens family legacy.[17]

Because of their work, the Clemens home still stands, massive and majestic, a mansion of brick and limestone as grand as any plantation home in the South. But this house sits among rolling cornfields in Ohio.

This was the home of James Clemens, who bought his first three hundred acres in Ohio from the federal government in 1822. But the Clemens family was not content with mere economic success, for they held the ideals of the American Revolution close to their hearts and were willing to be revolutionaries in order to uphold liberty and equality. They started and supported the Union Literary Institute and were active conductors on the Underground Railroad.[18]

The Clemens home now stands empty, its big windows shuttered with plywood as it patiently awaits renovations. Someday the house will be a museum, but for now it takes the generosity of a descendant of these pioneers to be invited in—to be able to witness the beauty and grandeur of a home that once belonged to a wealthy African American farming family in the Northwest Territory states.

First the door must be unlocked and pushed hard to open, the house breathing out a sigh of cool air smelling of old wood, dust, and damp stone.

There is no electricity, so it takes a flashlight's flickering light to reveal the evidence of great wealth, one grand room after another, with massive fireplaces decorated with intricately hand-carved surrounds. One of those surrounds mimics the tiered shape of a Yoruba crown, a shape that can be seen in Washington, DC, in the building that houses the Smithsonian's National Museum of African American History and Culture.

In the gracious central entry hall of the Clemens home there is a slight roughness in the smooth plaster of the wall. This is where James Clemens scrawled his name in flowing script into the fresh plaster upon his home's completion.

This home stands as a witness to a lost chapter of this nation's past—the story of tens of thousands of African American pioneers making their way in the Northwest Territory states.

This book is their story, but only a tiny portion of it. There were so many other mansions, many now destroyed or lost.[19]

But there are still other communities, other home places, whether the homes are still there or not. Reunions are still held, and people are working to preserve the past and hold on to farms in the present. And they often call those places the "home place" because that is what they are. These are their roots, their land, where their ancestors settled generations before.[20]

Lyles Station is one of these communities. Frequent flooding has long since washed away many of the oldest buildings in the area, but Stanley Madison, a fifth-generation farmer in Gibson County, is continuing the long tradition started by Keziah and Charles Grier over two hundred years ago. He and the African American farmers around him work the good earth that their families have been working for generations, planting their seeds every spring in hope, despite all the many challenges they have faced.

And Stanley Madison has been working hard to preserve the history of that community.

Sometimes he visits Charles Grier's grave. It is in a small cemetery on a windy rise surrounded by farm fields. The stone is old and worn, but the beautifully carved weeping willow can still be seen. Was it chosen by Keziah, grieving the loss of Charles? They had been married for over fifty years when he died.

From that rise Stanley Madison can see for miles, the cleared fields stretching into the distance. Charles and Keziah Grier helped make that land, that county, that state, and the nation. As Stanley Madison says, "The soil, the land, is what we make it."[21]

Notes

African American Farming Settlements in the
Northwest Territory States, 1800–1860

1. Ancestry.com, *1830 United States Federal Census* [database online] (Provo, UT: Ancestry.com Operations, Inc., 2010). Images reproduced by FamilySearch. Original data: Fifth Census of the United States, 1830 (National Archives and Records Administration [NARA] microfilm publication M19, 201 rolls). Records of the Bureau of the Census, Record Group 29 (National Archives, Washington, DC); Ancestry.com, *1850 United States Federal Census* [database online] (Provo, UT: Ancestry.com Operations, Inc., 2009). Images reproduced by FamilySearch. Original data: Seventh Census of the United States, 1850 (National Archives Microfilm Publication M432, 1009 rolls); Records of the Bureau of the Census, Record Group 29 (National Archives, Washington, DC); Ancestry.com, *1860 United States Federal Census* [database online] (Provo, UT: Ancestry.com Operations, Inc., 2009). Images reproduced by FamilySearch. Original data: 1860 US census, population schedule (NARA microfilm publication M653, 1,438 rolls. Washington, DC: NARA, n.d.). [All regular population census schedules were accessed online on Ancestry.com, starting in January 2013 through to October 2017. A shortened citation format will be used for the rest of the book.]; Emma Lou Thornbrough, *The Negro in Indiana Before 1900* (Bloomington: Indiana University Press, 1993); Cheryl Janifer LaRoche, *Free Black Communities and the Underground Railroad: The Geography of Resistance* (Urbana: University of Illinois Press, 2013); Juliet Walker, *Free Frank: A Black Pioneer on the Antebellum Frontier* (Lexington: University Press of Kentucky, 1983); Stephen A. Vincent, *Southern Seed, Northern Soil: African-American Farm Communities in the Midwest, 1765–1900* (Bloomington: Indiana University Press, 1999); Coy Robbins, *Forgotten Hoosiers: African Heritage in Orange County, Indiana* (Bowie, MD: Heritage Books, 1994); Deborah Rotman, *African-American and Quaker Farmers in East Central Indiana: Social, Political and Economic Aspects of Life in Nineteenth-Century Rural Communities: Randolph County, Indiana* (Muncie, IN: Archaeological Resources Management Service, Ball State University, 1998); Xenia Cord, "Black Rural Settlements in Indiana Before 1860,"

in *Indiana's African-American Heritage*, ed. Wilma Gibbs (Indianapolis: Indiana Historical Society Press, 1993); Coy Robbins, *Reclaiming African Heritage at Salem, Indiana* (Bowie, MD: Heritage Books, 1995); "Enoch Harris," obituary, *Kalamazoo Telegraph*, March 25, 1870; Keith Griffler, *Front Line of Freedom: African Americans and the Forging of the Underground Railroad in the Ohio Valley* (Lexington: University Press of Kentucky, 2004); Aimee Lee Cheek and William Cheek, *John Mercer Langston and the Fight for Black Freedom, 1829–65* (Urbana: University of Illinois Press, 1996); Wayne L. Snider, *All in the Same Spaceship: Portions of American Negro History Illustrated in Highland County, Ohio, U.S.A.* (New York: Vantage Press, 1974); David Gerber, *Black Ohio and the Color Line, 1860–1915* (Urbana: University of Illinois Press, 1976); J. H. Battle and William Lerner, *History of Morrow County and Ohio* (Chicago: O. L. Baskin, 1880); William Katz, *Black Pioneers: An Untold Story* (New York: Atheneum Books for Young Readers, 1999); Mary Ann Brown, "Vanished Black Rural Communities in Western Ohio," in *Perspectives in Vernacular Architecture, I*, ed. Camille Wells (Columbia: University of Missouri Press, 1987); Zachary Cooper, *Black Settlers in Rural Wisconsin* (Madison: State Historical Society of Wisconsin, 1994).

Author's Note

1. I am thankful for my research intern, Alexandra Piper, whose dedication and hard work helped me to find many of these settlements.

2. William F. Cheek and Aimee Lee Cheek, *John Mercer Langston and the Fight for Black Freedom, 1829–65* (Urbana: University of Illinois Press, 1996), 179–180, 199. My research into a small sample of census reports comparing local land deed and tax records shows this pattern to hold true, but further research is essential to recover a full picture of the wealth of African American farmers in this region before the Civil War.

Introduction

1. "Visit to the West," *Liberator*, September 30, 1853, 154. Accessed on Ebscohost.

2. Christian Wolmar, *The Great Railroad Revolution: The History of Trains in America* (New York: PublicAffairs, 2013); Henry Mayer, *All on Fire: William Lloyd Garrison and the Abolition of Slavery* (New York: St. Martin's Press, 1998), 199–210. See Chapter 9 in this book for a full discussion of tarring and feathering as a tool of pro-prejudice organizers.

3. "Tour to Ohio and Michigan," *Liberator*, December 2, 1853. Accessed on Ebscohost.

4. Ibid.

5. A few works have looked at African Americans in the rural antebellum Northwest Territory and states, although most have assumed that the

settlements they covered were unusual or unique. However, these books have been invaluable in laying the groundwork for this book. They include Cheryl Janifer LaRoche, *Free Black Communities and the Underground Railroad: The Geography of Resistance* (Urbana: University of Illinois Press, 2013); Stephen Vincent, *Southern Seed, Northern Soil: African-American Farm Communities in the Midwest, 1765–1900* (Bloomington: Indiana University Press, 1999); Juliet E. K. Walker, *Free Frank: A Black Pioneer on the Antebellum Frontier* (Lexington: University Press of Kentucky, 1983); Sundiata Keita Cha-Jua, *America's First Black Town: Brooklyn, Illinois, 1830–1915* (Urbana: University of Illinois Press, 2002); Leslie Schwalm, *Emancipation's Diaspora: Race and Reconstruction in the Upper Midwest* (Chapel Hill: University of North Carolina Press, 2009); Leon Litwack, *North of Slavery: The Negro in the Free States, 1790–1860* (Chicago: University of Chicago Press, 1970); Wilma Gibbs, *Indiana's African-American Heritage: Essays from Black History News & Notes* (Indianapolis: Indiana Historical Society Press, 2007); William Loren Katz, *Black Pioneers: An Untold Story* (New York: Atheneum Books for Young Readers, 1999); Emma Lou Thornbrough, *The Negro in Indiana Before 1900: A Study of a Minority* (Indianapolis: Indiana Historical Bureau, 1957); David Gerber, *Black Ohio and the Color Line, 1860–1915* (Urbana: University of Illinois Press, 1991); Benjamin Wilson, *The Rural Black Heritage Between Chicago and Detroit, 1850–1929: A Photograph Album and Random Thoughts* (Kalamazoo, MI: New Issues Press, Western Michigan University, 1985).

6. Stephen Vincent, *Southern Seed, Northern Soil: African-American Farm Communities in the Midwest, 1765–1900* (Bloomington: Indiana University Press, 1999), Table 1, xii; "Negro Population: 1790–1915," US Department of Interior, Census Office, Federal Census Report, Washington, DC, 1918, 44–45, www.census.gov/prod2/decennial/documents/00480330ch02.pdf.

7. "Negro Population: 1790–1915," 44–45; Clayton E. Cramer, *Black Demographic Data, 1790–1860: A Sourcebook* (Westport, CT: Greenwood Press, 1997), 149; James Campbell, *Middle Passages: African American Journeys to Africa, 1787–2005* (New York: Penguin Books, 2007), 57–98, 243; Antonio McDaniel, *Swing Low, Sweet Chariot: The Mortality Cost of Colonizing Liberia in the Nineteenth Century* (Chicago: University of Chicago Press, 1995); Bronwen Everill, "'Destiny Seems to Point Me to That Country': Early Nineteenth-Century African American Migration, Emigration, and Expansion," *Journal of Global History* 7, no. 1 (2012): 53–77.

8. Leslie Schwalm, *Emancipation's Diaspora: Race and Reconstruction in the Upper Midwest* (Chapel Hill: University of North Carolina Press, 2009), 34; Vincent, *Southern Seed*, xiii–xiv; Juliet E. K. Walker, *The History of Black Business in America: Capitalism, Race, Entrepreneurship*, vol. 1: *To 1865* (Chapel Hill: University of North Carolina Press, 2009), 95–96.

9. The idea that this region could be home to a "middle ground" between various cultures was first proposed by Richard White in *The Middle Ground: Indians, Empires, and Republics in the Great Lakes Region, 1650–1815*

(New York: Cambridge University Press, 1991). His theories of settlement and cultural accommodation could well bear rich harvest if applied to African-descended people in the Northwest Territory states.

10. See Chapter 1 for more on the African Americans at Fort Allison in the Indiana Territory and those who fought in the War of 1812 in that region; see Chapter 5 for African Americans manning forts along the Arkansas territorial border.

11. For more on the concept of freedom as applied to African Americans and property ownership in the early republic, see Eric Foner's excellent *The Story of American Freedom* (New York: W. W. Norton, 1998), which informed my use of "freedom" as thought of by African Americans in the antebellum Northwest territories and states. See Chapter 2 for more on the creation of the Northwest Ordinance and its ties to the time and ideals of its creation.

12. "National Convention of Colored Men—Negro Colony in Ohio," *Cleveland Daily Herald*, August 26, 1843, n.p. President Andrew Jackson coined the phrase "bone and sinew" during his famous farewell speech in March 1837: "The planter, the farmer, the mechanic, and the laborer all know that their success depends upon their own industry and economy, and that they must not expect to become suddenly rich by the fruits of their toil. Yet these classes of society form the great body of the people of the United States; they are the bone and sinew of the country—men who love liberty and desire nothing but equal rights and equal laws" (Andrew Jackson and Martin Van Buren, *Farewell Address of Andrew Jackson to the People of the United States; and the Inaugural Address of Martin Van Buren, President of the United States* [Washington City: Blair and Rives, 1837]). The term was then used by African American leaders frequently in the 1840s as a way of appropriating language meant to be applied only to white men.

Chapter 1: "Life, Liberty"

1. Tract Book of Gibson County, Indiana, for the NE 1/4 of the NE 1/4 of section 21, township 3S, range 12W (40 acres), August 15, 1815, Charles Grier purchaser, Princeton Public Library, Princeton, Indiana.

2. Allan Bogue, *From Prairie to Corn Belt: Farming on the Illinois and Iowa Prairies in the Nineteenth Century* (Chicago: University of Chicago, 1963), 73–74.

3. For more on the desirability of Wabash River valley land and land sales of the Northwest Territory lands, see Malcolm J. Rohrbough, *The Land Office Business: The Settlement and Administration of American Public Lands, 1789–1837* (New York: Oxford University Press, 1968).

4. I am indebted to Richard Roosenberg, president and founder of Tillers International, for sharing his experiential and research-based knowledge of frontier farming in the antebellum Northwest Territory states. Original notes from May 15, 2015, meeting in author's possession, along with follow-up email communications.

5. A young woman called Eliza Little, who—like Keziah—had been born and raised in bondage until her teens, reported on her satisfaction at owning and working the land of her frontier farm with her husband, from clearing it to finally being able to farm it. As she explained, "I could handle an axe, or plow or, any thing. I felt proud to be able to do it—to help get cleared up, so that we could have a home, and plenty to live on." Benjamin Drew, *A North-Side View of Slavery. The Refugee: or, The Narratives of Fugitive Slaves in Canada. Related by Themselves, with an Account of the History and Condition of the Colored Population of Upper Canada* (New York: Negro Universities Press, 1968), 163.

6. Gibson County Negro Registry, Princeton Public Library, Princeton, Indiana, 1851. Like many of these early settlers, Keziah and Charles are both described as very dark skinned or "black."

7. Andrew R. L. Cayton, *Frontier Indiana* (Bloomington: Indiana University Press, 1996), 188–193.

8. M. Scott Heerman, "In a State of Slavery: Black Servitude in Illinois, 1800–1830," *Early American Studies: An Interdisciplinary Journal* 14, no. 1 (2016): 114–139.

9. Margaret Cross Norton, *Illinois Census Returns, 1810–1818* (Springfield: Illinois State Historical Library, 1935), xi; Alan Taylor, *The Civil War of 1812: American Citizens, British Subjects, Irish Rebels, and Indian Allies* (New York: Alfred A. Knopf, 2011).

10. W. Faux, *Memorable Days in America: Being a Journal of a Tour to the United States Principally Undertaken to Ascertain, by Positive Evidence, the Condition and Probable Prospects of British Emigrants; Including Accounts of Mr. Birkbeck's Settlement in the Illinois, and Intended to Show Men and Things as They Are in America* (London: Printed for W. Simpkin and R. Marshall, 1823), quoted in Denise Gigante, *The Keats Brothers: The Life of John and George* (Cambridge, MA: Belknap Press of Harvard University Press, 2011), 286.

11. Paul Finkelman, "Evading the Ordinance: The Persistence of Bondage in Indiana and Illinois," *Journal of the Early Republic* 9, no. 1 (spring 1989): 21–51, doi:10.2307/3123523.

12. William K. Klingaman and Nicholas P. Klingaman, *The Year Without Summer: 1816 and the Volcano That Darkened the World and Changed History* (New York: St. Martin's Press, 2013).

13. "Communicated," *Princeton Clarion*, May 30, 1872, front page. This narrative of how Charles Grier arrived in Indiana is from his own obituary. This is how he and his family wanted his story told. The details may turn out to be slightly different, but for the purposes of this book I am honoring the way that Charles Grier wanted the story of his coming to the Indiana Territory to be known.

14. Ibid.

15. Ibid.

16. Loren Schweninger, "The Fragile Nature of Freedom: Free Women of Color in the U.S. South," in *Beyond Bondage: Free Women of Color in the*

Americas, ed. David Gaspar and Darlene Hine (Urbana: University of Illinois, 2004), 106; Ellen Eslinger, "Liberation in a Rural Context," in *Paths to Freedom: Manumission in the Atlantic World*, ed. Rosemary Brana-Shute and Randy J. Sparks (Columbia: University of South Carolina Press, 2009), 363–379.

17. Indiana would soon enough pass similar laws, as well as prejudiced laws barring service in the militia and the ability to testify in court. But these were early days on the frontier, and many laws were ignored or lightly adhered to, including the ban on slavery. Still, any of these laws would hang as a threat over settled African American pioneers. Newly arrived whites could use the Black Code laws to force them to leave. There were many examples of this. See Nikki Taylor, *Frontiers of Freedom: Cincinnati's Black Community, 1802–1868* (Athens: Ohio University Press, 2005); Ross Bagby, "The Randolph Slave Saga: Communities in Collision" (PhD diss., Ohio State University, 1998), 153; Stephen Middleton, *The Black Laws in the Old Northwest: A Documentary History* (Westport, CT: Greenwood Press, 1993).

18. "Communicated," *Princeton Clarion*, May 30, 1872, front page; "Black History/Little Africa," Lawrence County Historical Society, accessed July 13, 2016, www.lawrencelore.org/blackhistory.

19. Annelise Morris, "Jumping the Legal Color Line: Negotiating Racial Geographies in the 19th Century" (paper presented at the annual meeting of the Society of Historical Archaeology, Seattle, Washington, January 6–11, 2015), accessed April 2, 2016, www.academia.edu/11559423/Jumping_the _Legal_Color_Line_Negotiating_Racial_Geographies_in_the_19th _Century. Pioneers and frontiers are not uncomplicated things in America. Even as the Morrises, Griers, and other pioneers of African descent were trying to make a new start and build a new nation, they were also a part of the destruction of other nations. For while the church at Fort Allison wanted to see freedom and equality grow, its vision did not encompass the Native peoples who were already there. This system of forts was put into place specifically to assist in settling a region that was not yet even officially in the hands of the United States. This was the region that saw Tecumseh rise to resist the unjust and brutal killing of people and theft of land in the Northwest Territory.

20. For more on this Evangelical abolitionist movement in the Northwest Territory, see James David Essig, "Break Every Yoke: American Evangelicals Against Slavery, 1770–1808" (PhD diss., Yale University, 1978).

21. *Lawrence County, Illinois* (Lawrence County Historical Society, 1995), 325; *Combined History of Edwards, Lawrence and Wabash Counties, Illinois: With Illustrations . . . and Biographical Sketches of Some of Their Prominent Men and Pioneers* (Philadelphia: J. L. McDonough & Co., 1883), 70–72, 270; "Fort Allison," Lawrence County Historical Society, accessed June 16, 2016, www .lawrencelore.org/fort-allison.

22. Emma Lou Thornbrough, *The Negro in Indiana Before 1900: A Study of a Minority* (Indianapolis: Indiana Historical Bureau, 1957), 11–12.

23. Cayton, *Frontier Indiana*, 188–193; "Communicated," *Princeton Clarion*, May 30, 1872, front page.

24. Some travelers from the urban areas of the Northeast expressed surprise at the amount of work women were doing alongside men on frontier farms in the Northwest territories and states at this time. See Samuel Bernard Judah, "A Journal of Travel from New York to Indiana in 1827," *Indiana Magazine of History* 17, no. 4 (December 1921): 338–352.

25. John Wood Sweet, *Bodies Politic: Negotiating Race in the American North, 1730–1830* (Baltimore: Johns Hopkins University Press, 2003), 251–253; Roger Kennedy, *Mr. Jefferson's Lost Cause: Land, Farmers, Slavery and the Louisiana Purchase* (New York: Oxford University Press, 2003), 149–151.

Chapter 2: Interlude

1. Paul Finkelman and Tim A. Garrison, "French and Indian War (1754–1763)," in *Encyclopedia of United States Indian Policy and Law*, ed. Paul Finkelman and Tim A. Garrison (Washington, DC: CQ Press, 2009), 323–324, doi: 10.4135/9781604265767.n228. For more on Native Americans and the fur trade in this area, see Richard White, *The Middle Ground: Indians, Empires, and Republics in the Great Lakes Region, 1650–1815* (New York: Cambridge University Press, 1991); John Timothy Fierst, "The Struggle to Defend Indian Authority in the Ohio Valley–Great Lakes Region, 1763–1794" (master's thesis, University of Manitoba, Canada, 2000).

2. For more on how this loss angered colonists, especially George Washington, see Taylor Alan, *American Revolutions: A Continental History, 1750–1804* (New York: W. W. Norton & Company, 2016). Malcolm J. Rohrbough, *The Land Office Business: The Settlement and Administration of American Public Lands, 1789–1837* (New York: Oxford University Press, 1968), 3–25.

3. Peter H. Wood, "From Estaban to York: African Americans in the Purchase Territory During Three Centuries," in *The Louisiana Purchase and Its Peoples: Perspectives from the New Orleans Conference*, ed. Paul E. Hoffman (Lafayette: Louisiana Historical Association and Center for Louisiana Studies, University of Louisiana, Lafayette, 2004), 9. My thanks to Peter Wood for this citation, information, and his encouragement.

4. Mattie Marie Harper, "French Africans in Ojibwe Country: Negotiating Marriage, Identity and Race, 1780–1890" (PhD diss., University of California, Berkeley, 2012); Kenneth W. Porter, "Negroes and the Fur Trade," *Minnesota History* 15, no. 4 (1934): 421–433.

5. Section 3 of Indiana Territory survey, Township No. 5 north of the Base Line, No. 10 west of the 2nd meridian, surveyed by Daniel Sullivan in 1807, under the authority of Ebenezer Buckingham in 1805. "Indiana Township Maps, Facsimiles 1805–1807 Surveys," Byron R. Lewis Historical Library at Vincennes University. From photostats in the Indiana Division of the Indiana State Library, Indiana. I am grateful to Lishawna Taylor and Richard Day for sharing this information with me.

6. "Primary Documents in American History: Northwest Ordinance," Library of Congress, www.loc.gov/rr/program/bib/ourdocs/northwest.html.

7. Rohrbough, *The Land Office Business*, 295.

8. Isabella Oliver, "On Slavery," 1805, reprinted in James G. Basker et al., *Early American Abolitionists: A Collection of Anti-slavery Writings, 1760–1820* (New York: Gilder Lehrman Institute of American History, 2005), 203–208.

9. Phillis Wheatley, "To the Right Honorable William—Earl of Dartmouth" (1773), in Phillis Wheatley, *The Poems of Phillis Wheatley*, ed. Julian D. Mason (Chapel Hill: University of North Carolina Press, 1989). It is important to note that while both Isabella Oliver and Phillis Wheatley were clear that freedom and equality should be the common rights of both the European and the African descended, they were still hostile toward Native Americans, whom they—and many Americans—viewed as savages fit only to be killed or violently removed from the land.

10. For more on Phillis Wheatley, see Henry Louis Gates Jr., *The Trials of Phillis Wheatley: America's First Black Poet and Her Encounters with the Founding Fathers* (New York: Basic Civitas Books, 2003). For more on pro-slavery patriots, see Alfred Blumrosen and Ruth Blumrosen, *Slave Nation: How Slavery United the Colonies and Sparked the American Revolution* (Naperville, IL: Sourcebooks, 2005). For the role of prejudice in binding together white Revolutionary War soldiers, see the excellent book by Robert Parkinson, *The Common Cause: Creating Race and Nation in the American Revolution* (Chapel Hill: University of North Carolina Press, 2016).

11. I am grateful to Danielle Allen's insights into the Declaration of Independence and its support of equality, brilliantly explored in *Our Declaration: A Reading of the Declaration of Independence in Defense of Equality* (New York: Liveright, 2015), which informed both this chapter and this book.

12. The study of slavery and race during the American Revolution is a large field of study. Some of the sources that have informed this section are Manisha Sinha, *The Slave's Cause: A History of Abolition* (New Haven, CT: Yale University Press, 2016); John Wood Sweet, *Bodies Politic: Negotiating Race in the American North, 1730–1830* (Baltimore: Johns Hopkins University Press, 2003); Stephen Middleton, *The Black Laws: Race and the Legal Process in Early Ohio* (Athens: Ohio University Press, 2005); Paul Finkelman, *Slavery and the Founders: Race and Liberty in the Age of Jefferson* (Armonk, NY: M. E. Sharpe, 1996); Charles Rappleye, *Sons of Providence: The Brown Brothers, the Slave Trade, and the American Revolution* (New York: Simon & Schuster, 2006); Gary B. Nash, *Race and Revolution* (Madison, WI: Madison House, 1990); Stephen David Kantrowitz, *More Than Freedom: Fighting for Black Citizenship in a White Republic, 1829–1889* (New York: Penguin Press, 2012); Robin D. G. Kelley and Earl Lewis, eds., *To Make Our World Anew: A History of African Americans* (Oxford: Oxford University Press, 2000); Sylvia R. Frey, *Water from the Rock: Black Resistance in a Revolutionary Age* (Princeton, NJ: Princeton University Press, 1991); Gene A. Smith, *The Slaves' Gamble: Choosing Sides in the War of 1812* (New York: Palgrave Macmillan, 2013); Laurent Dubois, *Avengers*

of the New World: The Story of the Haitian Revolution (Cambridge, MA: Belknap Press of Harvard University Press, 2004).

13. I use the word "prejudice" instead of "racism" to be historically accurate. "Prejudice" was the most common term used in the late 1700s and early 1800s to describe the problem of discrimination against people of African descent, or discrimination and unjust treatment—especially disenfranchisement—of any group of people. We might use the term "racism" today, but it was a word invented in the twentieth century and was created to describe damaging ideas about supposed essential and negative differences in people that would warrant their segregation or even extermination. See Francisco Bethencourt, *Racisms: From the Crusades to the Twentieth Century* (Princeton, NJ: Princeton University Press, 2013).

14. James Otis and Richard Dana, *The Rights of the British Colonies Asserted and Proved* (Boston: Printed and sold by Edes and Gill, in Queen-Street, 1764), Evans Early American Imprint Collection, accessed October 4, 2016, https://quod.lib.umich.edu/e/evans/N07655.0001.001/1:5?rgn=div1;view=fulltext.

15. Charles de Secondat Montesquieu et al., *The Spirit of the Laws* (New York: D. Appleton and Co., 1900), 284–285.

16. Ibid., 284–286. Montesquieu presents this story as a way of explaining why skin color should not be used as an excuse to enslave people. Given that his experience of people with red hair in Europe would have been of people with very pale skin, this story almost certainly implies that it was people with white skin who were killed out of prejudice.

17. Henry Louis Gates Jr. and William L. Andrews, *Pioneers of the Black Atlantic: Five Slave Narratives from the Enlightenment, 1772–1815* (Washington, DC: Civitas, 1998), 210.

18. For more on the creation of the idea of human and equal rights, including during this revolutionary period, see Lynn Avery Hunt, *Inventing Human Rights: A History* (New York: W. W. Norton, 2008).

19. Sweet, *Bodies Politic*, 251–253; Middleton, *The Black Laws*, 10.

20. Thomas Jefferson, *The Writings of Thomas Jefferson: Being His Autobiography, Correspondence, Reports, Messages, Addresses, and Other Writings, Official and Private. Published by the Order of the Joint Committee of Congress on the Library, from the Original Manuscripts, Deposited in the Department of State*, ed. H. A. Washington (Washington, DC: Taylor & Maury, 1853), 23; Sean Wilentz, *The Rise of American Democracy: Jefferson to Lincoln* (New York: Norton, 2005), 34–35; John Hope Franklin and Alfred A. Moss, *From Slavery to Freedom: A History of African Americans* (New York: McGraw-Hill, 1994), 79–81. For more on Thomas Jefferson and his many contradictions on the subject of slavery and racial equality, see Annette Gordon-Reed, *The Hemingses of Monticello: An American Family* (New York: W. W. Norton, 2009); Annette Gordon-Reed and Peter S. Onuf, *"Most Blessed of the Patriarchs": Thomas Jefferson and the Empire of the Imagination* (New York: Liveright Publishing Corporation, 2017).

21. Paul Finkelman, *Slavery and the Founders: Race and Liberty in the Age of Jefferson* (Armonk, NY: M. E. Sharpe, 1996); Parkinson, *The Common Cause*; Sinha, *The Slave's Cause*, 34–64.

22. Sinha, *The Slave's Cause*, 65–76, quote from p. 43. While there have been many good books written on African-descended people during the revolutionary period, Manisha Sinha's offers a detailed and compelling overview of the struggle for freedom and equality during the Revolution and afterward, and I am indebted to her excellent work. See also Daniel Littlefield, "Revolutionary Citizens," in Kelley and Lewis, *To Make Our World Anew*; Gates and Andrews, *Pioneers of the Black Atlantic*.

23. Sinha, *The Slave's Cause*, 12–24; James Birney, "American Churches, the Bulwarks of American Slavery," *Philanthropist (1836–1843)*, November 18, 1840, 1. James Birney also published this information in a pamphlet, and it was later reprinted in England.

24. For an important study of the importance of the slave trade in New York compared to Charleston, see Melissa Maestri, "The Atlantic Web of Bondage: Comparing the Slave Trades of New York City and Charleston, South Carolina" (PhD diss., University of Delaware, 2015). For more on the length and results of this early emancipation, see Ira Berlin, *The Long Emancipation: The Demise of Slavery in the United States* (Cambridge, MA: Harvard University Press, 2015).

25. Sinha, *The Slave's Cause*, 86; John Hope Franklin, *The Free Negro in North Carolina, 1790–1860* (New York: Russell & Russell, 1969), 14–15. The number of people freed during this period is very difficult to gauge accurately. For more on the difficulty of counting manumitted people during this period, see Andrew Levy, *The First Emancipator* (New York: Random House, 2005).

26. Littlefield, "Revolutionary Citizens," 103–168.

27. Middleton, *The Black Laws*, 25.

28. This understanding of voting rights is also clear in that the wordings were changed in subsequent years as whites decided to exclude African Americans from the vote.

29. Franklin, *The Free Negro in North Carolina*, 12–13; C. Perry Patterson, *The Negro in Tennessee, 1790–1865* (Austin: University of Texas, 1922), 163–166. In 1776 North Carolina opened the vote to free people of color; Tennessee followed suit in 1796.

30. Alexander Keyssar, *The Right to Vote: The Contested History of Democracy in the United States* (New York: Basic Books, 2009), Table A.4. I have not included Georgia in this total, even though it removed "white" from the definition of who could vote in 1789, out of an excess of caution. Keyssar notes that he was not able to find any evidence in secondary sources of African Americans voting in that state. However, given that there were wealthy African-descended plantation owners in Georgia at this time, further research is needed on voting rights in Georgia during this early period when they were granted.

31. Sinha, *The Slave's Cause*, 65–96.

32. Laurent Dubois, *Avengers of the New World: The Story of the Haitian Revolution* (Cambridge, MA: Belknap Press of Harvard University Press, 2004), 1–7, 168–169, 142, 163–164.

33. Ibid., 169.

34. Ibid.

35. Ibid., 170.

36. Jennifer Randazzo, "Introduction," in Basker et al., *Early American Abolitionists*, 217–220.

37. Basker et al., *Early American Abolitionists*, 234.

38. Basker et al., *Early American Abolitionists*, 235, 237.

39. Ibid.

40. Randazzo, "Introduction," 217–241.

41. "Northern Involvement in the Slave Trade," Tracing Center, accessed July 10, 2017, www.tracingcenter.org/resources/background/northern-involvement-in-the-slave-trade. For more on the financial power and importance of the Rhode Island slave trade in the early United States, see Charles Rappleye, *Sons of Providence: The Brown Brothers, the Slave Trade, and the American Revolution* (New York: Simon & Schuster, 2006).

42. Keyssar, *The Right to Vote*, Table A.4.

43. Middleton, *The Black Laws*, 7–40; Jacob Piatt Dunn, *Slavery Petitions and Papers* (Indianapolis: Bowen-Merrill Company, 1894), 74.

44. Middleton, *The Black Laws*, 14; John D. Barnhart and Dorothy Lois Riker, *Indiana to 1816: The Colonial Period* (Indianapolis: Indiana Historical Bureau, 1971), 347; Robert M. Owens, *Mr. Jefferson's Hammer: William Henry Harrison and the Origins of American Indian Policy* (Norman: University of Oklahoma Press, 2007), 68–72. Robert Owens's book offers an excellent overview of William Henry Harrison's petitions and actions during this territorial period.

45. Dubois, *Avengers of the New World*, 196.

46. Ibid., 4, 284–286.

47. Ibid., 284–286. My grateful thanks to Michael Rapport and Jonathan Sperber for their generous assistance in helping me to connect the various revolutions in the United States, France, and Haiti, the advancements within those revolutions toward ending slavery and moving toward racial equality, and the subsequent backlash against those advancements.

48. Keyssar, *The Right to Vote*, Table A.4. Also in 1802, Thomas Jefferson made sure that Washington, DC, barred African Americans from voting; see Franklin and Moss, *From Slavery to Freedom*, 153.

49. It was exceeded only by the island of Saint-Domingue, otherwise known as Haiti, whose enslaved people had waged a successful revolutionary war to free themselves. See Dubois, *Avengers of the New World*.

Chapter 3: "The pursuit of Happiness"

1. Census records for this period of early statehood are often incomplete and full of errors. Census takers in southern Indiana working on the 1820 census would often separate African Americans entirely from the regular census pages, placing them at the end on a separate sheet and categorizing them as indentured/enslaved and free. See pp. 256–257 of Gibson County, Indiana Federal Census for 1820 (where the website Ancestry.com mistakenly records Charles Grier as white). Because of these irregularities, it is difficult to know just how many children the Griers had at this time, especially since death was common among infants and children on the frontier during this period. But the 1840 census shows that the Griers had nine children still living, four boys and five girls. And the 1850 census shows that Malinda was their eldest child, born in 1818 (US Census Bureau, 1840 Federal Census Records, Montgomery Township, Gibson County, 107). All US federal census records accessed through the website Ancestry.com, January 1, 2015, to October 1, 2017.

2. Denise Gigante, *The Keats Brothers: The Life of John and George* (Cambridge, MA: Belknap Press of Harvard University Press, 2011), 226. Gigante offers a fascinating and detailed account of how English pioneers viewed the Old Northwest frontier region in the early 1800s.

3. US Census Bureau, 1850 Federal Census, Patoka Township, Gibson County, Indiana.

4. E. S. Abdy, *Journal of a Residence and Tour in the United States of North America, from April, 1833, to October, 1834* (London: J. Murray, 1835), 2:366. Abdy recorded a thriving African American farming settlement just outside Madison, Indiana, where African Americans settled on some of the best land in the region in the 1810s. He writes, "While they were clearing their farms of the timber, they were unmolested; but now that they have got the land into a good state of cultivation, and are rising in the world, the avarice of the white man casts a greedy eye on their luxuriant crops; and his pride is offended at the decent appearance of their sons and daughters."

5. Benjamin Lundy, Letter Box 1, Folder 4, *Benjamin Lundy Papers, 1821–1904* (MSS 112, Ohio History Center, Columbus).

6. Emma Lou Thornbrough, *The Negro in Indiana Before 1900: A Study of a Minority* (Indianapolis: Indiana Historical Bureau, 1957), 21.

7. Morris Birkbeck and George Flower, *History of the English Settlement in Edwards County, Illinois, Founded in 1817 and 1818* (Chicago: Fergus Print. Co., 1882); Nathan Jérémie-Brink, "Transnational Frontiers of Freedom: An 1823 Black Emigration from the Illinois Prairie to the Republic of Haiti" (paper presented at the African Americans in the Nineteenth-Century West Research Symposium, Saint Louis University, Saint Louis, Missouri, May 20–21, 2016).

8. Birkbeck and Flower, *History of the English Settlement*, 258–260.

9. Ibid., 265.

10. For a good overview of the creation of the ACS and its various motivations, see Nicholas Guyatt, *Bind Us Apart: How Enlightened Americans Invented Racial Segregation* (New York: Basic Books, 2016). For more on African Americans' resistance to the colonization movement and the movement's rise in the Northwest Territory states, see Ousmane K. Power-Greene, *Against Wind and Tide: The African American Struggle Against the Colonization Movement* (New York: New York University Press, 2014). For the colonization movement in Indiana, see Racquel Henry, "The Colonization Movement in Indiana, 1820–1864: A Struggle to Remove the African American" (PhD diss., Indiana University, 2008).

11. Lacy K. Ford, *Deliver Us from Evil: The Slavery Question in the Old South* (New York: Oxford University Press, 2009), 70–73; Cheryl J. LaRoche, *Free Black Communities and the Underground Railroad: The Geography of Resistance* (Urbana: University of Illinois Press, 2014), 106–110.

12. Ford, *Deliver Us from Evil*, 9–10.

13. Jérémie-Brink, "Transnational Frontiers of Freedom"; Birkbeck and Flower, *History of the English Settlement*, 266.

14. David Walker and Peter P. Hinks, *David Walker's Appeal to the Coloured Citizens of the World* (University Park: Pennsylvania State University Press, 2000), 59.

15. Jérémie-Brink, "Transnational Frontiers of Freedom"; Birkbeck and Flower, *History of the English Settlement*, 269–273.

16. David Fiske, *Solomon Northup's Kindred: The Kidnapping of Free Citizens Before the Civil War* (Santa Barbara, CA: Praeger, 2016); George Rogers Taylor, *The Transportation Revolution, 1815–1860* (New York: Harper & Row, 1951), 56–69.

17. For excellent overviews of this forced migration west, see Ira Berlin, *The Making of African America* (New York: Viking, 2010); Walter Johnson, *River of Dark Dreams: Slavery and Empire in the Cotton Kingdom* (Cambridge, MA: Belknap Press of Harvard University Press, 2013). For more on the importance of the Ohio River as a border between slavery and freedom, see Matthew Salafia, *Slavery's Borderland: Freedom and Bondage Along the Ohio River* (Philadelphia: University of Pennsylvania Press, 2013).

18. John Wood Sweet, *Bodies Politic: Negotiating Race in the American North, 1730–1830* (Baltimore: Johns Hopkins University Press, 2003), 251–253. For more on the growth of slavery during this period, see Edward E. Baptist, *The Half Has Never Been Told: Slavery and the Making of American Capitalism* (New York: Basic Books, 2014).

19. Keziah Grier is listed as being unable to read and write on the 1850 federal census.

20. Senator William Pinkney, quoted in Jeremy Tewell, *A Self-Evident Lie: Southern Slavery and the Threat to American Freedom* (Kent, OH: Kent State University Press, 2013), 131–132.

21. Ibid.

22. Henry Barnard and Moses B. Goodwin, *History of Schools for the Colored Population* (New York: Arno Press, 1969), 195–199.

23. For more on African-descended people in South Carolina, see Peter Wood's groundbreaking work, *Black Majority: Negroes in Colonial South Carolina from 1670 Through the Stono Rebellion* (New York: Alfred A. Knopf, 1974).

24. Thornbrough, *The Negro in Indiana*, 11–12; John D. Barnhart and Dorothy Lois Riker, *Indiana to 1816: The Colonial Period* (Indianapolis: Indiana Historical Bureau, 1971), 347.

25. Raymond H. Hammes, ed., *Cahokia, St. Clair County Record Book B, 1800–1813* (Springfield: Illinois Research Center for Colonial and Territorial Studies, 1982), 13; Robert Owens, *Mr. Jefferson's Hammer: William Henry Harrison and the Origins of American Indian Policy* (Norman: University of Oklahoma Press, 2007), 68–72.

26. Paul Finkelman, "Evading the Ordinance: The Persistence of Bondage in Indiana and Illinois," *Journal of the Early Republic* 9, no. 1 (spring 1989): 33–34.

27. Indenture Deed Book, 1806, McGrady-Brockman House Archive, Knox County Public Library, Vincennes, Indiana. My grateful thanks to Ann Hecht at the McGrady-Brockman House Archive for her invaluable research assistance.

28. Ibid.

29. For a comparison of indenture bonds for white indentured servants in the Indiana Territory at this time, see Deed Book 1, Harrison County, Harrison County Courthouse, Corydon, Indiana.

30. Indenture Deed Book, 1806, Knox County Public Library, Indiana.

31. "[They were] mustered into the service of the United States by Gen. Harrison who formed a colored company to aid in defending the frontier." Birkbeck and Flower, *History of the English Settlement*, 266.

32. *Liberty Hall* newspaper, Cincinnati, Ohio, October 29, 1830, from Audrey C. Werle Papers, "Research Notes on Indiana African American History," M 792, William Henry Smith Memorial Library, Indiana Historical Society, Indianapolis, Indiana. The overseer of the poor was often the official responsible for enforcing Black Laws. If free African Americans entered the state and could not pay their $500 bond, they could be forced by the overseer of the poor to do six months of forced labor as a punishment.

33. *History of Knox and Daviess Counties, Indiana: From the Earliest Time to the Present; with Biographical Sketches, Reminiscences, Notes, etc.; Together with an Extended History of the Colonial Days of Vincennes, and Its Progress Down to the Formation of the State Government* (Chicago: Goodspeed, 1886), 600–601.

34. Courtney Bettner, *Polly v. Lasselle: Slavery in Early Indiana* (Muncie, IN: Ball State University, 2012).

35. Thornbrough, *The Negro in Indiana*, 25–26; Paul Finkelman, "Almost a Free State: The Indiana Constitution of 1816 and the Problem of Slavery," *Indiana Magazine of History* 111, no. 1 (March 2015): 64–95; Bettner, *Polly v.*

Lasselle; Malcolm Maurice Hodges, "A Social History of Vincennes and Knox County, Indiana from the Beginning to 1860" (Muncie, IN: Ball State University, 1968); Jacob Piatt Dunn, *Indiana: A Redemption from Slavery* (Boston and New York: Houghton, Mifflin and Co., 1905).

36. Thornbrough, *The Negro in Indiana*, 121; Stephen Middleton, *The Black Laws in the Old Northwest: A Documentary History* (Westport, CT: Greenwood Press, 1993); Randall T. Shepard, *Slavery Cases in the Indiana Supreme Court: Where Slaves and Former Slaves Found Hope* (Indianapolis: Indiana Supreme Court, 2007).

37. M. Scott Heerman, "In a State of Slavery: Black Servitude in Illinois, 1800–1830," *Early American Studies: An Interdisciplinary Journal* 14, no. 1 (winter 2016): 137.

38. Ibid.

39. Unfortunately, those same voters who included this as section 1 in their constitution thought this statement should extend not to equality, only to freedom: *The State v. Lasselle*, (Supreme Court of Indiana 1820). Lasselle, it seems, tried to appeal this decision to the Federal Supreme Court but was rejected. See *Polly v. Lasselle*, Assignment of Errors, US (July 27, 1820), Indiana State Library Digital Collection, accessed July 7, 2017, http://cdm16066 .contentdm.oclc.org/cdm/ref/collection/p16066coll38/id/26.

40. For more on enslaved women bringing suits for freedom during this period, see Manisha Sinha, *The Slave's Cause: A History of Abolition* (New Haven, CT: Yale University Press, 2016).

41. *History of Knox and Daviess Counties*, 660–601; L. Rex Myers, *Daviess County, Indiana: History* (Paducah, KY: Turner Publication Co., 1991), 37. My thanks to Ken Graves at the Daviess County Historical Society for his generous research assistance. There are haunting similarities between the widowed Mrs. Hawkins and Dred Scott's case many years later, in which a widowed enslaver insisted upon her right to keep people enslaved in the Northwest Territory states.

42. *History of Knox and Daviess Counties, Indiana*, 769.

43. Ibid., 600–601; Myers, *Daviess County, Indiana*, 37.

44. Myers, *Daviess County, Indiana*, 37.

45. *History of Knox and Daviess Counties, Indiana*, 769–771.

46. *The Vincennes Gazette*, October 9, 1830, vol. 1, no. 2, from McGrady-Brockman House Archive, Knox County Public Library, Vincennes, Indiana.

47. Benjamin Drew, *A North-Side View of Slavery. The Refugee: or, The Narratives of Fugitive Slaves in Canada. Related by Themselves, with an Account of the History and Condition of the Colored Population of Upper Canada* (New York: Negro Universities Press, 1968), 139–163.

48. Ibid.

49. Ibid., 148; "Deeply Interesting Facts," *Philanthropist (1836–1843)*, December 24, 1839, accessed October 2, 2017.

50. For more on the important role of African American Underground Railroad agents in Indiana and the Northwest Territory states, see Cheryl

LaRoche's excellent *Free Black Communities and the Underground Railroad: The Geography of Resistance*.

51. Thornbrough, *The Negro in Indiana*, 19.

52. Abdy, *Journal of a Residence and Tour in the United States of North America*, 360–370.

53. Laurel Thatcher Ulrich, *The Age of Homespun: Objects and Stories in the Creation of an American Myth* (New York: Vintage Books, 2001).

Chapter 4: "And secure the blessings of Liberty"

1. George W. Smith, "The Salines of Southern Illinois," in *Transactions of the Illinois State Historical Society for the Year 1904*, ed. Illinois State Historical Society (Springfield, IL: Phillips Bros., State Printers, 1904), 245–258.

2. Jacob Myers, "History of the Gallatin County Salines," *Journal of the Illinois State Historical Society (1908–1984)* 14, no. 3/4 (1921): 337–350.

3. Robert Martin Owens, "William Henry Harrison's Indiana: Paternalism and Patriotism on the Frontier, 1795–1812" (PhD diss., University of Illinois at Urbana–Champaign, 2003), 245–255; Myers, "History of the Gallatin County Salines," 342–343.

4. Smith, "Salines," 246.

5. M. Scott Heerman, "In a State of Slavery: Black Servitude in Illinois, 1800–1830," *Early American Studies: An Interdisciplinary Journal* 14, no. 1 (2016): 130; Anne Silverwood Twitty, "Slavery and Freedom in the American Confluence, from the Northwest Ordinance to Dred Scott" (PhD diss., Princeton University, 2010), 28–29.

6. Charles Noye Zucker, "The Free Negro Question: Race Relations in Ante-Bellum Illinois, 1801–1860" (PhD diss., Northwestern University, 1973), 57–61; Yvonne Blackmore, "African-Americans and Race Relations in Gallatin County, Illinois, from the Eighteenth Century to 1870" (PhD diss., Northern Illinois University, 1996), 16–19; Twitty, "Slavery and Freedom in the American Confluence," 26–27; Heerman, "In a State of Slavery," 121–122.

7. Heerman, "In a State of Slavery," 129–130; Blackmore, "African-Americans and Race Relations in Gallatin County," 116–117.

8. Smith, "Salines," 255; Mary Prince and Sara Salih, *The History of Mary Prince: A West Indian Slave* (London: Penguin Books, 2004), 7.

9. Smith, "Salines," 256.

10. Ibid., 251; US Department of the Interior, Census Office, *Population Schedules of the Seventh Census of the United States, 1850*, Gallatin County, Illinois.

11. H. Obert Anderson, comp., *Register of Slaves (Indentures) and Emancipation of Slaves from the Gallatin County Clerk's Office, Shawneetown, Illinois*, 125–126, from the Shawneetown Public Library History Collection, Shawneetown, Illinois. See also "New African-American Genealogy Data at ISGS Website," Illinois State Genealogical Society Blog, July 4, 2011, accessed

June 12, 2017, https://ilgensoc.blogspot.com/2011/07/new-african-american
-genealogy-data-at.html (the deed was recorded in 1829, but the actual trans-
action occurred on August 4, 1821); Smith, "Salines," 251; Samuel Bernard
Judah, "A Journal of Travel from New York to Indiana in 1827," *Indiana Magazine of History* 17, no. 4 (1921): 347; Samuel H. Williamson, "Measuring
Slavery in 2016 Dollars," MeasuringWorth.com, www.measuringworth.com
/slavery.php; Scott Derks and Tony Smith, *The Value of a Dollar, 1600–1865:
The Colonial Era to the Civil War* (Millerton, NY: Grey House Publishing,
2005), 363.

12. James Penick, *The New Madrid Earthquakes of 1811–1812* (Columbia:
University of Missouri Press, 1976).

13. Ibid.

14. Benjamin Drew, *A North-Side View of Slavery. The Refugee: or, The
Narratives of Fugitive Slaves in Canada. Related by Themselves, with an Account
of the History and Condition of the Colored Population of Upper Canada* (New
York: Negro Universities Press, 1968), 49.

15. Paul Finkelman, "Evading the Ordinance: The Persistence of Bondage
in Indiana and Illinois," *Journal of the Early Republic* 9, no. 1 (spring 1989):
33–34; Matthew Salafia, *Slavery's Borderland: Freedom and Bondage Along the
Ohio River* (Philadelphia: University of Pennsylvania Press, 2013), 67–68. For
more on the conflict between pro- and antislavery forces in early Illinois, see
Suzanne Cooper Guasco, *Confronting Slavery: Edward Coles and the Rise of
Antislavery Politics in Nineteenth-Century America* (DeKalb: Northern Illinois
University Press, 2013).

16. Anderson, *Register of Slaves (Indentures)*, 125–126.

17. Drew, *North-Side*, 106–107.

18. Ibid.

19. Roy Finkenbine, "A Beacon of Liberty on the Great Lakes: Race, Slav-
ery and the Law in Antebellum Michigan," in *The History of Michigan Law*,
ed. Paul Finkelman, Martin J. Hershock, and Clifford W. Taylor (Athens:
Ohio University Press, 2006), 84; James Oliver Horton and Lois E. Horton, *In
Hope of Liberty: Culture, Community, and Protest Among Northern Free Blacks,
1700–1860* (New York: Oxford University Press, 1998), 102–103; Eugene
Berwanger, *The Frontier Against Slavery: Western Anti-Negro Prejudice and the
Slavery Extension Controversy* (Urbana: University of Illinois Press, 2002), 32;
Coy Robbins, *Forgotten Hoosiers: African Heritage in Orange County, Indiana*
(Bowie, MD: Heritage Books, 1994), 52–65.

20. Anderson, *Register of Slaves (Indentures) and Emancipation of Slaves*,
169.

21. Campbell Gibson and Kay Jung, "Historical Census Statistics on Population Totals by Race, 1790 to 1990, and by Hispanic Origin, 1970 to 1990,
for Large Cities and Other Urban Places in the United States" (Working Paper Series No. 56, Population Division, US Census Bureau, September 2002),
www.census.gov/population/www/documentation/twps0076/twps0076.html;

Stephen Middleton, *The Black Laws in the Old Northwest: A Documentary History* (Westport, CT: Greenwood Press, 1993), 291–294.

22. Anderson, *Register of Slaves (Indentures)*.

23. Ibid., 125–126.

24. Illinois State Archives, Servitude Database, www.ilsos.gov/isa /servEmanSearch.do?nameNo=1604.

25. Robert Scott Davis, "Free but Not Freed: Stephen Deane's African Family in Early Georgia," *Georgia Historical Quarterly* 97, no. 1 (2013): 61–72. For more on African Americans who chose to own enslaved people who were not kin, see Loren Schweninger, *Black Property Owners in the South, 1790–1915* (Urbana: University of Illinois Press, 1997).

26. Alexandra Piper, "Ruthless, Lawless, and Defiant: The Unbelievable Life of Freed Slave Armistead Lawless in Nineteenth Century St. Louis," Special Research Project, Hope College, Holland, Michigan, 2016. Unpublished paper, in author's possession.

27. Cheryl LaRoche, *Free Black Communities and the Underground Railroad: The Geography of Resistance* (Urbana: University of Illinois Press, 2014), 113–117; David Gerber, in *Black Ohio and the Color Line, 1860–1915* (Urbana: University of Illinois Press, 1976), 19, noted that as many as 20 percent of African Americans in two southern Ohio African American communities had bought their own freedom or been bought into freedom by kin or loved ones; Juliet E. K. Walker, *Free Frank: A Black Pioneer on the Antebellum Frontier* (Lexington: University Press of Kentucky, 1983), 1–7; Christopher Valvano, "'Some Day on American Soil': The Material Record of New Philadelphia and the Middle Class on the American Prairie" (PhD diss., Michigan State University, 2015), 36–50.

28. Valvano, "'Some Day,'" 36–50.

29. Walker, *Free Frank*, 1–7.

30. Anderson, *Register of Slaves (Indentures)*.

31. Ellen Eslinger, "Liberation in a Rural Context," in *Paths to Freedom: Manumission in the Atlantic World*, ed. Rosemary Brana-Shute and Randy J. Sparks (Columbia: University of South Carolina Press, 2009), 363–381.

32. For a comprehensive look at the various conflicts in the Great Lakes region of the Northwest Territory, see Larry L. Nelson and David Curtis Skaggs, *Sixty Years' War for the Great Lakes, 1754–1814* (East Lansing: Michigan State University Press, 2001).

33. Anderson, *Register of Slaves (Indentures)*, 61.

34. Deed Book K, Gallatin County Courthouse, Shawneetown, Illinois, 66–67. Land Deed 1, July 6, 1829. Elliott bought numerous plots of land starting in 1829, which are recorded in this deed book on pp. 64–69. While the deeds were recorded in the late 1830s, they are clearly records of land deeds for land purchased by Elliott between 1829 and 1839. Other historians have merely stated the date the deeds were recorded rather than the actual sale date of the land. This confusion between actual deed dates and when those deeds were recorded by the county clerk also includes deeds of sale and freedom for

Elliott and his family members, which has resulted in some unfortunate confusion in later historical works about Elliott.

35. Smith, "Salines," 255–256; US Department of the Interior, Census Office, *Population Schedules of the Seventh Census of the United States, 1850,* Gallatin County, Illinois. Later local historians have made claims that Elliott purchased the freedom of over a dozen family members, but his son and daughter stated that it was around four, and the known historic record shows much fewer. It is my hope that more research into records in Tennessee, Kentucky, and other states may find more people whom Elliott purchased and freed.

Chapter 5: "To secure these rights, ..."

1. It is important to note that various branches of the Lyles family in Indiana have preserved different oral traditions about their background before coming to the region. And these oral traditions are important to the ways they identify themselves. In the last few decades, however, there has been growing interest in the Lyles family's background, and a few scholars have discovered that some of the oral traditions preserved within the Gibson County branch were not entirely accurate. In most cases, scholars try to share information and work with others to build an accurate record of the past. Unfortunately, this information about the Lyles family was used in a way that was—at a minimum—disrespectful to that family. It ended up bringing into question their entire history and distracting attention from all the extraordinary accomplishments of these highly successful rural entrepreneurs in nineteenth-century Indiana. This is not the first time this has happened to families from some of the pioneering settlements that still exist in the Northwest Territory states. And since this incident, members of the Lyles family itself have done excellent research of their own, discovering important and noteworthy facts about their background. It is important for historians to remember that successful African American pioneering families in the Northwest Territory states were—and sometimes still are—surrounded by prejudice. Scholars need to understand the power that they themselves hold and should try to be respectful and careful when dealing with these pioneering families' sense of self and identity. Surprising them in public with information intended to expose them as holding myths about their past, without at least first sharing information with them in a collegial, quiet, and respectful way, distracts from these pioneering families' actual accomplishments on the frontier and can have a harmful effect. For more on the damage that such actions can do, see Arlene Blanks Polk, "The Truth About Joshua Lyles: A Free African American Settler of Lyles Station, Indiana," *Traces of Indiana & Midwestern History* 25, no. 4 (October 2013): 32–37.

2. Ibid., 32–37.

3. Billy D. Higgins, *A Stranger and a Sojourner: Peter Caulder, Free Black Frontiersman in Antebellum Arkansas* (Fayetteville: University of Arkansas Press, 2004), xi, xii–xiii.

4. Gibson County Negro Registry, 1851, Princeton Public Library, Princeton, Indiana.

5. William Imes, "The Legal Status of Free Negroes and Slaves in Tennessee," *Journal of Negro History* 4, no. 3 (July 1919): 254–272. For an excellent overview of the debates in Tennessee over slavery and the status of free African Americans during this period, see Lacy K. Ford, *Deliver Us from Evil: The Slavery Question in the Old South* (New York: Oxford University Press, 2009).

6. Polk, "The Truth About Joshua Lyles," 32–37.

7. Deed Book W, Vanderburgh County Recorder's Office, Evansville, Indiana, 235. My gratitude to Stanley Schmitt at the Willard Library in Evansville for his extraordinary research and assistance in locating these and other documents connected to the Lyles family in Vanderburgh County, Indiana.

8. Polk, "The Truth About Joshua Lyles," 32–37.

9. Ibid.

10. Ibid.

11. Ibid.

12. Ford, *Deliver Us*, 394.

13. Caleb Perry Patterson, *The Negro in Tennessee, 1790–1865* (Austin: University of Texas, 1922), 153–175.

14. A man who had fled enslavement and was living in Canada in the 1850s recounted how the most helpless members of slave coffles were treated by drivers on these long marches: "killing babes—I have seen one with its brains dashed out against a red oak tree. Tired of carrying it . . . they put it out of the way." Benjamin Drew, "Mr. ____," in *Refugees from Slavery: Autobiographies of Fugitive Slaves in Canada*, ed. Tilden G. Edelstein (Mineola, NY: Dover Publications, 2004), 197–199.

15. David F. Allmendinger, *Nat Turner and the Rising in Southampton County* (Baltimore: Johns Hopkins University Press, 2014); Patrick Breen, *The Land Shall Be Deluged in Blood: A New History of the Nat Turner Revolt* (New York: Oxford University Press, 2015).

16. Ford, *Deliver Us*, 343–356; John Hope Franklin, *The Free Negro in North Carolina,1790–1860* (New York: Russell & Russell, 1969), 73–74; *The Western Freeman*, September 6, 1831, Shelbyville, Tennessee, quoted in Patterson, *The Negro in Tennessee*, 154.

17. *Liberator*, January 7, 1832, viewed on Accessible Archives; Manisha Sinha, *The Slave's Cause: A History of Abolition* (New Haven, CT: Yale University Press, 2016), 210–213.

18. Edward Rugemer, "Caribbean Slave Revolts and the Origins of the Gag Rule: A Contest Between Abolitionism and Democracy, 1797–1835," in *Contesting Slavery: The Politics of Bondage and Freedom in the New American Nation*, ed. John Craig Hammond and Matthew Mason (Charlottesville: University of Virginia Press, 2011), 93–114. While Rugemer does an excellent job researching the ties between abolitionist activities and revolution, as well as describing the fears that enslavers had about abolitionist activities in the United

States, he misses the point that most enslavers understood and debated at this time: that the best way to avoid the risk of revolution was to end slavery.

19. Herbert Aptheker, *American Negro Slave Revolts* (New York: Columbia University Press, 1963); Walter C. Rucker, "'I Will Gather All Nations': Resistance, Culture, and Pan-African Collaboration in Denmark Vesey's South Carolina," *Journal of Negro History* 86, no. 2 (spring 2001): 132–147; Adalberto Aguirre Jr. and David V. Baker, "Slave Executions in the United States: A Descriptive Analysis of Social and Historical Factors," *Social Science Journal* 36, no. 1 (1999): 1–31; Ford, *Deliver Us*, 361–375, 390–417.

20. Governor John Floyd Diary, November 21, 1831, quoted in Ford, *Deliver Us*, 362.

21. For more on the rhetoric and actions of prejudiced whites in the North during this period, see Chapter 6.

22. Antonio T. Bly, "Slave Literacy and Education in Virginia," *Encyclopedia Virginia*, last modified July 11, 2017, accessed October 8, 2017, www.encyclopediavirginia.org/Slave_Literacy_and_Education_in_Virginia; Hilary Moss, *Schooling Citizens: The Struggle for African American Education in Antebellum America* (Chicago: University of Chicago Press, 2009), 2–5.

23. Imes, "The Legal Status of Free Negroes," 264; Ford, *Deliver Us*, 343–357, 390–417.

24. Imes, "The Legal Status of Free Negroes," 262–264.

25. Leonard H. Sims, quoted in Ford, *Deliver Us*, 392.

26. Alexander Keyssar, *The Right to Vote: The Contested History of Democracy in the United States* (New York: Basic Books, 2000), Table A.4.

27. For a brilliant overview of the contentious debate over prejudice and equality in the Old Northwest Territory state constitutional conventions, see Silvana Siddali, *Frontier Democracy: Constitutional Conventions in the Old Northwest* (New York: Cambridge University Press, 2016), 265–308; Stephen Middleton, *The Black Laws in the Old Northwest: A Documentary History* (Westport, CT: Greenwood Press, 1993), 18–41.

28. Patterson, *The Negro in Tennessee*, 156.

29. Philip Foner and George Walker, *Proceedings of the Black State Conventions, 1840–1865* (Philadelphia: Temple University Press, 1979), 1:233.

30. Keyssar, *The Right to Vote*, Table A.4.

31. Franklin, *The Free Negro in North Carolina*, 12–13, 18, 112–113.

32. John Chavis, quoted in Franklin, *The Free Negro in North Carolina*, 106.

33. More research is needed on how these Black Code bonds were used to strengthen inequality and unfairly target successful African Americans. A number of such incidents were recorded in various cities of the Northwest Territory states, including in Cincinnati and Detroit. Less research has been done on rural areas, although Ross F. Bagby in his PhD dissertation found the bonds being used as an excuse for organized mob violence against African Americans in rural Mercer County, Ohio, in the 1840s. See Ross Bagby, "The

Randolph Slave Saga: Communities in Collision" (PhD diss., Ohio State University, 1998), 59–108.

34. Jefferson County, Indiana Deed Book P, 355, in Audrey C. Werle, "Research Notes on Indiana African American History," M 792, William Henry Smith Memorial Library, Indiana Historical Society, Indianapolis, Indiana.

35. Abraham Bishop, quoted in Sinha, *The Slave's Cause*, 59–60.

36. The census data in Indiana would seem to show that the Lyles family moved in waves over five years. Based on birth places, John and his family seem to have arrived first, around 1837, with Daniel and Nancy coming in the early 1840s. But given the inaccuracy of this census data, especially concerning birth information, they may all have come together.

37. For more on the challenges free African American farmers faced in Canada in the first half of the 1800s, see Anna-Lisa Cox, *A Stronger Kinship: One Town's Extraordinary Story of Hope and Faith* (New York: Little, Brown and Co., 2006).

38. See Chapter 6 for more on the violence rising in northern cities. For more on the creation of ghettos in cities of the Western world as a means of controlling and disempowering minority groups, see Mitchell Duneier, *Ghetto: The Invention of a Place, the History of an Idea* (New York: Farrar, Straus and Giroux, 2016).

39. "Resolution from Michigan's Black Convention of 1843," in Foner and Walker, *Proceedings of the Black State Conventions*, 1:189.

40. Ira Berlin termed these early Americans "Atlantic Creoles." Ira Berlin, *Many Thousands Gone: The First Two Centuries of Slavery in North America* (Cambridge, MA: Harvard University Press, 1998), 15–77. Toni Morrison's novel *A Mercy* gives a masterful description of what life was like for the people from many lands and of many ancestries living in seventeenth-century Virginia.

41. John Finger, *Tennessee Frontiers: Three Regions in Transition* (Bloomington: Indiana University Press, 2001).

42. While free African Americans had been moving onto the Old Northwest frontier since the 1700s, the majority did so between 1830 and 1850. In some areas of North Carolina and Virginia the number of people leaving during the height of this diaspora was notable. Stephen Vincent, in *Southern Seed, Northern Soil: African-American Farm Communities in the Midwest, 1765–1900* (Bloomington: Indiana University Press, 1999), 38–39, describes this extraordinary out-migration and its local effects in North Carolina, noting that over half of free African American families left Greenville County between 1833 and 1835. Luther Porter Jackson, in *Free Negro Labor and Property Holding in Virginia, 1830–1860* (New York: Atheneum, 1969), 25, gives evidence of a clear period of out-migration from Virginia in the 1830s.

A large percentage of these free black pioneers seem to be free blacks from North Carolina and Virginia. By the early nineteenth century, Maryland, Virginia, and North Carolina had the highest number of free blacks of any of the southern slaveholding states. It could be that African Americans in Maryland did not move onto the frontier in such large numbers because they were primarily urban, while North Carolina's African American population was primarily rural and Virginia also had a large rural African American population, but further research is needed on this question. See Loren Schweninger, "Prosperous Blacks in the South, 1790–1880," *American Historical Review* 95, no. 1 (February 1990): 41–44; Vincent, *Southern Seed*, 13; Roger Peterson, *African Americans Found in Owen County, IN Records, 1819–1880* (self-published, 1996), 27, 48; William Katz, *Black Pioneers: An Untold Story* (New York: Atheneum, 1999), 29; Franklin, *The Free Negro in North Carolina*, 7. For more on life for free African Americans in rural antebellum Virginia, see Melvin Ely, *Israel on the Appomattox: A Southern Experiment in Black Freedom from the 1790s Through the Civil War* (New York: Knopf, 2004).

43. For more on the integrated nature of this pioneering movement to the Northwest territories and states, as well as the southern and northern whites who were coming to this region to fight for equality and freedom, see Vincent, *Southern Seed*; Brian Hackett, "'Harboring Negroes': Race, Religion, and Politics in North Carolina and Indiana" (PhD diss., Middle Tennessee State University, 2009); Lynn Marie Getz, "Partners in Motion: Gender, Migration, and Reform in Antebellum Ohio and Kansas," *Frontiers* 27, no. 2 (2006): 102–135, 163.

44. Prejudice in the Northwest Territory states has often been blamed on southern whites. True, some white southern yeoman farmers seem to have come to the Northwest territories looking to escape the company of African Americans. And some wealthy and powerful southern whites worked hard to spread slavery across the Northwest Territory states. But an alternate southern culture—both black and white—was settling the Northwest Territory states. These southerners must also be considered when thinking about the identity of this region. My grateful thanks to Brother Abraham, OSB, for his thoughtful challenges to my assumptions about region, identity, and politics in antebellum America, which led me to explore this issue more thoroughly throughout this book.

45. Drew, "Mr. ____," in *Refugees from Slavery*, 193–196.

46. Augustus Wattles, "Communications," *Philanthropist (1836–1843)* 2, no. 25 (August 4, 1837): 1 (article was originally accessed on Proquest, October 11, 2013).

47. Vincent, *Southern Seed*, xi–xvii, 26–45.

48. Juliet E. K. Walker, *The History of Black Business in America: Capitalism, Race, Entrepreneurship* (Chapel Hill: University of North Carolina Press, 1998), 95.

49. Darrel Dexter, "Free and American: A Study of Eleven Illinois Families of Color," *Free African Americans of Virginia, North Carolina, South Carolina, Maryland and Delaware*, last modified September 14, 2001, accessed October 8, 2017, www.freeafricanamericans.com/Illinois.htm.

50. US Department of the Interior, Census Office, *Population Schedules of the Seventh Census of the United States, 1850, Ohio, Delaware County, Concord Township*, 252; Fred Fowler and H. Georgiana Whyte, "Some Undistinguished Negroes," *Journal of Negro History* 5, no. 4 (October 1920): 484–485.

51. US Department of the Interior, Census Office, *Population Schedules of the Seventh Census of the United States, 1850, Ohio, Franklin County, Perry Township*, 239; Fowler and Whyte, "Some Undistinguished Negroes," 484–485. "Litchford" is the spelling of the name given by Georgiana Whyte, who knew the family, although "Letchford" is the spelling of the name in the convention records, while "Leitchford" is the spelling on the 1850 census.

52. Walker, *Black Business*, 95. For more on the corruption common in these federal land offices during this period, see Malcolm J. Rohrbough, *The Land Office Business: The Settlement and Administration of American Public Lands, 1789–1837* (New York: Oxford University Press, 1968).

53. Loren Schweninger, "The Fragile Nature of Freedom: Free Women of Color in the U.S. South," in *Beyond Bondage: Free Women of Color in the Americas*, ed. David Gaspar and Darlene Hine (Urbana: University of Illinois Press, 2004), 109. Kidnapping of free African Americans was a threat in both the North and the South. See Carol Wilson, *Freedom at Risk: The Kidnapping of Free Blacks in America, 1780–1865* (Lexington: University Press of Kentucky, 1994); Wilma King, *Stolen Childhood, Second Edition: Slave Youth in Nineteenth-Century America* (Bloomington: Indiana University Press, 2011), 212–261; Walter Johnson, *Soul by Soul: Life Inside the Antebellum Slave Market* (Cambridge, MA: Harvard University Press, 1999), 140–141.

54. Thomas P. Weaver, "Life and Works," *Free African Americans of Virginia, North Carolina, South Carolina, Maryland, and Delaware*, 1922, www.freeafricanamericans.com/19th_4.htm.

55. Vincent, *Southern Seed*, 26–27. This story was passed down as an oral narrative within the settlement in Indiana. Oral narratives have especial potency within the African American community, particularly in the Northwest Territory states. Because the truth of their history was denied or ignored, these oral narratives kept important truths alive within these pioneering families and settlements, often with an astonishing level of accuracy. See my previous book *A Stronger Kinship* for a full discussion on the use of African American oral narratives.

56. Vincent, *Southern Seed*, 26–27.

57. Cox, *Stronger Kinship*, 53–54.

58. Foner and Walker, *Proceedings of the Black State Conventions*, 1:234.

Chapter 6: "Burnt our towns, and destroyed the lives of our people"

1. The details of this Cincinnati race war of 1841 are drawn from Nikki Taylor, *Frontiers of Freedom: Cincinnati's Black Community, 1802–1868*

(Athens: Ohio University Press, 2005), 20–25; John Langston, *From the Virginia Plantation to the National Capital; or, The First and Only Negro Representative in Congress from the Old Dominion* (New York: Johnson Reprint Corp., 1968 [1894]), 64; William F. Cheek and Aimee Lee Cheek, *John Mercer Langston and the Fight for Black Freedom, 1829–65* (Urbana: University of Illinois Press, 1996), 59–63; Leonard Richards, *Gentlemen of Property and Standing: Anti-abolition Mobs in Jacksonian America* (New York: Oxford University Press, 1971), 122–129; "Riot at Cincinnati," *Liberator*, September 4, 1841; "Riot, Mob, Confusion and Bloodshed," *Liberator*, September 17, 1841; "The Mob," *Liberator*, September 17, 1841; "The Riot in Cincinnati," *Liberator*, September 24, 1841; "Reign of Terror Again in Cincinnati," *Liberator*, September 24, 1841; "Cincinnati Riot," *Liberator*, October 1, 1841; "Selections from the Cincinnati Philanthropist," *Liberator*, October 1, 1841. In all, William Lloyd Garrison published over twenty-four articles in 1841 about the battle in Cincinnati. In some of these cases Garrison was reprinting articles originally published in Ohio and New York papers, doing his best to get the information to his readers and spread word of the attack on African Americans in Cincinnati. On October 1 he posted an article stating that he, Wendell Phillips, and their Massachusetts Anti-slavery Society had raised and sent $100 to the Cincinnati abolitionist newspaper the *Philanthropist*, whose press had been destroyed by the mob. (All *Liberator* articles accessed on Ebscohost's website between 2015 and 2017. Grateful thanks to my research intern, Miriam Roth, who helped me find many of these articles.)

2. Steve C. Gordon, "From Slaughterhouse to Soap-Boiler: Cincinnati's Meat Packing Industry, Changing Technologies, and the Rise of Mass Production, 1825–1870," *IA: The Journal of the Society for Industrial Archeology* 16, no. 1 (1990): 55–67; Margaret Walsh, "Pork Packing as a Leading Edge of Midwestern Industry, 1835–1875," *Agricultural History* 51, no. 4 (1977): 702–717.

3. Taylor, *Frontiers*, 28–79. Nikki Taylor shows that African American leaders courageously managed extraordinary levels of organizing in the face of white threats of violence in order to make escape plans to Canada for many of the African American citizens of Cincinnati.

4. Numerous historians over the years have identified these patterns of white prejudice against African Americans, most recently Ibram X. Kendi in his magisterial *Stamped from the Beginning: The Definitive History of Racist Ideas in America* (New York: Nation Books, 2016).

5. Shane White, *Prince of Darkness: The Untold Story of Jeremiah G. Hamilton, Wall Street's First Black Millionaire* (Gordonsville, VA: Palgrave Macmillan, 2016); Edward Williams Clay, engraver, "Life in Philadelphia, Plate 4 / C. fecit," Philadelphia, published by W. Simpson, 1828, Library of Congress, www.loc.gov/item/2012647352. For more on the earliest northern roots of bigoted American cartoons, see John Wood Sweet, *Bodies Politic: Negotiating Race in the American North, 1730–1830* (Baltimore: Johns Hopkins University Press, 2003), 365–392.

6. Taylor, *Frontiers*, 28–79.

7. Langston, *From the Virginia Plantation to the National Capital*, 64; Major James Wilkerson, "The Midnight Cry: The Parable of the Great Supper" (Philadelphia: Quinn, Card and Job Printer, 1859), accessed on Readex, Series: American Broadsides and Ephemera. First series: no. 10550.

8. Wilkerson, "The Midnight Cry"; James Wilkerson, *Wilkerson's History of His Travels and Labors, in the United States, as a Missionary, in . . . Particular, That of the Union Seminary* (Columbus, Ohio, 1861).

9. Wilkerson, "The Midnight Cry"; Wilkerson, *History of His Travels*.

10. For more on James Wilkerson's grandfather, see Andro Linklater, *An Artist in Treason: The Extraordinary Double Life of General James Wilkinson* (New York: Walker, 2009).

11. Wilkerson, *History of His Travels*, 36; Wilkerson, "The Midnight Cry."

12. Wilkerson would mention his connection to the Joseph story often in his writings and wrote a hymn on the theme. See Wilkerson, "The Midnight Cry"; Major James Wilkerson, *The Midnight Cry & Millennium Dawn: A Cry from the Forest or Wilderness—Prepare to Meet Thy God, O Israel!* (New Orleans, 1865), Houghton Library, Harvard University.

13. Wilkerson, *History of His Travels*, 36.

14. Ibid., 13.

15. Wilkerson, "The Midnight Cry."

16. Richard Anthony Lewis, "Richard Clague Jr," *Encyclopedia of Louisiana*, ed. David Johnson, Louisiana Endowment for the Humanities, 2010–, last modified January 11, 2011, accessed June 30, 2017, www.knowlouisiana.org/entry/richard-clague-jr.

17. Ibid.

18. Ibid.; Wilkerson, "The Midnight Cry."

19. Much has been written on large-scale manumissions in antebellum America, but as late as the 1850s, southern enslavers continued trying to personally end enslavement. See Ross Bagby, "The Randolph Slave Saga: Communities in Collision" (PhD diss., Ohio State University, 1998), 59–108; Carrie Eldridge, *Cabell County's Empire for Freedom: The Manumission of Sampson Sanders' Slaves* (Bowie, MD: Willow Bend Books, 1999).

20. Wilkerson, "The Midnight Cry."

21. Ibid.

22. Undated petition by the residents of Cass and Van Buren counties (c. 1835), Box 223, File 7, Group 44, State of Michigan Archives, Lansing, Michigan. I am deeply grateful to Debian Marty for the extraordinary work she has done to tell the history of abolitionism in Michigan and who kindly identified and dated this document I found in an uncatalogued collection.

23. Lacy K. Ford, *Deliver Us from Evil: The Slavery Question in the Old South* (New York: Oxford University Press, 2009), 496–497.

24. Ibid., 481–503.

25. Wilkerson, "The Midnight Cry."

26. Ibid. For the full record of Clague's work with Pollock, see "Pollock, Carlile Indexes, 1817–1845," Research Center and Historical Documents, Clerk of the Civil District Court for the Parish of Orleans, www.orleanscivilclerk.com/pollock.htm.

27. Wilkerson, "The Midnight Cry."

28. Ibid.; Wilkerson, *History of His Travels*.

29. Augustus Wattles, "Communications," *Philanthropist (1836–1843)* 2, no. 25 (August 4, 1837): 1 (article was originally accessed on Proquest, October 11, 2013).

30. Langston, *From the Virginia Plantation to the National Capital*, 64.

31. Wilkerson, *History of His Travels*, 18.

32. Taylor, *Frontiers*, 50–79; Richards, *Gentlemen*, 34–35, 92–100. William Lloyd Garrison made sure that the events in Cincinnati in the summer of 1841 were well covered by his Boston-based newspaper, the *Liberator*. Before the battle broke out in August, Garrison had already been covering more personal attacks in the city starting in July. "A Mob in Cincinnati," *Liberator*, July 16, 1841.

33. Henry Barnard and Moses B. Goodwin, *History of Schools for the Colored Population* (New York: Arno Press, 1969), 200.

34. Harry Reed, *Platform for Change: The Foundations of the Northern Free Black Community, 1775–1865* (East Lansing: Michigan State University Press, 1994), 127–161.

35. Ford, *Deliver Us*, 484. For more on Bishop Allen and the AME Church and its schools, see Richard Newman, *Freedom's Prophet: Bishop Richard Allen, the AME Church, and the Black Founding Fathers* (New York: New York University Press, 2008).

36. For use of the term "human rights" among early American abolitionists at this time, see Manisha Sinha, *The Slave's Cause: A History of Abolition* (New Haven, CT: Yale University Press, 2016).

37. Phillip Lapsansky, Richard S. Newman, and Patrick Rael, *Pamphlets of Protest: An Anthology of Early African-American Protest Literature, 1790–1860* (New York: Routledge, 2001), 111; John Hope Franklin and Evelyn Brooks Higginbotham, *From Slavery to Freedom: A History of African Americans* (New York: McGraw-Hill, 2011), 165–166.

38. John Wood Sweet, *Bodies Politic: Negotiating Race in the American North, 1730–1830* (Baltimore: Johns Hopkins University Press, 2003), 395; Richards, *Gentlemen*, 34.

39. Karolyn Smardz Frost, *I've Got a Home in Glory Land: A Lost Tale of the Underground Railroad* (New York: Farrar, Straus and Giroux, 2007), 163–190.

40. Ibid.

41. Richards, *Gentlemen*, 9; Andrew Neilly, "The Violent Volunteers: A History of the Volunteer Fire Department of Philadelphia, 1736–1871" (PhD diss., University of Pennsylvania, 1959), 63–69.

42. For more on the riots of this period, see Richards's groundbreaking *Gentlemen of Property and Standing.*

43. Ibid., 3–19.

44. For an important work on pro-slavery and prejudice in the North, see Leon Litwack, *North of Slavery: The Negro in the Free States, 1790–1860* (Chicago: University of Chicago Press, 1961).

45. While Thomas Morris started out as a supporter of Andrew Jackson in the late 1820s, in 1844 he ran for vice president on a Liberty Party ticket with James Birney as an abolitionist and equal rights advocate. Stephen Middleton, *The Black Laws: Race and the Legal Process in Early Ohio* (Athens: Ohio University Press, 2005), 124; "Thomas Morris," Supreme Court of Ohio, www .supremecourt.ohio.gov/SCO/formerjustices/bios/morris.asp.

46. Silvana Siddali, "'The Language of Wrath': Race, Violence, and Civil Rights in Western State Constitutional Conventions, 1835–1865" (paper presented at the African Americans in the Nineteenth-Century West Research Symposium, Saint Louis University, Saint Louis, Missouri, May 21, 2016).

47. Ibid.

48. Quoted in Richards, *Gentlemen*, 95. Richards suggests that Lytle probably used a more obscene term than "castrate."

49. Ibid., 93–100; Taylor, *Frontiers*, 109–112.

50. Andrew Judson to Reverend Samuel May, March 1833, quoted in Diana Ross McCain, *To All on Equal Terms: The Life and Legacy of Prudence Crandall* (Hartford: Connecticut Commission on Arts, Tourism, Culture, History and Film, 2004), 29.

51. John Melvin Werner, "Race Riots in the United States During the Age of Jackson: 1824–1849" (PhD diss., Indiana University, 1972); Sinha, *The Slave's Cause*, 232–239.

52. Richards, *Gentlemen*, 101. For more on Elijah Lovejoy's activities in Saint Louis, including his educating of African Americans there, see Christopher Hamilton's interview in Benjamin Drew's *A North-Side View of Slavery.*

53. Richards, *Gentlemen*, 103–104, 106.

54. Charles Noye Zucker, "The Free Negro Question: Race Relations in Ante-Bellum Illinois, 1801–1860" (PhD diss., Northwestern University, 1971), 123–124, 129. Zucker's dissertation offers an excellent overview of the anti-slavery movement and the rise of white supremacy in antebellum Illinois.

55. Quoted in Richards, *Gentlemen*, 109; Zucker, "The Free Negro Question," 184. For a full exploration of the way in which Lovejoy fit into the larger abolitionist movement in Illinois, see Dana Elizabeth Weiner, *Race and Rights: Fighting Slavery and Prejudice in the Old Northwest, 1830–1870* (DeKalb: Northern Illinois University Press, 2013), 100–110.

56. "Colonization," *Liberator*, October 1841.

57. Quoted in Ford, *Deliver Us*, 501.

58. For more on African American presses at this time, see Todd Vogel, *The Black Press: New Literary and Historical Essays* (New Brunswick, NJ: Rutgers University Press, 2001). During my research I have been surprised by how well

connected the *Liberator* was, becoming a clearinghouse for other newspapers and republishing articles about violence rising across the country at this time, from an attack against an African American physician in Detroit to each of the Cincinnati riots. And Garrison was far from alone. A study of the Carl Bajema clippings collection (Grand Rapids Public Library, African Americans, 1830–1856, Folder 1) in Grand Rapids, Michigan, revealed a variety of newspapers covering issues surrounding prejudice and violence against African Americans during this period. A broader study of how newspapers across the United States focused on prejudiced violence during the 1830s is worth further study.

59. Taylor, *Frontiers*, 109–115.

60. Richards, *Gentlemen*, 92–100; Taylor, *Frontiers*, 109–112; "Mob in Cincinnati. Destruction of Mr. Birney's Press," *Liberator*, August 13, 1836; "The Cincinnati Riot," *Liberator*, August 27, 1836; "Mr. Birney," *Liberator*, September 17, 1836.

61. D. Laurence Rogers, *Apostles of Equality: The Birneys, the Republicans, and the Civil War* (East Lansing: Michigan State University Press, 2011), xi–xiii. See this volume for more on James Birney's life before coming to Cincinnati.

62. Ibid., 107–117; Clayton Douglas Cormany, "Ohio's Abolitionist Campaign: The Study of Rhetoric of Conversion" (PhD diss., Ohio State University, 1981), 30–33.

63. James Birney, *The American Churches: The Bulwarks of American Slavery* (London, 1840), 8.

64. Ibid., 24–25. For an excellent summation of the religious dialogue over slavery during the revolutionary period, see Mark A. Noll, *In the Beginning Was the Word: The Bible in American Public Life, 1492–1783* (Oxford: Oxford University Press, 2016).

65. Birney, *American Churches*, 6.

66. Ibid., 5, 32.

67. Neilly, "The Violent Volunteers," 63–69; Alexander Keyssar, *The Right to Vote: The Contested History of Democracy in the United States* (New York: Basic Books, 2000), 53–76.

68. Emma Lou Thornbrough, *The Negro in Indiana Before 1900: A Study of a Minority* (Indianapolis: Indiana Historical Bureau, 1957), 58.

69. Taylor, *Frontiers of Freedom*, 188–193.

70. Drew, *A North-Side View of Slavery*, 199.

71. Cheek and Cheek, *John Mercer Langston*, 62.

72. Taylor, *Frontiers*, 118; Richards, *Gentlemen*, 123. There was also a "Captain Brough" mentioned as leading the white militia in Cincinnati, who became notorious for his unwillingness to keep the peace or defend African American lives and homes during the 1841 race war. See *Liberator* articles cited in note 1 of this chapter.

73. As Robert Parkinson points out in his excellent book *The Common Cause: Creating Race and Nation in the American Revolution* (Chapel Hill: University of North Carolina Press, 2016), using the press to prejudice, divide,

and bring people to violence was an American tradition dating back to the Revolutionary War. But by the 1830s there were many more newspapers and more readers. And newspapers had gained even more power. For the role of newspapers in fomenting these attacks, see Richards, *Gentlemen*.

74. For a strong recent critique of the "uplift" argument, see Ibram Kendi, *Stamped from the Beginning: The Definitive History of Racist Ideas in America* (New York: Nation Books, 2016). For a critique of "uplift" written at the time of these battles against equality, see Hosea Easton's brilliant *A Treatise on the Intellectual Character and Civil and Political Condition of the Colored People of the U. States and the Prejudice Exercised Towards Them* (Philadelphia: Rhistoric Publications, 1969 [1837]).

75. The riots in Hartford, Connecticut, in 1834 and 1835 hit Hosea Easton close to home. For more on Easton and his family, see George R. Price, "The Easton Family of Southeast Massachusetts: The Dynamics Surrounding Five Generations of Human Rights Activism, 1753–1935" (PhD diss., University of Montana, 2006); Hosea Easton, George R. Price, and James Brewer Stewart, *To Heal the Scourge of Prejudice: The Life and Writings of Hosea Easton* (Amherst: University of Massachusetts Press, 1999).

76. Easton, *A Treatise*, 43.

77. Ibid.

78. Information and quote from Richards, *Gentlemen*, 123.

79. See note 1 in this chapter for full citation of sources for this section on the actions of the mob and Wilkerson's defense against them in 1841.

80. Taylor, *Frontiers*, 20–25; John Langston, *From the Virginia Plantation to the National Capital; or, The First and Only Negro Representative in Congress from the Old Dominion* (New York: Johnson Reprint Corp., 1968 [1894]), 64; Cheek and Cheek, *John Mercer Langston*, 59–63; Richards, *Gentlemen*, 122–129; "Riot at Cincinnati," *Liberator*, September 4, 1841; "Riot, Mob, Confusion and Bloodshed," *Liberator*, September 17, 1841; "The Mob," *Liberator*, September 17, 1841; "The Riot in Cincinnati," *Liberator*, September 24, 1841; "Reign of Terror Again in Cincinnati," *Liberator*, September 24, 1841; "Cincinnati Riot," *Liberator*, October 1, 1841; "Selections from the Cincinnati Philanthropist," *Liberator*, October 1, 1841.

Chapter 7: "The right of the people peaceably to assemble"

1. I acknowledge with gratitude the support of the Spencer Foundation in funding this research on integrated and African American educational opportunities in the rural antebellum Northwest Territory states.

2. Union Literary Institute Preservation Society (ULIPS), *Union Literary Institute Board of Managers' Secretary Book: From Original Book Housed at the Indiana Historical Society*, (Indiana: ULIPS, 2001), 39. My grateful thanks to Roane Smothers and the Board of the ULIPS for their tireless efforts to

preserve the history of this extraordinary school and their willingness to share their research with me.

3. ULIPS, "Constitution," *Board of Managers' Secretary Book*, 26–45.

4. The board members in the first few years of the Union Literary Institute's founding changed pretty frequently, but core members included Thornton Alexander (African American, Virginia), William R. J. Clemens (African American and the first board president, born in Indiana but father born in Virginia), Levi Coffin, Nathan Thomas (Quaker, born in Indiana in 1811, but his parents were from the South), David Willcutt (North Carolina, Quaker); ULIPS, *Board of Managers' Secretary Book*, 14–16; Center for Historic Preservation (Ball State University), Randolph County (Indiana), and ULIPS, *Preservation Plan for the Union Literary Institute Building, Randolph County, Indiana* (Muncie, IN: Ball State University, 2010), 13–49; Roane Smothers, "Union Literary Institute National Register of Historic Places Nomination" (unpublished, in author's possession, 2014); US Department of the Interior, Census Office, *Population Schedules of the Seventh Census of the United States, 1850, Indiana, Randolph County and Ohio, Darke County*. For more on the relationship between Quakers and these early African American pioneers to the Northwest Territory states, see Stephen Vincent, *Southern Seed, Northern Soil: African-American Farm Communities in the Midwest, 1765–1900* (Bloomington: Indiana University Press, 1999).

5. ULIPS, "Constitution," *Board of Managers' Secretary Book*, 26–45.

6. Ibid.

7. Valerie Scura Trovato, "Slate Pencils? Education of Free and Enslaved African American Children at the Bray School, Williamsburg, Virginia, 1760–1774" (master's thesis, The College of William and Mary, 2016).

8. Maurice Jackson, *Let This Voice Be Heard: Anthony Benezet, Father of Atlantic Abolitionism* (Philadelphia: University of Pennsylvania Press, 2010), ix–xv, 1–30, 57–70.

9. Ibid., 1–30.

10. For a good overview of the education of free African American children in the antebellum South, see Loren Schweninger, *Black Property Owners in the South, 1790–1915* (Urbana: University of Illinois Press, 1997).

11. David Kantrowitz, *More Than Freedom: Fighting for Black Citizenship in a White Republic, 1829–1889* (New York: Penguin Books, 2012), 26.

12. Leslie Harris, *In the Shadow of Slavery: African Americans in New York City, 1626–1863* (Chicago: University of Chicago Press, 2004), 64–66.

13. Henry Barnard and Moses B. Goodwin, *History of Schools for the Colored Population* (New York: Arno Press, 1969 [1871]), 195.

14. John Hope Franklin, *The Free Negro in North Carolina, 1790–1860* (New York: Russell & Russell, 1969), 171.

15. Barnard and Goodwin, *History of Schools for the Colored Population*, 196; Russell Irvine, *The African American Quest for Institutions of Higher Education Before the Civil War: The Forgotten Histories of the Ashmun Institute,*

Liberia College, and Avery College (Lewiston, NY: Edwin Mellen Press, 2010), 436; "Building to Be Renamed for Pioneer Black Educator Anne Marie Becraft," Georgetown University, www.georgetown.edu/news/anne-marie -becraft-hall; Lacy K. Ford, *Deliver Us from Evil: The Slavery Question in the Old South* (New York: Oxford University Press, 2009), 183–184.

16. See C. L. Glenn, "Enslaved and Free Blacks Before 1862," in *African-American/Afro-Canadian Schooling* (New York: Palgrave Macmillan, 2011).

17. For more on the intersections between education in America and concepts of citizenship, see Carolyn Eastman, *A Nation of Speechifiers: Making an American Public After the Revolution* (Chicago: University of Chicago Press, 2009); Kim Warren, *The Quest for Citizenship: African American and Native American Education in Kansas, 1880–1935* (Chapel Hill: University of North Carolina Press, 2010); Hilary Moss, *Schooling Citizens: The Struggle for African American Education in Antebellum America* (Chicago: University of Chicago Press, 2009).

18. Diana Ross McCain, *To All on Equal Terms: The Life and Legacy of Prudence Crandall* (Canterbury, CT: Prudence Crandall Museum, 2004), 13–15. For more on Prudence Crandall and the work of other women on the antebellum East Coast to educate African American children, see Philip Foner and Josephine F. Pacheco, *Three Who Dared: Prudence Crandall, Margaret Douglass, Myrtilla Miner: Champions of Antebellum Black Education* (London: Greenwood, 1984).

19. Quoted in McCain, *To All*, 27.

20. Ibid., 32–34.

21. Ibid.

22. Ibid., 36–39.

23. Ibid., 40.

24. Irvine, *The African American Quest*, 165–184; Russell Irvine and Donna Zani Dunkerton, "The Noyes Academy, 1834–35: The Road to the Oberlin Collegiate Institute and the Higher Education of African-Americans in the Nineteenth Century," *Western Journal of Black Studies* 22, no. 4 (winter 1998): 260.

25. Irvine, *The African American Quest*, 172–175.

26. "Colored School at Canaan," *Liberator*, September 5, 1835 (accessed on Accessible Archives, August 12, 2016); Manisha Sinha, *The Slave's Cause: A History of Abolition* (New Haven, CT: Yale University Press, 2016), 231; Irvine, *The African American Quest*, 176–177.

27. For more on African Americans achieving higher levels of education in the early years of the United States, see Daniel Harrison, "Southern Presbyterians and the Negro in the Early National Period," *Journal of Negro History* 58, no. 3 (1973): 291–312; ULIPS, *Preservation Plan*, 13–49.

28. "Deeply Interesting Facts," *Philanthropist (1836–1843)*, December 24, 1839, 2. Clarissa Wright's story is drawn from this long and detailed article.

29. Clarissa Wright's report is featured in Susan Wattles, "Education Among Colored People—Report," *Philanthropist (1836–1843)*, November 26,

1839, 1. For more on Clarissa Wright and other Garrisonian white female abolitionists and their teaching roles in African American schools in antebellum Ohio, see Douglas Gamble, "Moral Suasion in the West: Garrisonian Abolitionism, 1831–1861" (PhD diss., Ohio State University, 1973), 143–144. Gamble makes clear that he never found a school where women were on the board, as they were at the Union Literary Institute.

30. For more on Clarissa Wright and her family's abolitionist activities, see Lawrence Goodheart, *Abolitionist, Actuary, Atheist: Elizur Wright and the Reform Impulse* (Kent, OH: Kent State University, 1990).

31. John Melvin Werner, "Race Riots in the United States During the Age of Jackson: 1824–1849" (PhD diss., Indiana University, 1972), 103, 172, 177; Goodheart, *Abolitionist*, 37–39.

32. Northwest Ordinance, July 13, 1787; (National Archives Microfilm Publication M332, roll 9); Miscellaneous Papers of the Continental Congress, 1774–1789; Records of the Continental and Confederation Congresses and the Constitutional Convention, 1774–1789, Record Group 360; National Archives, www.archives.gov/historical-docs/todays-doc/?dod-date=713. Note that this clause in Article 3 of the Ordinance is directly followed by clear proscriptions that "the utmost good faith shall always be observed towards the Indians." Clearly many of the intentions of the 1787 Ordinance were broken where both African-descended and indigenous peoples were concerned. For more on the history of indigenous peoples in the Northwest Territory, see Richard White, *The Middle Ground: Indians, Empires, and Republics in the Great Lakes Region, 1650–1815* (New York: Cambridge University Press, 1991).

33. "Deeply Interesting Facts."

34. Ibid.

35. Taylor, *Frontiers*, 94; "Deeply Interesting Facts." For more on Amzi Barber and the Wright family's involvement in the struggle for equality in Cincinnati and Ohio, see Stacey Robertson, *Betsy Mix Cowles: Champion of Equality* (Boulder, CO: Westview Press, 2014).

36. David Reynolds, *John Brown, Abolitionist: The Man Who Killed Slavery, Sparked the Civil War, and Seeded Civil Rights* (New York: Vintage, 2006), 60.

37. "Deeply Interesting Facts"; Goodheart, *Abolitionist*, 68.

38. Given Clarissa Wright's standing within the Ohio and national abolitionist movement, as well as the fame of the Wright family in general within this movement, news of her murder would have been covered by those presses, and there are no such reports.

39. Blanche Coggan, *Prior Foster, Pioneer Afro-American Educator, First Afro-American to Found and Incorporate an Educational Institution in the Northwest Territory, Woodstock Manual Labor Institute, Addison, Lenawee County, Michigan* (Lansing, MI: J. P. Kaechele, 1969); Richard Sisson, Christian K. Zacher, and Andrew R. L. Cayton, *The American Midwest: An Interpretive Encyclopedia* (Bloomington: Indiana University Press, 2007), 854. Prior Foster opened his school close to the white abolitionist Laura Smith Haviland, who was also planning on opening a school for African Americans. Unfortunately,

allies of Haviland seem to have spread rumors about Foster's school and its finances. These rumors were later proven untrue but did irreparable damage to Foster's school (Coggan, *Prior Foster*, 7–8). See also Shelly McCoy Grissom, "An Examination of a Woman's Life Work: Laura Smith Haviland and the Founding of the Raisin Institute" (PhD diss., Cappella University, 2007).

40. *African Methodist Episcopal Church Review* 8, no. 4 (April 1892), accessed October 17, 2017, http://dbs.ohiohistory.org/africanam/html /page4c71-2.html?ID=2372&Current=P394&View=Text; William Thompson, "Eleutherian Institute," *Indiana Magazine of History* 19, no. 2 (1923): 109–131. Founded around 1849 the Eleutherian Institute was for African Americans only, but it was mixed gender. It faced violent opposition, and some of its first buildings were burned by local prejudiced whites. A mixed-race couple who moved from Mississippi and started supporting the school also found themselves under attack. However, the school's founders and funders persevered, and by 1860 the school was teaching around 150 students. M. W. Montgomery, *History of Jay County, Indiana* (Chicago: Printed for the author by Church, Goodman & Cushing, 1864), 191–195; Carter G. Woodson, *The Education of the Negro Prior to 1861* (New York: Arno Press, 1968), 294. While some historians have made much of Liber College as a pioneering integrated school, founded in Jay County, Indiana, in 1853, records from the time reveal that the school only ever accepted one African American student. When that student was accepted, most of the school's board members and donors were so opposed to his admission that they resigned and withdrew their funding.

41. J. S. H., "Our Coloured Population," *Friend; a Religious and Literary Journal* (December 1840), 100; Richard Folk, "Black Man's Burden in Ohio, 1849–1863" (PhD diss., University of Toledo, 1972), 8–14; Mary Ann Brown, "Vanished Black Rural Communities in Western Ohio," *Perspectives in Vernacular Architecture, I*, ed. Camille Wells (Columbia: University of Missouri Press, 1987), 97–113. Unfortunately, as Augustus Wattles tried to raise funds for their school, he or his allies seem to have decided it would help their cause if they asserted that it was Augustus Wattles himself who had founded the settlement. Land deeds showing African Americans buying land there long before Wattles did disprove this. Other white abolitionists who visited Mercer County and some contemporary newspaper editors also corrected this claim. As the editor of the *Massachusetts Abolitionist* wrote in May 1839, "We presume the *Witness* is not exactly correct here. The colored people have purchased land *for themselves* [original emphasis]. . . . The 'tract' which we think cannot be extensive is solely for the manual labor school. Brother Wattles encourages individuality and independence, and not a common-stock settlement or any thing of the sort" ("Anchoring in the Soil," *Massachusetts Abolitionist*, May 30, 1839, accessed via the Slavery and Abolition, 1789–1887 website of the University of Arkansas). Later historians seem not to have recognized these facts or corrections, however, and some perpetrated the myth of a "utopian" community for African Americans paternalistically founded by the white Wattles.

42. Woodson, *The Education of the Negro*, 294; J. S. H., "Our Coloured Population," 100.

43. Ross Bagby, "The Randolph Slave Saga: Communities in Collision" (PhD diss., Ohio State University, 1998). Because of the amount of attention paid to the Underground Railroad and the communities that whites tried to create as homes for large groups of people newly released from bondage, this study avoids focusing on those two aspects of life for African Americans in the Northwest Territory states. For overviews of two manumission settlements, see Ross Bagby, "The Randolph Slave Saga," and Carrie Eldridge, *Cabell County's Empire for Freedom: The Manumission of Sampson Sanders' Slaves* (Bowie, MD: Willow Bend Books, 1999). For African Americans' role in the Underground Railroad in the Northwest Territory states, see Cheryl LaRoche, *Free Black Communities and the Underground Railroad: The Geography of Resistance* (Urbana: University of Illinois Press, 2013); Keith Griffler, *Front Line of Freedom: African Americans and the Forging of the Underground Railroad in the Ohio Valley* (Lexington: University Press of Kentucky, 2004).

44. Quoted in Bagby, "The Randolph Slave Saga," 164–165. Bagby points out that while the white men who wrote this document claimed first right and settlement to that county, most of them had only settled there after 1840, including the two county officials and Congressman Sawyer, long after the African American pioneers had settled that frontier and established good farms there. This pattern of prejudiced whites asserting their roots in a community and attacking white and black equal rights proponents as "outsiders," even though they were often there before the prejudiced whites, has a long history in the North in both the nineteenth and twentieth centuries. It is a social pattern well worth more study.

45. Frazer Wilson, *History of Darke County, Ohio: From Its Earliest Settlement to the Present Time in Two Volumes: Also Biographical Sketches of Many Representative Citizens of the County* (Greenville, OH: Darke County Genealogical Society, 1997 [1914]), 554–555; ULIPS, *Preservation Plan*, 13–49; Smothers, "Union Literary Institute National Register of Historic Places Nomination"; US Department of the Interior, Census Office, *Population Schedules of the Seventh Census of the United States, 1850, Indiana, Randolph County and Ohio, Darke County*; Deborah Rotman, *African-American and Quaker Farmers in East Central Indiana: Social, Political and Economic Aspects of Life in Nineteenth-Century Rural Communities: Randolph County, Indiana* (Muncie, IN: Archaeological Resources Management Service, Ball State University, 1998), 46–48.

46. While the mechanical reaper/harvester machines were invented in the United States in the 1830s, they were not utilized in the Northwest Territory states until the 1850s, which meant that there was an intensive need for labor during harvest time, especially for grain. For more on farming in Ohio and the Northwest Territory states at this time, see Graeme Quick and Wesley Fisher Buchele, *The Grain Harvesters* (St. Joseph, MI: American Society

of Agricultural Engineers, 1978); C. H. Danhof, *Change in Agriculture: The Northern United States, 1820–1870* (Cambridge, MA: Harvard University Press, 1969), 228–250. My thanks to Richard Roosenberg of Tillers International for sharing this secondary information and for the generous sharing of his hands-on research into the labor involved in harvesting grain with a variety of scythes.

47. Darrel Dexter, "Arthur and Patience Hawley Allen," *Free African Americans*, last modified November 2004, accessed October 17, 2017, www .freeafricanamericans.com/free_AAllen.htm.

48. "Conventions by Year," Colored Conventions: Bringing Nineteenth-Century Black Organizing to Life, accessed October 17, 2017, http:// coloredconventions.org/convention-by-year. For more information on these conventions, please see this excellent website. I am very grateful to the team at the University of Delaware for creating this important website on the antebellum black convention movement—they are truly continuing the work of these early American activists.

49. Derrick Spires, "Imagining a State of Fellow Citizens: Early African American Politics of Publicity in the Black State Conventions," in *Early African American Print Culture*, ed. Lara Langer Cohen and Jordan Alexander Stein (Philadelphia: University of Pennsylvania Press, 2012), 274–289.

50. Ibid.

51. "Address of the State Convention," *Palladium of Liberty*, Columbus, Ohio, November 13, 1844, front page, accessed at http://coloredconventions .org/files/original/945c2778ed57366af6d37c528e85f036.pdf.

52. While by no means complete, this table gives a sense of the involvement of African American farmers as leaders in state conventions. Attendees were rarely mentioned by name, so these are only people in leadership positions. I am greatly grateful to Tsione Wolde-Michael for her assistance in researching these convention attendees.

Cursory List of African American Leaders of Midwestern Black State Conventions with Land Holdings Worth More Than $1,000

Name	Town/Township/County	Value of Land (Census Year)	Conventions Attended
Rev. William Chandler	Lost Creek, Vigo	$3,000 (1850)	Indiana, 1851
Noah Nooks	Milton/Jackson	$3,000 (1850)	Ohio, 1849
Lewis Adams	Concord/Champaign	$1,500 (1850)	Ohio, 1849, 1852
John Mercer Langston	Brownhelm/Lorain	$4,590 (N/A*)	Ohio, 1849–1865

Name	Town/Township/County	Value of Land (Census Year)	Conventions Attended
Thomas Brown	Russia/Lorain	$1,000 (1850)	Ohio, 1850
George Adams	Wayne/Pickaway	$1,800 (1850)	Ohio, 1850
P. Letchford/Plesant Leitchford	Perry/Franklin	$8,000 (1850)	Ohio, 1850
Cyrus King	Green/Clinton	$4,120 (1850)	Ohio, 1852
David Barnett	Pebble/Pike	$1,000 (1860)	Ohio, 1852
William Morgan	Monroe/Logan	$1,160 (1860)	Ohio, 1852

*John Mercer Langston is not recorded in the 1850 or the 1860 census in Lorain County, so land values are taken from local records found in William F. Cheek and Aimee Lee Cheek, John Mercer Langston and the Fight for Black Freedom, 1829–65 (Urbana: University of Illinois Press, 1996), 179–180, 244.

Sources: Philip Foner and George Walker, ed., Proceedings of the Black State Conventions, 1840–1865 (Philadelphia: Temple University Press, 1979), 1:176–177, 218–238, 241–256, 274–294; US Department of the Interior, Census Office, Population Schedules of the Seventh Census of the United States, 1850, Ohio, Vigo County, Lost Creek Township, 174; Ohio, Jackson County, Milton Township, 314; Ohio, Champaign County, Concord Township, 318; Ohio, Lorain County, Russia Township, 259; Ohio, Pickaway County, Wayne Township, 127; Ohio, Perry County, Franklin Township, 239; US Department of the Interior, Census Office, Population Schedules of the Eighth Census of the United States, 1860, Ohio, Clinton County, Green Township, 166; Ohio, Pike County, Pebble Township, 428; Ohio, Logan County, Monroe Township, 179. (All census records were sourced from Ancestry.com [Provo, Utah], Ancestry.com Operations, Inc., 2009, http://search.ancestrylibrary.com/group/usfedcen/US_Federal_Census_Collection.aspx.)

53. Foner and Walker, Proceedings of the Black State Conventions, 1:232–233.

54. Ibid.; North Star, November 10, 1848, in Smothers, "Union Literary Institute National Register of Historic Places Nomination." For more on Douglass's daughter, Rosetta, and her experience in the schools of Rochester, New York, see Leigh Fought, Women in the World of Frederick Douglass (New York: Oxford University Press, 2017), 156–158.

55. See map at the beginning of this book.

56. Dana Weiner, Race and Rights: Fighting Slavery and Prejudice in the Old Northwest, 1830–1870 (DeKalb: Northern Illinois University Press, 2013), 159.

57. Weiner, Race and Rights, 151–162; "Madison County," Early Black Settlements, Indiana Historical Society, accessed September 13, 2017, www.indianahistory.org/our-collections/reference/early-black-settlements/madison-county#.WkvFZsaZM0Q; US Department of the Interior, Census Office, Population Schedules of the Sixth Census of the United States, 1840, Indiana, Madison County. As these sources make clear, there were a few African

Americans living in Madison County by 1840, but none of them were land-owning farmers, and one was actually held enslaved. By 1840 African Americans had proven themselves eager to settle and farm good land in the lower Northwest Territory states of Ohio, Indiana, and Illinois. Research in Indiana on rural African American antebellum settlements has shown that if, by 1850, a county in that state did not have any African American farmers, it was because of the concerted effort of whites in those counties to use the prejudiced laws of their state—and often violence as well—to drive out the African Americans who were there when the prejudiced whites arrived and to repel any further African American settlers. Further research in local records for the enforcement of prejudiced Black Code laws, as well as the use of violence, is needed to determine the extent of this pattern. However, historians of this region during this settlement period should assume that if by 1850 a rural county in Ohio, Indiana, or Illinois had no African American residents, some form of prejudice was at work during a period when so many African American farmers were intent upon integrating those states. I am grateful to Wilma Gibbs Moore, head archivist of the Indiana Historical Society's African American collection, for spearheading this important research in Indiana and making this point to me.

58. ULIPS, "Constitution," *Board of Managers' Secretary Book*, 26–45.

59. Ibid.

60. Genevieve Haas, "The Brief, but Courageous Life of the Noyes Academy," *Dartmouth Life*, December 2005, accessed October 17, 2017, www .dartmouth.edu/~dartlife/archives/15-5/noyes.html.

61. ULIPS, "Constitution," *Board of Managers' Secretary Book*, 44.

62. Ibid.

63. Ibid., 42.

Chapter 8: "For taking away our Charters, …"

1. Cheryl LaRoche, *Free Black Communities and the Underground Railroad: The Geography of Resistance* (Urbana: University of Illinois Press, 2013), 53–54, 76–77, 118–121; William Still, *The Underground Rail Road: A Record of Facts, Authentic Narratives, Letters, &c.* (Philadelphia: Porter & Coates, 1872), 27–29 (accessed via HathiTrust on the Harvard HOLLIS website).

2. Emma Lou Thornbrough, *The Negro in Indiana Before 1900: A Study of a Minority* (Bloomington: Indiana University Press, 1957), 114–115.

3. LaRoche, *Free Black Communities*, 118–121; Thornbrough, *The Negro in Indiana*, 114–115.

4. Thornbrough, *The Negro in Indiana*, 106–118; Silvana Siddali, *Frontier Democracy: Constitutional Conventions in the Old Northwest* (New York: Cambridge University Press, 2016), 161, 240, 283, 378. There has long been an assumption among most historians that these prejudiced laws in the Northwest Territory states did not matter very much or had little effect on African Americans in those states. To be fair, many of these historians assumed that there

were very few African Americans living in that region, so there were few people to be affected by these laws. Others have argued that since state populations of African Americans did not massively decline in response to these laws, these prejudiced laws must not have been upheld very consistently. But historians have not fully investigated just how many people were discouraged or actually prohibited from settling in those states and can never know how many more may have come if those laws had not been passed. Until the local records of antebellum African American settlements can be carefully studied in the Northwest Territory states, we cannot assume that these laws were not used and did not have a powerful impact. For excellent and well-researched exceptions to this stance among historians, see Stephen Vincent, *Southern Seed, Northern Soil: African-American Farm Communities in the Midwest, 1765–1900* (Bloomington: Indiana University Press, 1999), and LaRoche, *Free Black Communities*.

5. Frederick Douglass, November 27, 1851, quoted in Leon Litwack, *North of Slavery: The Negro in the Free States, 1790–1860* (Chicago: University of Chicago Press, 1971), 249. For more on the effects of the Fugitive Slave Law of 1850 on African American equal rights advocates in the Northwest Territory, see Aimee Lee Cheek and William F. Cheek, *John Mercer Langston and the Fight for Black Freedom, 1829–65* (Urbana: University of Illinois Press, 1996), 169–174, 183–189. For more on its effects in the Northeast, see Eric Foner's excellent *Gateway to Freedom: The Hidden History of the Underground Railroad* (Oxford: Oxford University Press, 2015).

6. Philip Foner and George E. Walker, *Proceedings of the Black State Conventions, 1840–1865* (Philadelphia: Temple University Press, 1979), 1:262, 1:256.

7. Arlene Polk, "The Truth About Joshua Lyles: A Free African American Settler of Lyles Station, Indiana," *Traces of Indiana & Midwestern History* 25, no. 4 (2013): 32–37. "America: History and Life with Full Text," EBSCO, www.ebsco.com/products/research-databases/america-history-and-life-with-full-text; US Department of the Interior, Census Office, *Population Schedules of the Seventh Census of the United States, 1850, Indiana, Gibson County.*

8. Gil R. Stormont, *History of Gibson County, Indiana: Her People, Industries and Institutions, with Biographical Sketches of Representative Citizens and Genealogical Records of Many of the Old Families* (Indianapolis: B. F. Bowen, 1914), 236–238.

9. Ibid., 231–232.

10. While it is true that there are many myths surrounding the Underground Railroad in the Northwest Territory states, I am somewhat at a loss to understand why some historians have argued that the African American abolitionist William Still partly or wholly fictionalized the account of Seth Concklin's rescue of Peter Still's family, when there is so much evidence to corroborate the event. This could be because some of the evidence comes from local and fairly obscure sources, such as local Evansville newspapers, the Gibson County history written by the Stormonts' son Gil, and the personal autobiography later published by the Reverend Johnston. The fact that both Seth

Concklin and the Reverend Johnston separately name Charles Grier as the "colored" conductor who brought Concklin and the Still family to the Stormonts is also strong evidence that the story is true, for the Griers had been able to protect the secret of their activities up until that point, and it is unlikely that William Still would have known of Charles Grier unless Seth Concklin had indeed written to him about Charles Grier.

11. US Department of the Interior, Census Office, *Population Schedules of the Seventh Census of the United States, 1850, Indiana, Gibson County.*

12. Still, *The Underground Rail Road*, 27; Stormont, *History of Gibson County*, 224–225, 232.

13. For Concklin's frustration in arranging help north of the Ohio River, see Seth Concklin, letter sent from Princeton, Indiana, February 18, 1851, quoted in Still, *The Underground Rail Road*, 28–29; Nathan R. Johnston, *Looking Back from the Sunset Land; or, People Worth Knowing* (Oakland, CA, 1898), 120–121.

14. Kate Pickard and William Henry Furness, *The Kidnapped and the Ransomed: Being the Personal Recollections of Peter Still and His Wife "Vina," After Forty Years of Slavery* (Syracuse, NY: W. T. Hamilton, 1856), 245–255.

15. For more on the growing restrictions on freeing enslaved people in the slave South in the 1850s, see Thomas Morris, *Southern Slavery and the Law, 1619–1860* (Chapel Hill: University of North Carolina Press, 1999).

16. Still, *The Underground Rail Road*, 24.

17. Ibid.

18. Ibid., 25.

19. Seth Concklin, letter sent from Princeton, Indiana, February 18, 1851, quoted in Still, *The Underground Rail Road*, 28–29; Johnston, *Looking Back*, 120–121.

20. Siddali, *Frontier*, 298–299; Thornbrough, *The Negro in Indiana*, 64–69.

21. Siddali, *Frontier*, 306–308; Stephen Middleton, *The Black Laws in the Old Northwest: A Documentary History* (Westport, CT: Greenwood Press, 1993), 291–294.

22. Quoted in Siddali, *Frontier*, 274, 278.

23. Thornbrough, *The Negro in Indiana*, 79–80, 144–146. See map for African American landowning farmers in Indiana during the period this new state constitution was being drafted. For other entrepreneurs in Indiana, see Thornbrough, *The Negro in Indiana*, 139–142; Joe William Trotter Jr., *River Jordan: African American Urban Life in the Ohio Valley* (Lexington: University Press of Kentucky, 2015), 37–42.

24. Foner and Walker, *Proceedings of the Black State Conventions*, 176–177; Vincent, *Southern Seed*, xii.

25. "At a Called Meeting for Sufferings of Indiana Yearly Meeting Held 25th of 11th Month 1850," Indiana Yearly Meeting for Sufferings Minutes, Indiana Yearly Meeting Archives, Friends Collection and College Archive, Earlham College, Richmond, Indiana. My grateful thanks to Dr. Thomas Hamm

for his able assistance and extraordinary efforts to preserve and disseminate the history of Quakers in the Northwest Territory states.

26. Lacy K. Ford, *Deliver Us from Evil: The Slavery Question in the Old South* (New York: Oxford University Press, 2009), 9–10; Siddali, *Frontier*, 270–272.

27. Still, *The Underground Rail Road*, 28–29.

28. Johnston, *Looking Back*, 119–131.

29. Charles Grier, Census of Agriculture, 1850, Franklin-Hamilton Counties, reel 3890, Indiana State Archives, Indianapolis, Indiana.

30. Pickard and Furness, *The Kidnapped and the Ransomed*, 281, 286.

31. Still, *The Underground Rail Road*, 30.

32. Ibid., 24, 30.

33. Seth Concklin, letter sent from Princeton, Indiana, February 18, 1851, quoted in Still, *The Underground Rail Road*, 28–29. Seth Concklin consistently misspelled the Stormonts' last name as "Stormon" in his letters to William Still, just as he often misspelled the Griers' last name as "Greer."

34. Johnston, *Looking Back*, 121.

35. Ibid., 121–122.

36. Pickard and Furness, *The Kidnapped and the Ransomed*, 402.

37. Still, *The Underground Rail Road*, 26–31; Pickard and Furness, *The Kidnapped and the Ransomed*, 402–409.

38. Pickard and Furness, *The Kidnapped and the Ransomed*, 400; Still, *The Underground Rail Road*, 34. The Evansville press would later praise Sheriff Gavitt for his role in capturing the "slave stealer" Seth Concklin; see Chapter 9.

39. N. R. Johnston, letter, Evansville, Indiana, March 31, 1851, quoted in Still, *The Underground Rail Road*, 30–31.

40. LaRoche, *Free Black Communities*, 6.

41. Johnston, letter, Evansville, Indiana, March 31, 1851, quoted in Still, *The Underground Rail Road*, 30–31; Pickard and Furness, *The Kidnapped and the Ransomed*, 400–408. Of course, the irony of this (as abolitionists who came down to Evansville to investigate the incident later pointed out) was that Sheriff Gavitt was willing to use the "testimony" of an African American, Levin Still, against a white man, Seth Concklin, which was technically illegal in Indiana at that time.

42. Johnston, letter, Evansville, Indiana, March 31, 1851, quoted in Still, *The Underground Rail Road*, 31.

43. Still, *The Underground Rail Road*, 31.

44. Pickard and Furness, *The Kidnapped and the Ransomed*, 339–342.

45. Ibid., 349–352.

46. Ibid.

47. Ibid., 307–362, 366–367.

48. Thornbrough, *The Negro in Indiana*, 69–70. These registries are a painful part of Indiana's past. When I first did research in Gibson County, Indiana, the "Negro Registry" book—a beautifully bound volume—was hidden

away in a broom closet under a stack of old phone books in the basement of the Princeton library. I will always be deeply grateful to the library volunteer who showed it to me when I asked if they had such a registry. She admitted that it had long been hidden away. A few years later the library staff had the courage to face the past and make the book public, having it scanned and put online for all to see.

49. Gibson County Negro Registry, Princeton Public Library, Princeton, Indiana, 1851.

50. Ibid.

51. 1850 Agricultural Census, Daviess County, Indiana, US Seventh Census of Agriculture, Indiana–1850, 401-E-4, Clark-Dearborn Counties, Reel 3888, State of Indiana Archives, Indianapolis, Indiana.

52. *History of Knox and Daviess Counties, Indiana: From the Earliest Time to the Present; with Biographical Sketches, Reminiscences, Notes, etc.; Together with an Extended History of the Colonial Days of Vincennes, and Its Progress Down to the Formation of the State Government* (Chicago, IL: Goodspeed Pub. Co., 1886), 769. Accessed on HathiTrust website via the Harvard HOLLIS website.

53. Lori Jacobi, "More Than a Church: The Educational Role of the African Methodist Episcopal Church in Indiana, 1844–1861," *Indiana's African-American Heritage: Essays from Black History News & Notes*, ed. Wilma Gibbs (Indianapolis: Indiana Historical Society, 1993), 3–18; Thornbrough, *The Negro in Indiana*, 151; LaRoche, *Free Black Communities*, 30, 134–137, 139–140, 142, 165; Sundiata Keita Cha-Jua, *America's First Black Town: Brooklyn, Illinois, 1830–1915* (Urbana: University of Illinois Press, 2002), 37–39; Vincent, *Southern Seed*, 70; Coy Robbins, *Forgotten Hoosiers: African Heritage in Orange County, Indiana* (Bowie, MD: Heritage Books, 1994), 82–83.

54. Ronald Palmer, "History: AME Bishop William Paul Quinn: Notes Toward a Biographical Chronology of an American Original," *African Methodist Episcopal Church Review* 120, no. 395 (July–September 2004): 40–61.

55. Vincent, *Southern Seed*, 70.

56. Palmer, "Bishop William Paul Quinn," 40–61.

57. "Communicated," *Princeton Clarion*, May 30, 1872, front page.

58. *History of Knox and Daviess Counties, Indiana*, 770–771.

59. Thornbrough, *The Negro in Indiana*, 72.

60. *History of Knox and Daviess Counties, Indiana*, 742.

61. 1850 Agricultural Census, Daviess County, Indiana.

62. Graeme Quick and Wesley Fisher Buchele, *The Grain Harvesters* (St. Joseph, MI: American Society of Agricultural Engineers, 1978), 39–62.

Chapter 9: "A history of repeated injuries and usurpations"

1. The following detailed narrative of this attack is drawn from Randy K. Mills, "'They Defended Themselves Nobly': A Story of African American

Empowerment in Evansville, Indiana, 1857," *Black History News & Notes* (August 2005): 2–8; Emma Lou Thornbrough, *The Negro in Indiana Before 1900: A Study of a Minority* (Bloomington: Indiana University Press, 1957), 130–131; *Daily Enquirer*, July 22, 24, 28, 29, 31, 1857, August 1, 2, 1857; *Daily Journal*, July 22, 23, 24, 27, 28, 29, 30, 1857, August 1, 1857 (microfilm newspaper collection, Willard Library, Evansville, Indiana). The details of this attack were well documented in local newspapers in Evansville at the time. The Democrat *Daily Enquirer* was overtly prejudiced and directly involved in fomenting these attacks on the Lyles family and other African Americans around them. The "Whig" *Daily Journal* was more moderate, making its insidious and prejudiced reporting on the Lyles family damaging in different ways from that of the *Daily Enquirer*, but still damaging. While both newspapers were prejudiced against African Americans, some details of the attack on the Lyles homestead seem fairly truthful based on corroboration by surviving subsequent court records. My thanks to Shannon Grayson at the Evansville Public Library for sharing Randy Mills's article from their collection, and an especial thanks to Stanley Schmitt at the Willard Library in Evansville for his heroic work in locating and preserving primary archival material on the Lyles family in Vanderburgh County, as well as generously sharing that material with me.

2. B. N. Griffing, "Union Township," in *Griffing's Atlas of Vanderburgh County* (Philadelphia: D. J. Lake & Co., 1880); Surveyor's Record Book B, p. 47, Vanderburgh County Courthouse, Evansville, Indiana.

3. "U.S., Indexed County Land Ownership Maps, 1860–1918," Ancestry.com, accessed 2010, https://search.ancestry.com/search/db.aspx?dbid=1127. Original data: Various publishers of county land ownership atlases, microfilmed by the Library of Congress, Washington, DC; US Department of the Interior, Census Office, *Population Schedules of the Seventh Census of the United States, 1850, Union Township, Vanderburgh County, Indiana*; Conevery Bolton Valenčius, *The Health of the Country: How American Settlers Understood Themselves and Their Land* (New York: Basic Books, 2004), 1–15.

4. Arlene Blanks Polk, "The Truth About Joshua Lyles: A Free African American Settler of Lyles Station, Indiana," *Traces of Indiana & Midwestern History* 25, no. 4 (October 2013): 32–37; Gibson County Negro Registry, 1851, Princeton Public Library, Princeton, Indiana. The Gibson County Negro Registry also shows that members of the Lyles family based in Gibson County and Vanderburgh County stayed for long visits with each other. The Evansville newspapers published bitter complaints against the whites around the Lyles family, furious that they were willing to move in around African Americans and work with them. See front page, first column of the *Daily Enquirer*, July 28, 1857.

5. Christian Bippus, Recorder, Register of Marks, Union Township, Daniel Lyles, Vanderburgh County Courthouse, Evansville, Indiana, 1854.

6. Mills, "'They Defended Themselves Nobly,'" 2.

7. For an excellent scholarly overview of the *Dred Scott* decision, see David Thomas Konig, Paul Finkelman, and Christopher Alan Bracey, *The Dred*

Scott Case: Historical and Contemporary Perspectives on Race and Law (Athens: Ohio University Press, 2010).

8. For an intimate and well-researched history of Harriet and Dred Scott and their trials during their fight for their family's freedom, as well as their life in the Northwest Territory states, see Lea VanderVelde, *Mrs. Dred Scott: A Life on Slavery's Frontier* (Oxford: Oxford University Press, 2009), which informs much of this section. For an overview of the lives of African Americans, both enslaved and free, in eighteenth- and nineteenth-century Saint Louis, see Julie Winch, *The Clamorgans: One Family's History of Race in America* (New York: Hill and Wang, 2011).

9. "The Dred Scott Decision: Opinion of Chief Justice Taney," Library of Congress, accessed August 18, 2017, www.loc.gov/resource/llst.022.

10. Gene A. Smith, *The Slaves' Gamble: Choosing Sides in the War of 1812* (New York: Palgrave Macmillan, 2013), 5–32; William Cooper Nell and Harriet Beecher Stowe, *The Colored Patriots of the American Revolution: With Sketches of Several Distinguished Colored Persons: To Which Is Added a Brief Survey of the Condition and Prospects of Colored Americans* (Santa Maria, CA: Janaway Publishing, 2010 [1855]); "The Dred Scott Decision: Opinion of Chief Justice Taney."

11. *Daily Enquirer,* July 22, 24, 28, 1857; *Daily Journal,* July 22, 23, 24, 27, 28, 1857 (microfilm newspaper collection, Willard Library, Evansville, Indiana). See note 1 in this chapter for sources.

12. Quoted in Brent Campney, "'The Peculiar Climate of This Region': The 1854 Cairo Lynching and the Historiography of Racist Violence Against Blacks in Illinois," *Journal of the Illinois State Historical Society (1998–)* 107, no. 2 (2014): 145, doi:10.5406/jillistathistsoc.107.2.0143Campney.

13. Joseph Spencer's death was reported in many newspapers, some calling it a "tragedy." This was a notable act of violence, and it was reported in papers from Saint Louis to Cleveland. Many report that he was suicidal at the time of the event, using a barrel of dynamite to threaten those who would attack him. However, further research into Joseph Spencer and this case in court and local records is called for to bring all the facts to light.

14. *Daily Journal,* July 29, 1857; Kate E. R. Pickard and William Henry Furness, *The Kidnapped and the Ransomed: Being the Personal Recollections of Peter Still and His Wife "Vina," After Forty Years of Slavery* (Syracuse, NY: W. T. Hamilton, 1856), 401–409; William Still, *The Underground Rail Road: A Record of Facts, Authentic Narratives, Letters, &c.* (Philadelphia: Porter & Coates, 1872), 26–31; Mills, "'They Defended Themselves Nobly,'" 2–5.

15. Horace Plummer, the Lyles family's lawyer, was excoriated in the Evansville newspapers for his belief in equality and his courageous defense of the Lyles men.

16. "Nigger vs. White Man," *Daily Enquirer,* July 24, 1857, front page (microfilm newspaper collection, Willard Library, Evansville, Indiana).

17. *Vanderburgh Circuit Order Book J,* Vanderburgh County Courthouse, Evansville, Indiana, 1857, 469, 485, 493–494, 497–498; *Vanderburgh Circuit*

Order Book K, Vanderburgh County Courthouse, Evansville, Indiana, 1858, 2, 57–58, 60, 61, 66, 68, 75, 82, 152. There seem to have been three separate hearings involving the Lyles family in 1857 and 1858 surrounding these incidents. The first was their initial hearing for bail. The second was a full trial involving Alexander Maddox/Maddux and five other men, with charges against the Lyles men for assault and battery with attempt to kill in which the Lyles men were found not guilty. The third seems to have involved the attack on the Lyles family home. According to Stanley Schmitt, head archivist and librarian of the Willard Library in Evansville, who has been working to locate and preserve these documents, the judge may have allowed the Lyles family to bring charges against the men who attacked them, although this would have broken Indiana law at this time. Further research is needed into these extensive court documents for the full story.

18. *Daily Enquirer*, July 24, 1857.

19. Darrel Bigham, *We Ask Only a Fair Trial: A History of the Black Community of Evansville, Indiana* (Bloomington: Indiana University Press, 1987), 15.

20. To this day oral traditions about this attack have been preserved among the African American families in Lyles Station. I am grateful to Stanley Madison for sharing this information.

21. Benjamin Drew, *A North-Side View of Slavery. The Refugee: or, The Narratives of Fugitive Slaves in Canada. Related by Themselves, with an Account of the History and Condition of the Colored Population of Upper Canada* (New York: Negro Universities Press, 1968), 189–191.

22. Ibid.

23. Ibid., 189–191. For more testimony from African Americans moving into Canada after the passing of the Fugitive Slave Law of 1850, see ibid., 276, 279–280.

24. Campney, "'The Peculiar Climate of This Region,'" 143–170; Dana Weiner, *Race and Rights: Fighting Slavery and Prejudice in the Old Northwest, 1830–1870* (DeKalb: Northern Illinois University Press, 2013), 209.

25. What happened to the Lyles family in Vanderburgh County does not seem to have been unique. There are troubling reports in both Indiana and Ohio of entire settlements disappearing or becoming much smaller during this time. While some African American farmers may have decided to leave voluntarily, mob violence often drove people from their homes. In Pebble Township, Pike County, Ohio, whites organized violent attacks against African American farmers at this time, including burning down the home of the African American farmer Minor Muntz. See "Pee Pee Settlement, Ohio History Central," Ohio History Connection, accessed October 12, 2017, www.ohiohistory central.org/w/Pee_Pee_Settlement.

Meanwhile, in Indiana, free African Americans residing in the large, established African American farming settlement on the Franklin and Decatur County line, who predated most white settlers in that area, were driven out by white violence. This settlement started close to the Whitewater River before statehood in 1816. By 1850, 270 African Americans were counted as living there. Around the time of the *Dred Scott* decision, the entire settlement was forced to leave. The Snellings were some of the most established families of that settlement, and by 1860 they were in Cass County, Michigan. See the excellent website by the Indiana Historical Society on African American rural communities. For Decatur County, see www.indianahistory.org /our-collections/reference/early-black-settlements/decatur-county#.WShm TBiZN8c; for Franklin County, see www.indianahistory.org/our-collections /reference/early-black-settlements/franklin-county#.WShnZhiZN8c.

For more on the rise of violence against African Americans in Illinois, see Campney, "'The Peculiar Climate of This Region'"; Christopher Hays, "Way Down in Egypt Land: Conflict and Community in Cairo, Illinois, 1850–1910" (PhD diss., University of Missouri, Columbia, 1996). For more on the importance of movement to freedom, see William Cohen, *At Freedom's Edge: Black Mobility and the Southern White Quest for Racial Control, 1861–1915* (Baton Rouge: Louisiana State University Press, 1997).

26. Eugene Berwanger, *The Frontier Against Slavery: Western Anti-Negro Prejudice and the Slavery Extension Controversy* (Urbana: University of Illinois Press, 2002), 60–67. For more on African Americans in the territories and states west of the Rockies in the nineteenth century, see Quintard Taylor's groundbreaking *In Search of the Racial Frontier: African Americans in the American West, 1528–1990* (New York: W. W. Norton, 1999).

27. Laurent Dubois, *Avengers of the New World: The Story of the Haitian Revolution* (Cambridge, MA: Belknap Press of Harvard University Press, 2004), 197.

28. John Quincy Adams, quoted in Clayton Cramer, *Black Demographic Data, 1790–1860: A Sourcebook* (Westport, CT: Greenwood Press, 1997). 44.

29. Cramer, *Black Demographic Data*, 44–45.

30. Ibid.

31. Cohen, *At Freedom's Edge*, 1–30. For more on the importance of landownership to this free black diaspora, see Stephen A. Vincent, *Southern Seed, Northern Soil: African-American Farm Communities in the Midwest, 1765–1900* (Bloomington: Indiana University Press, 1999); Cramer, *Black Demographic Data*, 113, 114. This free African American move to frontiers, or borderlands, of the nation in the 1850s in order to find a space for equality points to a rich vein within the academic field of borderland studies that could well produce interesting new findings.

32. Marcia Sawyer, "Surviving Freedom: African American Farm Households in Cass County, Michigan, 1832–1880" (PhD diss., Michigan State University, 1990), 85–86, 89; Anna-Lisa Cox, *A Stronger Kinship* (Boston, MA: Little, Brown, 2006), 47–48; Clarence Knuth, "Early Immigration and Current Residential Patterns of Negroes in Southwestern Michigan" (PhD diss., University of Michigan, 1969); "Chain Lake Missionary Baptist Church Records," Michigan State University Archives, Lansing, Michigan, http://archives.msu.edu/findaid/190.html.

33. Sawyer, "Surviving Freedom," 85–86, 89; Weiner, *Race and Rights*, 208–209; Thomas M. Cooley, *The Compiled Laws of the State of Michigan* (Lansing, MI: Hosmer & Kerr, State Printers and Binders, 1857); Roy Finkenbine, "A Beacon of Liberty on the Great Lakes: Race, Slavery and the Law in Antebellum Michigan," in *The History of Michigan Law*, ed. Paul Finkelman (Athens: Ohio University Press, 2006), 83–107. Note that the speech made just before this law was passed passionately opposed the 1850 Fugitive Slave Law, attacking it as trampling Michigan's state's rights. This suggests that the law granting African Americans this limited voting right may well have been a response to the 1850 Fugitive Slave Law.

34. US Department of the Interior, Census Office, *Population Schedules of the Eighth Census of the United States, 1860, Michigan, Cass County*; George Hesslink and Joanne M. Hesslink, *Black Neighbours: Negroes in a Northern Rural Community* (Indianapolis: Bobbs-Merrill, 1974), 31, 37; H. Robert Baker, *The Rescue of Joshua Glover: A Fugitive Slave, the Constitution, and the Coming of the Civil War* (Athens: Ohio University Press, 2007).

35. The African American Stewart family were the first pioneers to buy federal land in Forest Township, Bad Ax County, Wisconsin, quickly followed by many other long-free families, such as the Bartons, Robertses, Allens, and Nolcoxes. US Department of the Interior, Census Office, *Population Schedules of the Eighth Census of the United States, 1860, Wisconsin, Bad Ax, Forest*, 136; Lynne Heasley, *A Thousand Pieces of Paradise: Landscape and Property in the Kickapoo Valley* (Madison: University of Wisconsin Press, 2005), 98; Zachary Cooper, *Black Settlers in Rural Wisconsin* (Madison: State Historical Society of Wisconsin, 1977), 5–6; *History of Vernon County, Wisconsin* (Springfield, IL: Union Pub. Co., 1884), 508, 510; US Department of the Interior, Census Office, *Population Schedules of the Seventh Census of the United States, 1850, Illinois, St. Clair, Ridge Prairie*, 478; Jordon Dodd, "Illinois Marriages, 1790–1860," Ancestry Library Edition, accessed June 12, 2016, https://search.ancestry .com/search/db.aspx?dbid=2086. While Zachary Cooper claims that Wesley Barton became the first African American postmaster in the United States, the first African American postmaster was James Mason, who founded his post office in Sunnyside, Arkansas. See Deanna Boyd and Kendra Chen, "The History and Experience of African Americans in America's Postal Service," Smithsonian National Postal Museum, accessed November 9, 2015, https: //postalmuseum.si.edu/AfricanAmericanhistory/p16.html. And Post Office petition records at the National Archives show that it was not Wesley Barton who founded a post office in Wisconsin, but his son, in 1870.

36. US Department of the Interior, Census Office, *Population Schedules of the Eighth Census of the United States, 1860, Wisconsin, Oconto County, Peshtigo Township*. William Welch (from New York) married to Sarah (from Canada) in Brothertown Township, Calumet County; Pascal Menard (M from Wisconsin) married to Mary (W from Wisconsin), Prairie du Chien Township, Crawford County; Mather Robinson (M from Virginia) married to Emeline (W from Virginia), Plymouth Township, Rock County.

37. Ibid.

38. John Matsui, "'We See What Our Fathers Did Not': Interracial Friendship in the Millenarian Atlantic World, 1816–1866" (PhD diss., Johns Hopkins University, 2013). Matsui details the terrible attacks on Professor William Allen and Maria King when they were married in Fulton, New York, in 1852 (349–358).

39. Thornbrough, *The Negro in Indiana*, 125–126.

40. Quoted in Stephen Middleton, *The Black Laws in the Old Northwest: A Documentary History* (Westport, CT: Greenwood Press, 1993), 154.

41. Aimee Lee Cheek and William F. Cheek, *John Mercer Langston and the Fight for Black Freedom, 1829–65* (Urbana: University of Illinois Press, 1996), 177–197, 249–255.

42. Ibid., 244–245.

43. Macon Bolling Allen was appointed to the position of justice of the peace in Boston in 1847, but John Langston was the first African American on record to have been freely elected to a political position in the United States. See John Clay Smith, *Emancipation: The Making of the Black Lawyer, 1844–1944* (Philadelphia: University of Pennsylvania Press, 1993), 94–96. By May 18, John Langston had been invited to speak at a special celebration of the anniversary of the American Anti-slavery Society in New York City. This meeting was attended by some of the most noted antislavery politicians of the time. The news of his election was broadly publicized both at this meeting and in the reports of it published in the *Liberator* ("Anniversary of the American Anti-slavery Society," *Liberator*, May 18, 1855).

44. Quoted in Cheek and Cheek, *John Langston*, 260.

45. "Address of the State Convention," *Palladium of Liberty* (Columbus, Ohio), November 13, 1844, front page, accessed August 3, 2017, http://coloredconventions.org/files/original/945c2778ed57366af6d37c528e85f036.pdf.

46. "Report of the Proceedings of the Colored National Convention Held at Cleveland, Ohio, on Wednesday, September 6, 1848," Colored Conventions, accessed August 3, 2017, http://coloredconventions.org/items/show/280, 3.

47. *Daily Journal*, July 28, 1857.

48. Pickard and Furness, *The Kidnapped and the Ransomed*, 401–409.

49. Mills, "'They Defended Themselves Nobly,'" 2–8; *Daily Enquirer*, July 28, 29, 31, 1857, August 1, 2, 1857; *Daily Journal*, July 24, 27, 28, 29, 30, 1857, August 1, 1857.

50. See notes 1 and 17 in this chapter.

51. *Daily Journal*, July 29, 1857.

52. Mills, "'They Defended Themselves Nobly,'" 2–8.

53. *Vanderburgh Circuit Order Book K*, Vanderburgh County Courthouse, Evansville, Indiana, 1858, 105–108.

54. Philip Foner and George E. Walker, *Proceedings of the Black State Conventions, 1840–1865* (Philadelphia: Temple University Press, 1979), 2:70–71.

55. Ibid.

56. Cox, *A Stronger Kinship*, 55–62, 70–71. The existence of African Americans across the Northwest Territory states was so well known before the Civil War that recruiters for Civil War African American regiments came from the East Coast to recruit soldiers. The Lyles men and other African Americans in Gibson County were recruited by the Fourteenth Rhode Island Heavy Artillery USCT (*History of Gibson County, Indiana: With Illustrations Descriptive of Its Scenery, and Biographical Sketches of Some of Its Prominent Men and Pioneers* (Edwardsville, IL: Jas. T. Tartt & Co., 1884), 135.

57. Jennifer Weber, *Copperheads* (New York: Oxford University Press, 2008), 24; V. Jacque Voegeli, *Free but Not Equal: The Midwest and the Negro During the Civil War* (Chicago: University of Chicago Press, 1970), 8–9.

58. Voegeli, *Free but Not Equal*, 88, 170. See Jacque Voegeli for more on violence and prejudice against African Americans in the Northwest Territory states during the Civil War.

59. Foner and Walker, *Proceedings of the Black State Conventions*, 1: 181–182.

Conclusion: "All men are created equal"

1. For a full history of African Americans in the Civil War, see Noah Trudeau, *Like Men of War: Black Troops in the Civil War, 1862–1865* (Edison, NJ: Castle Books, 2002).

2. Darrel Bigham, *We Ask Only a Fair Trial: A History of the Black Community of Evansville, Indiana* (Bloomington: Indiana University Press, 1987), 15–16.

3. Emma Lou Thornbrough, *The Negro in Indiana Before 1900: A Study of a Minority* (Indianapolis: Indiana Historical Bureau, 1957), 231–287.

4. "Communicated," *Princeton Clarion*, May 30, 1872, front page.

5. "U.S., Indexed County Land Ownership Maps, 1860–1918," Ancestry .com, accessed 2013, https://search.ancestry.com/search/db.aspx?dbid=1127. Original data: Various publishers of county land ownership atlases, microfilmed by the Library of Congress, Washington, DC.

6. Cally L. Waite, *Permission to Remain Among Us: Education for Blacks in Oberlin, Ohio, 1880–1914* (Westport, CT: Praeger, 2002).

7. *Greenville Democrat*, October 1878, quoted in Stephen Miller, *The Palestine Book: History of Liberty (German) Township Darke County, Ohio.* Compiled for Palestine Sesqui-Centennial 1833–1983 (Defiance, OH: Hubbard Company, 1983), 253–255.

8. "District Rally of Klan Well Attended," *Arcanum Times*, June 19, 1924, front page. Greenville Public Library Genealogical Collection, Greenville, Ohio. My deepest thanks to Roane Smothers and Connor Keiser for their assistance and courageous research into the history of race relations in this region.

9. Dana M. Caldemeyer, "Conditional Conservatism: Evansville, Indiana's Embrace of the Ku Klux Klan, 1919–1924," *Ohio Valley History* 11, no. 4 (2011): 3–24.

10. Historians of the Ku Klux Klan in the twentieth-century Midwest have long assumed that there were very few African Americans in the rural Midwest during the rise of the Klan in the 1910s and 1920s. This is not the case. But due to this assumption, historians have tried to come up with various reasons why the Klan arose in Indiana, Ohio, Illinois, Michigan, and Wisconsin—and have argued that prejudice against African Americans was not a central focus of the Klan in these states. My cursory research into Klan violence against rural African American farming communities during this period has revealed that these communities were truly embattled and had to fight for their survival against attacks by the Klan. Further research is sorely needed in local records and with African Americans in the region to fully gauge the impact of the Klan on African Americans in the rural Midwest during this rise. But until this has been accomplished, the assumption should be that in these states, the Klan was racist toward people of African descent and reflected a continuation and growth of the type of prejudiced violence that had long wracked that region. See Kathleen Blee, "Book Review of *Citizen Klansmen: The Ku Klux Klan in Indiana, 1921–1928* by Leonard J. Moore and *The Dragon and the Cross: The Rise and Fall of the Ku Klux Klan in Middle America* by Richard K. Tucker," *Journal of American History* 79, no. 3 (1992): 1219–1221, doi:10.2307/2080914; Craig Fox, *Everyday Klansfolk: White Protestant Life and the KKK in 1920s Michigan* (East Lansing: Michigan State University Press, 2011); "Early Black Settlements, Grand County," Indiana Historical Society, accessed April 11, 2016, www.indianahistory.org/our-collections /reference/early-black-settlements/grant-county#.WQp2GxiZPos.

11. Elliott Jaspin, *Buried in the Bitter Waters: The Hidden History of Racial Cleansing in America* (New York: Basic Books, 2007).

12. In the 1920s children of African American farming families in Gibson County were horribly harmed by a radiation experiment illegally conducted on them in the local hospital. There has been a documentary made on the subject: *Hole in the Head: A Life Revealed* (www.holeinthehead.com). For the other injustices mentioned, see Valerie Grim, "Between Forty Acres and a Class Action Lawsuit: Black Farmers, Civil Rights, and Protests Against the US Department of Agriculture, 1997–2010," in *Beyond Forty Acres and a Mule: African American Landowning Families Since Reconstruction*, ed. Evan P. Bennett and Debra Ann Reid (Gainesville: University Press of Florida, 2012); Jasmine Melvin, "Black Farmers Win 2.5 Billion in Discrimination Suit," *Reuters*, February 18, 2010, www.reuters.com/article/us-usa-farmers-pigford/black-farmers-win -1-25-billion-in-discrimination-suit-idUSTRE61H5XD20100218; Greg Burns, "Farms Run by African-Americans in Illinois Are 'Mighty Few,'" *Chicago Tribune*, June 12, 2005, http://articles.chicagotribune.com/2005-06-12 /business/0506120151_1_national-black-farmers-association-african-american -calvin-beale. African American farmers in and around the Griers' home

county of Gibson, Indiana, were able to win some recompense for the Department of Agriculture's racist loan policies, but many had already lost their farms and could not buy them back.

13. W. E. B. Du Bois, "Negro Farmers," in *Department of Commerce and Labor Bureau of the Census Special Reports: Supplementary Analysis and Derivative Tables* (Washington, DC: Government Printing Office, 1906), 512–513. For an important discussion on the long-term effects of landownership on African Americans, see Henry Louis Gates Jr., "Forty Acres and a Gap in Wealth," *New York Times*, November 18, 2007, www.nytimes.com/2007/11/18/opinion /18gates.html.

14. Booker T. Washington, "Two Generations Under Freedom," *Outlook (1893–1924)* 73, no. 6 (February 7, 1903): 292. Washington asserted that the African Americans in Cass County had all arrived as enslaved people fleeing bondage, but the historical record and later research shows that most of the earliest settlers and landowning famers in Cass County had been free before coming to Michigan. See Marcia Renee Sawyer, "Surviving Freedom: African American Farm Households in Cass County, Michigan, 1832–1880" (PhD diss., Michigan State University, 1990); Anna-Lisa Cox, *A Stronger Kinship: One Town's Extraordinary Story of Hope and Faith* (Boston: Little, Brown, 2006).

15. "Address of the State Convention," *Palladium of Liberty* (Columbus, Ohio), November 13, 1844, front page, accessed July 4, 2017, http://colored conventions.org/files/original/945c2778ed57366af6d37c528e85f036.pdf.

16. John Wooden and Steve Jamison, *My Personal Best: Life Lessons from an All-American Journey* (New York: McGraw-Hill, 2004), 1–9; Zac Keefer, "Indiana Basketball Player Broke Racial Barrier," *IndyStar*, March 15, 2017, updated March 16, 2017, accessed August 20, 2017, www.indystar.com/story /sports/college/2017/03/15/private-paln-clarence-walker/99144560.

17. Annelise Morris, "Jumping the Legal Color Line: Negotiating Racial Geographies in the 19th Century" (paper presented at the annual meeting of the Society of Historical Archaeology, Seattle, Washington, January 6–11, 2015), accessed April 2, 2016, www.academia.edu/11559423/Jumping_the_Legal _Color_Line_Negotiating_Racial_Geographies_in_the_19th_Century; L. Rex Myers, *Daviess County, Indiana: History* (Paducah, KY: Turner Pub. Co., 1988). The Beulah AME Church that Jacob Hawkins founded in Washington, Indiana, is still an active church despite the fact that its building has been burned down at least twice, a fate that occurred to many AME churches across the rural Northwest Territory states, including the AME church founded by Charles Grier in Gibson County. See "Beulah AME Church," Facebook, www.facebook.com/Belah805Washington. My deepest gratitude to Brenda Jett and Roane Smothers for showing me around the Clemens home, as well as for their work with Dr. Jayne Beilke, Connor Keiser, and the many others who are researching and preserving the African American pioneer history of Darke County, Ohio. See Aileen LeBlanc, "Historic Ohio Town Fights 'Mega Dairy,'" NPR News and Notes, February 13, 2006, accessed

July 28, 2016, www.npr.org/templates/story/story.php?storyId=5203581; Kevin Williams, "An Ohio Town Where Races Mixed Freely," *Washington Post*, September 26, 2015, accessed August 21, 2017, www.washingtonpost .com/national/an-ohio-town-where-the-races-have-mixed-freely-for-more -than-200-years/2015/09/26/7ab3b250-4cfa-11e5-bfb9-9736d04fc8e4_story .html. (Kevin Williams seemed unaware of the prejudice and prejudiced violence that arose in Darke County after the Civil War.)

18. For more on the Clemens family's involvement in the Underground Railroad, see "A Free Black Settlement and the Underground Railroad," Ohio River National Freedom Corridor, accessed December 10, 2017, www.ohioriver nationalfreedomcorridor.org/a-free-black-settlement.html.

19. There continue to be challenges to preserving these very visible testimonies to African American wealth and success in the antebellum Northwest Territory states, and many homes have been lost. See Wayne L. Snider, *All in the Same Spaceship: Portions of American Negro History Illustrated in Highland County, Ohio, U.S.A.* (New York: Vantage Press, 1974), 34–36. While John Langston's farmhouse in Ohio has been destroyed, work is being done to preserve the home he and his family lived in, in Oberlin, Ohio, soon after he was elected to office in 1855. At the time it was built, it was considered one of the finer homes in the area. See "Introduction to John Mercer Langston," John Mercer Langston Historic Home, accessed July 23, 2017, www.johnmercer langstonhistorichome.org.

20. The Roberts settlement in central Indiana, the Cheyenne Valley settlement in Wisconsin, and the Longtown community that straddles the Indiana-Ohio border still have yearly reunions, as do many more of these early pioneering settlements.

21. Interview with Stanley Madison, July 12, 2017, cited with permission. My deepest gratitude to Professor Henry Louis Gates Jr., Professor Evelyn Brooks Higginbotham, Dr. Abby Wolf, Dr. Krishna Lewis, Dr. Kevin Burke, Dr. Donald Yacovone, Dr. Vera Ingrid Grant, Tom Wolejko, Shawn Lee, and all of the supportive staff and community at Harvard University's Hutchins Center for African and African American Research, which has been my academic "home place" while I wrote this book. I could not have written this book without their encouragement, advice, and help. My grateful thanks also to Michael Bourret, Brett Brinker, Martin Luchtefeld, Benjamin Adams, MAM, and the community of St. Gregory's Abbey for making the completion of this book possible. And finally, to my family and friends, who supported me in times of trial and rejoiced with me when times were good. I would not have made it without you.

Index

Anna-Lisa Cox is an award-winning historian of race relations in the Old Northwest Territory and states. She is currently a fellow at Harvard University's Hutchins Center for African and African American Research. She holds an MPhil from the University of Cambridge and a PhD in American history from the University of Illinois. She has been the recipient of numerous awards for her research, including the Gilder Lehrman Foundation Fellowship, a Sheila Biddle Ford Foundation Fellowship, and grants from the Spencer Foundation. She was a recent research associate at the Smithsonian National Museum of African American History and Culture, where her original research underpinned two historical exhibits, including the "Power of Place" exhibit on African American pioneers that is now the subject of this book. She is author of the award-winning *A Stronger Kinship: One Town's Extraordinary Story of Hope and Faith*. She lives in Michigan.

PublicAffairs is a publishing house founded in 1997. It is a tribute to the standards, values, and flair of three persons who have served as mentors to countless reporters, writers, editors, and book people of all kinds, including me.

I. F. STONE, proprietor of *I. F. Stone's Weekly*, combined a commitment to the First Amendment with entrepreneurial zeal and reporting skill and became one of the great independent journalists in American history. At the age of eighty, Izzy published *The Trial of Socrates*, which was a national bestseller. He wrote the book after he taught himself ancient Greek.

BENJAMIN C. BRADLEE was for nearly thirty years the charismatic editorial leader of *The Washington Post*. It was Ben who gave the *Post* the range and courage to pursue such historic issues as Watergate. He supported his reporters with a tenacity that made them fearless and it is no accident that so many became authors of influential, best-selling books.

ROBERT L. BERNSTEIN, the chief executive of Random House for more than a quarter century, guided one of the nation's premier publishing houses. Bob was personally responsible for many books of political dissent and argument that challenged tyranny around the globe. He is also the founder and longtime chair of Human Rights Watch, one of the most respected human rights organizations in the world.

· · ·

For fifty years, the banner of Public Affairs Press was carried by its owner Morris B. Schnapper, who published Gandhi, Nasser, Toynbee, Truman, and about 1,500 other authors. In 1983, Schnapper was described by *The Washington Post* as "a redoubtable gadfly." His legacy will endure in the books to come.

Peter Osnos, *Founder*